Date Due

THE WORLD'S GREAT AGE

THE MACMILLAN COMPANY
NEW YORK · BOSTON · CHICAGO · DALLAS
ATLANTA · SAN FRANCISCO

MACMILLAN & CO., Limited
LONDON · BOMBAY · CALCUTTA
MELBOURNE

THE MACMILLAN COMPANY
OF CANADA, Limited
TORONTO

THE WORLD'S GREAT AGE

The Story of A Century's Search for a Philosophy of Life

By
PHILO M. BUCK, JR.

Decorations by
NORMAN G. RUDOLPH

1936
THE MACMILLAN COMPANY

PRINTED IN THE UNITED STATES OF AMERICA
NORWOOD PRESS LINOTYPE, INC.
NORWOOD, MASS., U.S.A.

TO STUDENTS OF THE UNIVERSITY OF WISCONSIN,
WHO GAVE MUCH OF THE INSPIRATION; TO THE
SPECIAL COMMITTEE OF ITS GRADUATE FACULTY
ON RESEARCH, WHO PROVIDED THE NECESSARY
LEISURE; AND TO MY COLLEAGUES, MRS. HAZEL
STEWART ALBERSON AND MR. NEAL F. DOUBLEDAY,
WHO GENEROUSLY GAVE THEIR COÖPERATION, THIS
BOOK IS GRATEFULLY DEDICATED.

PREFACE

DOMINATING the square, named in honor of his great victory, is the pillared statue of Britain's greatest sailor, Lord Nelson. Only a few yards from this imperishable memorial to the nation's hero of a great war is the reminder of the cost of another great war, the grave of the Unknown Soldier. His martyrdom—or glory—is memorialized anew under Napoleon's Arc de Triomphe in Paris; and is again the central shrine in our own Arlington Cemetery. Scarce a country that took part in that conflict but has his precious and nameless memorial. Its generals and statesmen are not much more than incidental names; the hero is the soldier who did his bit and paid with his life and name. Such is the change in the bravest adventure in the world that has come in a scant century.

The change in all the manifoldness of life is no less startling. Only a few days ago a colleague, seeing the hundreds and thousands of new students pouring into one of our mid-western universities, and knowing his responsibilities, "what shall I tell them?" he asked. "The old formulas are attractive, and these young people would eagerly accept them; but will they work?" And he is a brave teacher who will return a complacent answer. Was it not Dostoevsky, that most contemporary of all nineteenth century artists, who once remarked that the confidence that two and two will always make four is a sign not of life but of death?

The nineteenth century—the century of change. To

tell its story in the pages of its literature has been a fascinating, and also a dangerous adventure. And as I lay aside
the manuscript, it is only too easy to see its shortcomings.
I have been arbitrary in my choice of authors—it is impossible to be otherwise. Only did I select the best, or
the most notable, the most typical? Was I arbitrary, too,
in the treatment of those I did select? But this was never
an effort to make a complete study of any one of the dozen
or more selected, only of the dominant idea of each, as it
contributed its share to the change in ideas of the century.
To do this sympathetically—as free from bias as each
author would have himself portrayed,—this has been
something more than an exercise in literary criticism.
There is in it also more than a trifle of personal confession.

For all of these authors from Rousseau to Thomas
Hardy have been heroes, in their day, to every right-
minded reader of their thoughtful pages. And yet, some
of them, how far away they seem in their serene confidence
or their passionate pleading. They are the epochs, not
only of the century, but of one's own search, hopeful or in
turn disillusioned and groping, for the clue to the meaning
of life. It is because one, during the process of writing this,
has lived again the years of enthusiasm, doubt, and new
fortitude, that in now laying the manuscript aside, there is
the pang of regret. There were so many other things that
clamored to be said, and so much further study that longed
to be made.

In comparing it with its predecessor, *The Golden
Thread*, there is one large difference. In the story from
Homer to Goethe there was one central theme that like a
golden clue gave direction and value from the beginning
to the end. Here there are many threads, and at times the
golden one seems lost, though it has never been broken.
The reason in part is that the perspective here is much

closer; and that the story of the century of change, this our "world's great-age," is not yet complete. Goethe marked the end of an epoch and was a summary of the best that had been until his time. We are not yet at the close of the epoch that began with Rousseau; and the story of the search during these our post-war days should also be told as the drama for which in a way the nineteenth century was the prelude.

P. M. B.

Madison, Wisconsin,
September, 1935.

ACKNOWLEDGMENT

The author is grateful for the privilege to use extracts from the following works covered by copyright:

Hebbell: *Three Plays Translated into English*, Everyman's Library —Dutton.

Tolstoi: *Anna Karenina, Childhood and Youth*, Everyman's Library —Dutton.

Dostoevsky: *Brothers Karamazov*—Grosset and Dunlap.

Crime and Punishment, Everyman's Library—Dutton.

Nietzsche: *So Spake Zarathustra*, and other works—Macmillan.

Zola: *Paris*—Macmillan.

Germinal—Knopf.

Hardy: *Collected Poems*, and *Dynasts*—Macmillan.

CONTENTS

THE WORLD'S GREAT AGE

I. A CENTURY OF SEARCH

"Ich verstehe die Welt nicht mehr!" HEBBEL, *Maria Magdalene*

IN an ancient storehouse of homely wisdom there is a pathetic ballad of a poor old woman who on her return from market fell asleep on the King's highway. During her slumbers a wicked pedlar cut her "petticoats all round about up to her knees." It was an awkward awakening full of bewilderment for the poor creature and doubts about her identity. But her sad heart had at least one comfort—

> "If I be I, as I hope it be,
> I've a little dog at home, and he'll know me."

But even this hope was vain, so sadly transformed was her appearance.

> "Home went the little woman all in the dark;
> Up got the little dog, and he began to bark.
> 'Lawk a mercy on me, this is none of I.'"

This our last century has more than once felt the same bewilderment.

Not that it has been a poor selection on our part of a century in which to live, for even bewilderment can be an exciting adventure—in retrospect. And there have been compensations too in our constant hope that the things brought home from the market would be received with

1

welcome recognition. But our transformations have been so persistent and make-ups so varied that the hundred and more years have been a bit breathless. One can't be forever changing rôles and lines without paying some price for one's dexterity. It may imply, in the last analysis, some want of faith in ourselves or in the world in which we live. One trying experience made the little old woman a confirmed sceptic; we in the past hundred years have had many. And the story of its scepticism and attempted faith makes it quite appropriately a century of search.

In a little manual gleaned by a soldier-disciple from the chance conversations of Epictetus there is this exquisite little paragraph:

> "As in a voyage, when the ship is at anchor, if you go on shore to get water you may amuse yourself with picking up a shellfish, or an onion, in your way, but your thoughts ought to be bent towards the ship, and perpetually attentive lest the captain should call, and then you must leave all these things, that you may not be thrown into the vessel, bound neck and heels like a sheep: thus likewise in life, if, instead of an onion or a shellfish, such a thing as a wife or a child be granted you, there is no objection; but if the captain calls, run to the ship, leave all these things, regard none of them. But if you are old, never go far from the ship: lest, when you are called, you should be unable to come in time."

It was spoken during the trembling before a new age in ancient Imperial Rome. Life then, as now, was full of change and bewilderment, and happiness seemed as illusory. But here at least is faith triumphant, pagan, to be sure, and none too easy. But how distant are its echoes today, and how they remind us that a long, a very long journey separates us from the ancient Stoic acceptance of a reliable Providence governing an evil and transitory world.

The eighteenth had been an eager century, busy with

the invention of scientific technique and enthusiastically thinking of the future triumph of science and the regeneration thereby of humanity. It was at this time that it was given to the human mind to think those long thoughts of the world of man and nature as a vast organization of glorious law, whose mathematical discovery and intelligible formulation were to be the glory of the newborn science and its newly acquired logic. Through these were to come the new ages of gold when man was to be intellectually freed, morally happy, and at his ease in a world subdued to his nature. Such were the distant dreams of those brilliant savants, who under d'Alembert and Diderot, contrived the *Great Encyclopedia*, that was to be the textbook of a new world.

Like Moses, to these, and to many like them, was given the glimpse from the lofty mountain of the Promised Land, a land flowing with milk and honey. And again, today only a scant century and a half from them, we are in spirit as far removed from their glowing optimism, and all else that characterized the second half of the Age of the Enlightenment, as we are from the genial Stoic of a long vanished empire.

And between us lies that age of transformation in make-up, of ruthless experiment and revolution, the nineteenth century, which began in war and revolution and closed in a greater war and revolution, whose reverberations yet leave us bewildered, and whose results we cannot even pretend to predict. These are revolutions that touch and transform almost every detail of our lives and thoughts. In material change we have progressed farther in a scant hundred years than the human race did between Waterloo and the days of Abraham. Noah and Ulysses are nearer to Lord Nelson and Captain Cook than these are to Admiral Jellicoe and Lindberg. For in this our own age a generation has been as a thousand years, and a century seems a history of the human race. It is scant wonder that each older generation, seeing the havoc the new is making with accepted custom and creed, shakes its head like the Father in Hebbel's *Maria Magdalene* and cries in tragic bewilderment: *"Ich verstehe die Welt nicht mehr!"* The poor little old lady and her dog.

At almost the very moment that the French Revolution was gathering for the "deluge," Goethe at the inn in Ilmenau composed the *Wanderer's Night Song:*

> Ueber allen Gipfeln
> Ist Ruh
> In allen Wipfeln
> Spuerest du
> Kaum einen Hauch.
> Die Voegelein schweigen im Walde
> Warte nur, balde
> Ruhest du auch.[1]

It is the restless wanderer's prayer for peace, and its promise. And though he lived through three revolutions and had seen a World War, for him the promise was kept. And even during its worst years he maintained his poise and looked with serenity to the future.

How distant, and perhaps foreign to our time, seems that composure of Germany's artist-scientist-poet. How strangely out of place he would again be found by any of those who are transforming our contemporary Europe and

---

[1] I add an attempt at translation; where hundreds have failed one more failure will not greatly discommode the company of those who have attempted the impossible.

> Peace o'er each mountain crest
> Broods low,
> The stately trees at rest
> Whisper slow,
> Then whispers cease.
> Hushed is the wood bird's song:
> Wait and for thee e'er long
> Rest, too, and Peace.

especially Germany. And yet the unrest of today is the child of the unrest of yesterday, with perhaps its parent's traits somewhat exaggerated, and that parent the restless child of restless parent, and so back to the restlessness that bred the French Revolution. Our century began with revolution and a world in turmoil, and it closed with a world in turmoil and fresh revolution.

Revolutions there have been uncounted in the long epochs of history, but never before so swift in succession, nor so thoroughgoing in scope. Had they involved only man's political and social creeds they would have been bad enough, for to change one's gestures in society and government is undoubtedly uncomfortable. But they have attacked man's economic life also, and transformed and continue to transform most intimate habits and associations. They have gone farther and in science overwhelmed us with an entirely transformed universe and threatened, and seemed to carry out the threat, to challenge man's unique reason and moral supremacy. And as if all this were not enough, the revolution has challenged, not only the reasonableness, but even the possibility of the basis of religion.

It has been difficult, trebly difficult in all these wars without and conflicts within to preserve the spirit of peace. But the story of them, their thrilling narrative, is the story of the rise and fall of faith in man and his institutions as we glean it best in nineteenth century literature, the story of the world's great age.

A century of search—a century adrift—the phrase does seem to give point to the restless bewilderment of the times that followed the cry Rousseau made to his contemporaries. "A spirit lost in this immensity"—I borrow his phrase—this is precisely what Rousseau felt himself to be, and after him the roll of his successors down to our own time. Immensity, the vast complexity of the world in which man lives and which the new science so remorselessly is exploring for his consciousness and his conscience. How to discover an adjustment in this new and expanding universe; how to live in it rightly and comfortably and justly; how to bring it into conformity with man's deepest desires; or, what seems much harder, how to bring one's deepest desires into conformity with it, these are perplexing problems. Science, the thing known and measurable, and human life, the thing so spontaneous and incalculable, how to bring these two apparent incompatibles to bed and board, this was the essential thought that inspired the prophetic Shelley. Only poetry could weave the magic bond between them. Without that "we want the creative faculty to imagine that which we know; we want the generous impulse to act that which we imagine; we want the poetry of life."

"A spirit lost in this immensity," this thought may lead to two quite different attitudes. The old mystic knew the immensity and felt the problem as he lifted his eyes to the blessed vision of a vast universe of divine plan in which man and nature, the human and the material and the divine were one; and only as he could look beyond the irrelevancies and inconsistencies and the discomforts and perplexities of the present to the spirit of unity that pervades all, only then could he discover the peace that his soul craved. There is not a little of this transcendental peace in Dante as he gazes upon the face of Deity itself. There is not a little of the same transcendental peace in this ecstasy of Wordsworth:

> "And I have felt
> A presence that disturbs me with the joy
> Of elevated thoughts; a sense sublime
> Of something far more deeply interfused,

Whose dwelling is the light of setting suns,
And the round ocean and the living air,
And the blue sky, and in the mind of man;
A motion and a spirit, that impels
All thinking things, all objects of all thought,
And rolls through all things."

To be sure there is a vast difference between Wordsworth and Dante in the preparation each underwent before he was ready for the blessed vision, and this discipline is something of a clue to their respective values. Dante had been through both Hell and Purgatory before he undertook the flight to the Heaven of Heavens, where the ineffable secrets were revealed. The lesser poet seems rather to take Heaven at a bound, as though it were man's rightful heritage and his easy refuge from the pains and disciplines of Hell and Purgatory. But be this as it may, there have been many poets, and even philosophers, in this our century who have found it a not too difficult feat to turn the back upon the world in which they seem forlorn, and to take refuge in a mystical immensity that is imaginatively so alluring; there, if they can lose themselves in an intoxication of sensibility, they may discover peace—our Babes in the Wood.

"Ich verstehe die Welt nicht mehr," I can no longer understand the world. After revolution and transformation upon transformation and revolution what more natural than this exclamation of despair; and what more natural after despair than to turn one's back upon revolution and transformation, to call it evil names and to retire to moral nudism in some Forest of Arden? What more natural and sometimes even more necessary? This world of science which has so transformed our lives and made them infinitely more complex, has it in sooth made man any the more happy or comfortable? Do we not all, on

occasion, repeat with fervor the simple lines of Wordsworth and go off for a vacation in the woods?

> "Enough of Science and of Art;
> Close up those barren leaves;
> Come forth, and bring with you a heart
> That watches and receives."

But most of us cannot be as fortunate as the poet, who
could live his life in the hills of Westmoreland. Life
which has been pushed off for a two week's vacation comes
flooding back like the immensity of the tide. The detached
serenity of the mystic is only for the chosen few. The
many take a healthy pleasure in the other and more
strenuous attitude of striving to comprehend and live in
accordance with a newly transformed world.

The place of man in the world, in nature and society,
this has been the fundamental human problem since man
was man, and it has from the beginning been the theme
of all literature in the small as in the large. It is an inescapable problem; for even the mystic, though he seems
to retire from the world, really does no more than to
create a new one in his own image. But in the earlier
centuries when changes came more slowly and grand-
parents could yet speak the language of their grandchil-
dren, there was at least the sense of one security, time.
If the answer to the problem could not be discovered
today, the problem at least would not change its denomina-
tor over night, and there was tomorrow and the day
after. "À demain les affaires." Given time the problem
could be solved. At least no one doubted—or few—the
ultimate solubility of the problem. In consequence there
is in the main a serene hopefulness in all the great literature of the past, a hopefulness in the essential worth of
human nature as human nature. It may exhibit its gro-

tesque comedies and its tragic horrors, but it is still the essential thing, the thing worthy of all respect and admiration, though it may find its way beset with grotesquerie and horror. So it appeared to Sophocles, and so later to Shakespeare.

But there has been no Shakespeare nor Sophocles, nor the splendid trust in human nature of a Sophocles or Shakespeare in the nineteenth century. Yet there is a compensation for this loss. There has been an earnestness and a whole-heartedness in the search, and a single-eyed pursuit of the main issue that we shall not find duplicated elsewhere. Never before has literature been so obsessed with the importance of its mission; never has the poet's warning, "we want the creative faculty to imagine that which we know," been more diligently heeded. The nineteenth century writers have nearly one and all felt the vital connection between poetry and literature and life. Not only must literature hold up the mirror to life, but it must like the scientist offer a formula for what it sees. Such was Shelley at the beginning of the century. Such were Tolstoi and Ibsen. Such are the writers of our own day. But whereas in the past a literary generation or school might be a thing of centuries, now the generations and schools are seen treading on each other's heels. Shakespeare, Cervantes, Montaigne were contemporaries, and all have much of their new age in common; and they sit comfortably side by side in the library. Nietzsche, Tolstoi, Zola are also contemporaries, but how strangely different and uncomfortable even in the same room; and their differences are the varied attitudes they have toward life.

Not that the writers of poetry and fiction are philosophers and scientists, in spite of Shelley's praise. Rather it has been their desire to see the significance of science to human nature in its relation to itself, to society, and to nature. Perhaps even to soften the impact of science on those who are bewildered by its bare formulas, a most necessary service, and one for which the scientist himself is of all people the least qualified. And this task the writers of the century have whole-heartedly accepted.

In consequence the pictures of human nature that are disclosed to us are not always complimentary or even pleasant; at times even, we revolt at their sordidness. The Greek even in the depth of tragedy at least preserves for us the ideal of human nature as a thing fundamentally sound and admirable. But science is cold and impersonal. To it atoms, quanta, germplasm, hormones, are interesting only as they can be measured or calculated. Why then should the novelist, who is dealing with human conduct with the same cool interest, show any illogical admiration for one group of protoplasm or another assortment of hormones? So Hauptmann's study of Emanuel Quint is not tragedy in the Greek sense at all, nor a comedy in the manner of *Don Quixote*, but an alienist's observation of a not uncommon species of *dementia*. And Zola's *Rougon-Macquart* series of novels are a sociological treatise on the effects of heredity and environment on indifferent moral character. To reply that this is neither pretty nor the old theme of fiction or drama is not quite relevant; for the modern replies that in the old days also there was no science as we today know science; and he might again in his defense quote Shelley. For the nineteenth century, in the main, has prided itself, and rightly, upon its intellectual honesty. It is a stubborn virtue, and none too common.

The place of man in relation to nature, to society, to himself, this has been the theme of literature from the beginnings, and modified only in the last century and a half by the new accumulations of science and industry and their effects on human institutions, and the rapid spread of new restless ideas. But as the dominant interest has shifted from this field to that, the theme of novels and dramas has tended to follow; sometimes in agreement, with the writer as it were the commentator and prophet, sometimes in horrified revolt, but always deeply convinced that man's knowledge and new appliances must somehow, somewhere, have a profound significance for his moral conduct, for the institutions of his society, and for his beliefs and creeds.

Dominating the century, therefore, and its symbol, is the figure of Tolstoi, a lonely figure, an agonized figure, seeing all that is passing around him, feeling all with an intenseness that reminds of Sophocles, knowing fully the significance of the new, loving the tradition of the old, yet searching painfully for a meaning for life, with life itself as the stake. Such will be the story of this our century of search.

By the end of the century it will have seemed as though man had lost himself, had, somehow, forfeited his privilege or uniqueness while making these prodigious advances in his knowledge. And the fact that he can summon to his laboratory the universe of the atom, or the universe of all intergalactic space, and make its reluctant members disclose their secrets, this fact will seem of small avail, if man the searcher be no more than one more remorseless and obedient flying cloud of electrons that conforms to no law of its own choosing. It may seem that in this abundance of knowledge, classified and ticketed and measured, the essential thing, human destiny, has somehow slipped out of range of the telescope or microscope. Where can it be found?

It is this profoundly moving and growing conviction

that runs like a scarlet clue through all of the greater works of the century of search, the search for human value. Even in works that are most profoundly sceptical, the search continues though there may be little hope for an answer. It is this same fact that gives something of a provisional character to the works, even the greatest, of our century. It will have few great affirmations, for as yet there is little to affirm. For even when it indulges in an orgy of optimism, there will be the ever present doubt, like the skeleton at the feast, to remind the banqueters of a day of conscious awakening. Yet withal, the story of the century of search has in it all the elements too of honest and downright adventure, of downright and adventurous honesty. The century of honest search, and as the poet Shelley at its beginning proudly proclaimed, the world's great age.

II. MY BROTHER'S KEEPER

ROUSSEAU

"On était loin de concevoir à que point je puis m'enflammer pour des êtres imaginaires."

Confessions

THE old geology had a most convenient cosmic date, an event as definite as the birth of Christ, a *terminus ad quem* or *a quo*, the Deluge. Everything before this catastrophe was labeled conveniently and dismissed to a dignified retreat among the interesting antiques of a mythical past; everything after was the tangible and inescapable fact of a world that demands practical consideration. There is something of the same obvious relevancy about the person of Jean Jacques Rousseau. He was: and then the order and value of things seemed to undergo a catastrophic change. It is not the French Revolution itself that counts so much today; it is the illuminating and transforming character of this man's personality and the new values he proclaimed. It is hardly unjust to say that our new age begins with Rousseau. Before him all things are classified and ticketed, after him all things yet seem in the process of becoming. A solvent that has not yet permitted recrystallization, a new magnetic pole not yet definitely located, a new map of man's universe in which

13

lines and boundaries are yet unsettled, Rousseau is all these, and something more. And the signs of all this uncertainty are the conflicts, bitter nearly always, that still rage over his personality and ideas.

To feel in an instant how modern he is, how restlessly modern, one needs only to set him against that other French writer who challenges comparison, Montaigne. Note the difference in tone in the opening words of the study each made of his own personality. Rousseau is never quite convinced, even of himself, and he challenges Deity for a verdict.

"I have entered upon a performance which is without example, whose accomplishment will have no imitator. I mean to present my fellow mortals with a man in all the integrity of nature, and this man shall be myself. I know my heart, and have studied mankind. I am not made like any one I have been acquainted with, perhaps not like any one in existence; if not better, I at least claim originality, and whether Nature did wisely in breaking the mold in which she formed me, can only be determined after reading this work.

"Whenever the last trumpet shall sound, I will present myself before the sovereign Judge with this book in my hand, and loudly proclaim: Thus have I acted; these were my thoughts; such was I. With equal freedom and veracity I have related what was laudable or wicked; I have concealed no crimes, added no virtues; and if I have sometimes introduced superfluous ornament, it was merely to occupy a void occasioned by defect of memory. I may have supposed certain that which I only knew to be probable, but I have never asserted as truth a conscious falsehood. Such as I was, I have declared myself; sometimes vile and despicable, at others virtuous, generous, and sublime. Even as Thou hast read my inmost soul, Power Eternal, assemble around Thy throne an innumerable throng of my fellow mortals, let them listen to my confessions, let them blush at my depravity, let them tremble at my sufferings; let each in turn expose with equal sincerity the failings, the wanderings of his heart, and, if he dare, aver, 'I was better than that man.' "

Montaigne is quietly assured, dismisses the jury, and renders the verdict himself.

"This is a sincere book, Reader. It forewarns you at the outset that in writing it I had no other than a private and family end in view. I thought neither of being serviceable to you, nor of my own fame. My powers are not equal to such a design. I intended it solely for the solace of my kinsfolk and friends: that, when they have lost me (as they must do before long), they may recover in it some lines of my character and humours, and by this means more fully and vividly cherish me in their memory.

"Had my intention been to court the world's favour, I should have trimmed myself more bravely, and stood before it in a studied attitude. I desire to be seen in my simple, natural, and everyday dress, without artifice or constraint; for it is myself I portray. My faults may therein be read to the life, and my native form, as far as my respect to the public has permitted.

"So, Reader, I am myself the subject of my books; it is not reasonable to expect you to waste your leisure on a matter so frivolous and empty."

Two such people could never be friends, or even peaceful acquaintances. But of the two Rousseau is much the more in attitude like to ourselves. One is respectful in the presence of Montaigne, but some would like to snuggle cozily into the lap of Rousseau—he is all lap.

Compared with Montaigne, Rousseau has no character, only sensitive impulses, like the restless, exploring tentacles of a polyp. He is by essence unstable, a perpetual vagabond in emotion and fancy. His life was a perpetual wandering for he knew not what goal; his imagination was always at odds with the present. "If I were to paint the spring, I could only do it in the winter." Montaigne studies himself coolly, objectively, that he may see himself as a symbol of human nature. What he wants is the universal, the general, the typically human, devoid of the accidental, the eccentric, the unique owing to time and circumstance. Know himself thus, and he will have the formula for human nature. By this he can judge at their true value the unique, the eccentric, the accidental, and give them the individual rôle their nature demands. Hence his large and life-long study of men and manners, in his own time and in history. Hence the tower from which he could look out on passing events, and the library which told him of the past.

But none of this sedentary aloofness from the sheer sensation of living for Rousseau. A half hour with a book gave him a headache unless it fired his heart and launched his imagination on a thousand adventures. A book, a person, a journey, not as food for thought or speculation, but only to send him into tears or, it mattered little, into ecstasies. Tears, ecstasies, these are the theme of his *Confessions,* and the manner of their coming, and the analysis of the process as their springs were unloosed. It is a book of self-portrayal, a study, if you will, of his inner life—a thing to rejoice the psychologist he unconsciously was. And he emerges from this self-study a thing unique, eccentric, an accidental sport. If God made him, then surely the Deity wisely broke the mold on his creation. There could be no two Rousseaus, not at least in the cosmos or consciousness of Jean Jacques.

And how like a new god he breaks with all previous moral obsessions and standards of value, or uses them for his own exaltation. No wonder he shocked his contemporaries and made good old Dr. Johnson long for his banishment to some penal colony. A new god, but a sad god, too, a melancholy god, who finds evidence for his godhead, not, as is orthodox, in his power, but in his impotence. And he is going to breed a huge spawn of melancholic godlings whose claim to divine parentage is going to be their moist irrelevancy.

For Rousseau's *Confessions* is by all odds the one really great book that owes its greatness to the power of tearful self-portrayal and self-judgment by self-lamentation. One can't do this sort of thing and score success, and great success, without at the same time having in one genuine greatness, not a positive greatness perhaps, but one none the less potent over one's generation and generations that succeed. Take this sentence, for example; not a chance, careless remark, but a deliberate expression of faith: "I have discovered this supreme maxim of morality, the only one perhaps of service in practice; avoid all situations which place our duty in opposition to our interests, and which show us our good in another's evil." Or this: "Were we always willing to be discreet, rarely would we need to be virtuous." Now no one would question the essential discretion that prompts these remarks; but how do they square with any theory of moral character that has to do with an active or practical life? They are at best a kind of moral camouflage. And is it not precisely because of this negative idea of virtue, that at the end he is forced to exclaim, "I was destined to become the most unhappy of mortals"; and glories in this his uniqueness, a modern contortion of the ideal of the man of sorrows?

He is convinced, as a necessary postulate, of his essential moral goodness, not necessarily of the goodness of his intentions—like the child who replies to an offended parent, "I didn't mean to do it"—these he frequently criticises freely; but of the goodness of soul that lies behind intention and will, of the thing that feels and judges and thus can deplore the errant intention and will. And his *Confessions* thus is the long story of the errancy of his active self that is always playing truant, and the pleas in extenuation of his agonizing self, that displays its highly moral nature in proportion as it suffers. This it is that would have shocked Montaigne. It would be as though man shows his most vigorous health at times when his body

is most racked by disease, and when his inner longing for
physical peace is most unbearable; and, on the other hand,
as though the man who has no bodily discomfort, and
hence is unconscious of health, is disqualified from dis-
cussing it. The greater the physical agony, the finer the
evidence for physical health. The more intense the moral
agony, the finer the moral nature.

For Rousseau, when his illness is at its worst, exclaims, "*mais je suis sublime.*" It is no wonder that Goethe
commenting on many of the little Rousseau-romantic godlings of his time impatiently broke out:

"All the poets write as if they were ill and the whole world a lazaretto. They all speak of the woe and misery of this earth, and of the
joys of a hereafter; all are discontented, and one draws another into a
state of still greater discontent. This is a real abuse of poetry, which was
given us to hide the little discords of life, and to make man contented
with the world and his condition. But the present generation is afraid
of all such strength, and is only poetical when it has weakness to deal
with."

Two illustrations out of a multitude. In his youth when
he was serving as lackey in a noble family in Italy he stole
a prized ribbon. He had fallen into the habit of petty
thievery in his untended childhood. He allowed the blame
to rest upon a poor, innocent maid, a girl too that he was
fond of and who had become fond of him. He allowed her
to bear the blame, as who in childhood perhaps has not,
and been troubled too in conscience? But Rousseau's response to the situation is unique. It was an opportunity
for him to show his essential goodness, not by the orthodox
method of coming forward at last and saving the poor
girl. This would have been far too obvious for his finer
nature, which by so gross an act would have been robbed
of an opportunity to show its true nobility. "The Count
de la Roque in bidding the two of us depart, contented

himself by saying that the conscience of the guilty one would sufficiently avenge the innocent. His prophecy was not vain, . . . and I am able to say that the desire in some way to escape has in a way had much to do with the writing of these *Confessions*."

But even better was the means he took to display to himself the noble sentiments of a father. True he goes about it in a way that orthodoxy or tradition hardly commends. He and Thérèse, whom he forgot to marry, were then just getting under way in Paris. The *ménage* was not quite regular, and not wholly comfortable; so he sent the babies one after the other away from the reluctant mother to the foundling asylum. Had this balancing of exigencies against instinct been all there would be little to be said about it, except perhaps a raising of the eyebrows at a bit of excellent scandal. But he is the Rousseau of the sanctity of childhood, the Rousseau that paints his own with such warm sentiment, the Rousseau of the *Émile*, and what better opportunity to show his own virtuous sublimity.

"Had I been one of those born to evil, deaf to the voice of nature, among whom no sincere feelings of justice or of humanity can ever take root, this hardness of heart might have been intelligible; but this warmth of heart, this keen sensitiveness, this readiness for affection, the power it has over me and the cruel pain when it is lost, this innate outpouring of heart for my fellows, this ardent love for the noble, the true, the beautiful, the just; this horror of evil of whatsoever sort, this inability to hate, to destroy, even to wish to destroy; this tenderness of heart, this overpowering and sweet emotion I feel on the approach of all that is virtuous, generous, lovable; could all these find themselves in the same soul with their opposites which would tread under foot without scruple the sweetest of all responsibilities? No, I know and I proclaim aloud its impossibility. Never for a moment of his life could Jean Jacques become a creature without feeling, without compassion, an unnatural father."

One is reminded of Dostoevsky's wastrel in *Crime and Punishment* who drank, not to drown his sorrows, and even stole from his prostitute daughter and starving family, that he might steep himself in an orgy of alcoholic remorse. This is to be titanically melancholy and maudlinly virtuous.

The old Greek myth of Prometheus Bound is going to receive a startlingly new moral significance with the age that follows. But with Rousseau the fact that he can thus suffer, distributes moral responsibility in a novel and curious way. The man, Rousseau, the individual, is wholly good; of this elemental fact the moral conscience that cries out in pain is *prima facie* evidence. The world in which his actions are so illogical, aberrant, or even criminal, is for the same reason wholly bad. And man's position like that of the old Titan is the tragic human paradox, a beautiful and divine pearl impotent in an oppressive and ugly oyster.

This is Rousseau's moral judgment on himself and the world—a judgment due to the discrepancies he himself discovered in his own life. It is not a judgment based upon what one might call a judicial or intellectual weighing of evidence. Much rather it is due to his sensitive awareness of discomfort, the discomfort of a vagabond in regions in which he never allowed himself to feel at home. He could not deny his own sincerity, nor the depth of his feelings of pain; these were spontaneous and hence must be good. The world because he could not spontaneously love it or even adjust himself to it must be bad. Hence his moral maxim: "Avoid all situations which place our duty in opposition to our interests"; for this is in effect an advice to cease from all moral endeavor. True virtue to him must be passive.

It is this moral point of view, drenched as it is with

tears and crowned with monuments of grief, that makes the *Confessions* so remarkable a book; unique of its kind, and potent to all later generations. It is as it were a *via crucis* of primal innocence, trodden by a supreme artist in feeling and words, innocence beguiled, mislead and crucified, a monument to all beholders. He is the sole subject of the book, full of sin but infinitely good; weak beyond the weakness of man, but radiant in purity. Venial faults are of no less significance than the heinous, criminal acts of no weightier charge than casual mistakes; for the index of all is the remorse they give rise to; and their end the opportunity for his virtue to shine the more brightly. All equally show his goodness defeated by his weakness; and in all it is his virtue that stands radiantly exonerated.

In a lesser man than Rousseau this virtue would look like the crafty mask of a Uriah Heep, and his forgiveness of the world that tormented him would be not different from Uriah's crawling humility. But not so. If he uses the incident of the stolen ribbon and his permitting the poor girl to carry the blame as an illustration of his love and sympathy for all creatures in distress, we must take him at his word.

Thus it is not his character that he is trying to present, but his plea in mitigation. Indeed character, as Montaigne understood character, or as Shakespeare presented character in his plays, it may even be doubted that he possessed. Much rather he is a complex of impulses and emotions, fluid always and unexpected. It was the world and other people that possessed character; and his design is to show how different he is from all others, how unique, spontaneous, just because he lacked the boundaries of fixed character. "The real purpose of my *Confessions* is to reveal precisely my inner response to all the situations of

my life. It is a history of my soul that I have promised."
It is this "inner life" precisely that has no limits or
imaginary lines. It was this, as he proclaimed, that made
him different from those that he knew. "I dare believe
that I am different from all creatures that ever existed."

Hence Rousseau is never quite able to recognize himself, either in his acts or in his memory. For his imagination, that lived in a world of its own dimensions, is constantly being surprised and shocked by the real world
when his foot slips. The imaginative world becomes for
such as he the real world. "Oh, if one could only keep a
record of the dreams of the feverish, what glorious and
sublime things would come at times from his delirium."
It is no wonder that when he tried to bring them to earth
and give them intelligible names that he became bewildered and lost his tongue. No wonder that he could never
recognize himself in his own everyday acts; when the
world in which he was at home was the fourth dimension
of his imagination. He is always at a stand with hands
raised in shocked surprise at the painful paradox of the
splendor of his imagination and the pitiful reality of
his sordid doings. He is the splendid prince set to a menial
task in which he is constantly blundering.

But he will never be other than convinced that the
world is interested in this prince, and will be edified by
his painful blunderings. And he calls for the world's pity
in the most melodious of music. His book has for its
subject his beautiful, battered, just self. His agony is
the result of the world's unfeeling obliquity. Now the
world must do him the belated justice of edified interest
and pity. If they will not hear, like Job he will rise and
present his indictment before the throne of the Almighty.
Even God may be "bluffed" by his unique importunity.
"Whenever the last trumpet shall sound, I will present

myself before the Sovereign Judge . . . and loudly proclaim, thus have I acted."

If he has not kept faith with life, at least he never faltered in his faith in his imagination. "One can never dream how my heart burns for the creatures of my imagination." If judged by the real he falls short, there has been no faltering in the ideal. There he will rest his case and be content. And the whole of the nineteenth century has heard the echoes of his voice.

A true appreciation of Rousseau in his relation to the coming century turns upon a definition of reality. The whole of the preceding century and much of the seventeenth had been diligently exploring the world of objective and tangible fact and science. Realities to these were the observable and measurable and partly controllable things of physics, social and economic science, and ethics, things that could be reduced to objective formulas. Here to the successors of Montaigne was the nature that could be carefully observed and disciplined to human uses. It was governed by common sense and intelligence, the thing Pascal defined as the *esprit géometrique* and the *esprit de finesse*, man's logic or man's more refined and disciplined intuition. But pure imagination this age learned by bitter experience to distrust; and I quote Pascal: "This is the deceptive faculty in man, the mistress of error and lies, and the more tricky because she is not so always; for she would be an infallible test of truth, if she were infallible against error."

Now it was precisely in this objective world of science and of economic society that Rousseau found himself a homeless and unwelcome vagabond. "My indifference for objective fact freezes my pen and silences my mind. . . . I never can write except as passion dictates." And when his imagination takes fire and soars, of what seventh heaven does it not feel itself native?

"A spirit lost in this immensity, I could not think, or reason, or philosophize, but with a kind of voluptuous delight I felt myself overwhelmed with the weight of this universe. I freed myself with rapture from the confusion of these great ideas; I loved in imagination to lose myself in space; my heart bound up in the confines of things found itself too straitened; I was suffocating in the universe. I longed to thrust myself into the infinite. I believe that if I had laid bare all the mysteries of nature I should have felt myself in a less delightful situation than this stupefying ecstasy, in which my spirit freed itself without restraint, and which in the agitation of my transport made me some times cry aloud, 'Presence ineffable!' without the power of farther speech or thought."

The ideal or the imaginative good, true, beautiful, these are the ultimate realities. They are the Absolute. In these there can be no evil. So he will not compromise with an objective world, association with which brings only pain, and which in consequence must be evil. The problem then for a genius, and of his uniqueness for the task he has no doubts, is to restore to humanity this absolute world of beauty, truth and goodness from which somehow human nature has allowed itself to be alienated. Evil has gained a tremendous headway; with every new victory of science its realms have been expanded. Can its ultimate triumph be arrested or delayed? Can man be spiritually rejuvenated? But all this calls for a revolution or even a series of revolutions, revolution guided by battle-cries of nobler and truer living. What shall be for him its leading motives?

I have called Rousseau an absolutist. First he is convinced of the absolute goodness of man at heart, the absolute goodness of nature, and the absolute nature of evil. Evil has gained a very large victory over good in human life, and above all in human institutions. The human heart, at least in its deepest instincts, is yet unspoiled, though its utterance has been choked by the lush weeds of evil. But nature is uncorruptible, and where man has not laid violent hands upon it can still offer its healing. Rousseau will therefore make his appeal to nature. Back then to nature. How often this cry is going to resound in the earlier decades of the century.

All of this study by Rousseau of what is implied by a return to nature is utterly different from the cool contemplation of an objective problem by an abstract philosopher. Rousseau is not a Plato or an Aristotle, far from it. In more than one place, as we have seen, he tells us how his mind works, not with thoughts but with passions. For example, "I never have thought things out, I have always felt them." And the next will tell you how he feels: "At the time when the noble prospect of liberty elevated my soul, those of equality, of brotherhood, of sweetness of manners, melted me to tears, and stirred me with keen regret to have lost all these blessings." This is hardly thinking by logic. If his work has a logic it is a logic of the emotions, and if it appears as a system it will be the result of a rationalization of his spontaneous moods.

Nothing in all literature is a more striking illustration of this fact than the story as he tells it of his first conversion to his faith. In its way it is as dramatic and as sudden as the conversion of Saint Paul. A vagabond musician and teacher of music, with an opera under his arm and the stirrings of nomadic discomfort in his heart, he is trying to find himself in Paris and its world of society, intrigue, and letters. Instinctively he hates the city. As instinctively he loves nature. He hates society as a denial of nature equally instinctively. Boiling always with emotional vagaries, he lights upon a notice of a prize which the Academy of Dijon is offering on the alluring theme, "Has the Restoration of the Arts and Sciences had a Purifying Effect upon Morals."

The question was like a flash of lightning. It clove the shadows, and in a moment everything stood for him clear and convincing. He had discovered the secret of life. The experience was overwhelming. Now for him, as for Saint Paul, God and Devil, man and nature, evil and good, guilt and innocence, stood forth clearly revealed in their own essence. There can be no compromise when a man thus in a supernal vision gets a witness of the truth. Feeling and knowing from now on to Rousseau were inseparable, and he must become the missionary, a bishop *in partibus infidelium*. It is not by way of jest that to this his book, that proved beyond a shadow of doubt that progress in the arts and in the sciences has contributed steadily to man's degeneration and unhappiness, he put as motto: *"Barbarus hic ego sum, qui non intelligor illis."* [1]

Civilization, then, as it has been practiced is bad, proud as it has been of its new arts and rapidly growing sciences.

"Let men learn for once that nature would have preserved them from science, as a mother snatches a dangerous weapon from the hands of her child. Let them know that all the secrets she hides are so many evils from which she protects them, and that the very difficulty they find in acquiring knowledge is not the least of her bounty towards them. Men are perverse; but they would have been far worse, if they had had the misfortune to be born learned."

Back then to nature, which has ever striven to protect man from the evils of science. All of his subsequent work is a prophetic making straight the way for the return.

[1] From Ovid. Here I stand a barbarian, because I am misunderstood by men. The account that Diderot gives of this 'conversion' differs in many important particulars. But of its being the critical moment in Rousseau's life there can be no doubt.

In all this Rousseau is the man of one motive, but a powerful one, a crystallization of all the doubts and bewilderments the new world of science and industry was gathering in its train. The rich with their new weapons of science were becoming richer, and the poor in their weakness poorer; greed, luxury, ambition were flourishing at the cost of the natural virtues of love and innocence that should be the motives of social life. Nature is affectionate and generous and naïve; but it has been displaced by hatred, greed and disingenuous sycophancy. How shall mankind return, or if return be impossible, can new institutions be devised that will be more in accord with nature? Karl Marx asked the same questions. And in one form or another the nineteenth century and our own time have been uncomfortably puzzling in the same search.

Rightly he begins with the individual. The individual is sacred, he is an absolute. He is convinced of this by the evidence of his own personality. But man can be so circumstanced as to respond morally, that is naturally instead of viciously. So Rousseau planned though he never executed a separate treatise on morals.

But morals are only half the story, and have to do only with the mechanics, the external form, of virtue. Below is the heart, the source of moral impulses, the feeling heart which with him responds with ecstasy at the vision of human happiness. Only put oneself and one's actions in accord with it and let its dictates become principles of action and the trick is turned. "Before," Rousseau confesses, "I had been good. After this I became virtuous, or at least intoxicated by virtue." The same thought is more gently insinuated in the *Profession of Faith of the Savoyard Vicar*. "They tell us that the conscience is the work of prejudice; but I know by my own experience that it struggles to follow Nature in preference to all the laws of man. . . . Oh, happy young man! She has not yet spoken in your ear! may you live long in this happy state where her voice is the voice of innocence." How often Wordsworth will repeat this poetic thought. The instincts of childhood, sacred childhood, and its "natural piety," how can they be rescued in childhood, fostered in youth, and preserved for mature age? So his most famous work is the *Émile*, not so much a book on education as a plea for the naïve and unspoiled in human nature, and the means of keeping it unsullied in an evil and machine age.

Compare it with Montaigne's essay on education, and one sees at a glance the glacial epoch that separates these two great men. They no longer speak the same language. They begin with wholly contradictory definitions of human nature. But each has behind him a life so utterly different from the other's. Montaigne, the boy reared so tenderly by an affectionate father, the success-crowned youth, the warm friendship with La Boétie, the rich experience in politics and at court, leisure, friendship, and wisdom born so lightly—what though the times were perilous?—he has learned to live secure with his home, his study, his friends. Rousseau, abandoned in his boyhood, with an imagination already on fire with the impossible, farmed out to inhospitables, a reluctant apprentice, with never a warm friend, a vagabond when most boys have not yet heard of the world, playing fast and loose at the deadly game of making a living, religion tossed at him like dice to be gambled with, meeting with generosity only once, and that neither intellectual nor moral, and never to know a secure home. The wisdom he learned was that of the protective coloring of the insect or of the cunning of the fox. What a different outlook on the world of these two men. No wonder the differences when they would train youth to meet life.

To Montaigne life is a thing that must be rightly understood; to Rousseau to be rightly transformed.

And in consequence the story of the *Émile* is that of the withdrawal of the child from the world, that his natural goodness might receive its richest development in harmonious surroundings. The teacher, like Nature, makes these to correspond with his advancing curiosity and aptitude. Everything not in harmony, every distraction, every real paradox or contradiction, is carefully put out of his little artifice of beauty, truth, goodness. Is not Rousseau thinking of the golden age his vagabond childhood never was allowed to know? [2]

Natural goodness, is not this to become the emotional motive for the renewed faith in democracy? Hence also for the largest possible degree of liberty, for liberty is the necessary corollary in a society where all are by nature good. But does not this also require the ultimate belief in human equality, that is, in the equal uniqueness and the equal rightness of the demands of human nature? Liberty, equality. The other word in the motto of the French Revolutionists is a necessary corollary. For if all are free and all equal in a state, and force can no longer be employed as a motive for social conduct, there is nothing left but love, fraternity.

Rousseau's doctrine of the absolute individual, though as a philosophical idea the thing may be much older, as an impelling motive completely transformed, not only the ideals of education, but went farther and gave the battle cry to the French Revolution, and to many a later revolution in the nineteenth century, as we shall note in the sequel. Rousseau's personal vagabond discomfort in

[2] I have refrained from an analysis of the *Émile*. There is not a course of lectures on Education that does not describe it minutely. There is not a kindergarten that does not caricature its ideal. It is nearly as obvious as romantic childhood; and nearly as convincing.

the complex life of his time brought on an emotional conversion, which became a philosophy, a settled conviction,
and a creed for much of the activity of the century and a
half that succeeded. In this respect at least Rousseau is the
Saint Paul of the new age.

And to give a picture of the ideal society, of man and
woman and friends, which might serve as the model for
the whole of perfect intercourse, when love and respect
and piety are the motives, he wrote the novel *The New
Heloïse*. This is the first time, I believe, in history that
the novel is used as an instrument of propaganda. But it
is going to breed a horde of successors; for its wide scope
and ample opportunity for comment and illustration is
going to show it to be the most powerful of weapons for
influencing and propagating ideas.

For his characters are not characters at all, but states
of emotion, as is the chief character, the only character, of
the *Confessions*. He is in no way attempting a picture of
life, but of an emotional conflict that led to peace. And
for a background there is nature, always in complete harmony with the chief character, like the accompaniment of
deep orchestral tones to the chant of the priest. Or to
change the figure, it is a series of pictures, such as one
long ago put up in nurseries—the good-morning, cheer-
ful smile of the awakening child, and the good-night of
the child peacefully asleep, as a memento to children of
the purpose of nurseries and the proper behavior of children therein.

But with all this, it is today an impossible book for any
except the scholarly student of Rousseau. In his own
time it was an amazing phenomenon, a best seller, and it
was followed by the horde of *Paul and Virginias*, and the
other sentimental stories of love and renunciation and of
nature ministering to the needy. But it is all so remote

today, for without a plot, in interminable letters of one character to another, in the manner Richardson made popular, and gushing an oil well of sentiment that today seems dry, it bores the modern reader, who lays the novel away before it is rightly begun.

The very object of the book, in the author's own words, seems today almost an indecent excursion into the author's own privacy. He wrote it "to give free wings to his desire to love which he had never been able to satisfy and by which he felt himself consumed." The frustration complex and compensation. The story is filled with the pictures of the women he loved, places he had known; and the chief place, Clarens, is the spot to which in imagination he was ever returning. It is in truth an autobiographical novel, but of the life which in his reveries he was ever pursuing and never, except for rarest moments, to capture.

Indeed St. Preux, the hero, is Rousseau, the affectionate, who has fallen in love with the forbidden, the unattainable; for to have captured love and to have domesticated it and breakfasted and supped with it would have soiled its celestial habiliments. Julie d'Etange is the lady of his dreams, the girl to whom St. Preux is tutor, and with whom he promptly falls in love. Had Rousseau studied the story of Abelard and Eloïse? The father, seeing the discrepancy in rank, makes light of romantic attachment and weds her to Wolmar. And now the impossible love story proceeds. The husband is generous, even when he learns of the inclinations of both. St. Preux is self-effacing, Julie, etherial always, dies that the romantic music might be low and sweet with melody. And the story ends with all romantically purged, all that are left alive, and purified.

There is no realism here. No real passion, no real character. Julie is not Juliet, least of all Eloïse. St. Preux is no Romeo, least of all Abelard. They are, as said before, personifications of virtuous and affectionate emotions. So is Wolmar, he is virtuous wisdom. It is really a morality play we have in these long letters, in which the author exploits the virtues that should exist in a regenerated society, when the golden age is renewed and men can live according to their inner goodness, and be bored by soft music and softer affection. It is Rousseau's own comment on his turbid youth and young manhood, when his virtue, forever thwarted, showed itself only in its remorse for its dirty hands and feet. But it is precisely because this book does postulate the humanly divine in human nature, that it was so potent, and became the ancestor of a long line of romantic novels and their heroes and heroines. Like St. Preux and Julie, the people of romance for some generations to come are going to be actors in morality rôles in edifying spectacles, instead of the real characters of Shakespeare or Fielding.

Man then is by nature good, if only a background can be discovered in which his goodness can be allowed to prevail. The order of nature is good. How can man find himself in coöperation with it? "Everything is good as it comes from the Author of all things, everything degenerates in the hands of man." It is human institutions then that have been sadly mishandled. For "man is born free; and everywhere he is in chains." Nor can man— Rousseau is clear sighted enough to perceive this—do as he or Wordsworth did, turn one's back and retire to Westmoreland and nature or the Hermitage, and become automatically restored. Can institutions be devised which will be more in accordance with nature? This problem Rousseau attacks in the *Social Contract*.

And the pattern for these, is it not to be discovered in

every happy family, or in such happy social units as the *New Heloïse?* Really the thing is absurdly easy, in theory, as every reformer since Rousseau has triumphantly proclaimed. Discover the general will, the *volonté general*, the absolute, elemental desire of all, stripping away the relative, the accidental, the *volonté de tous*, the selfish desire of the each or the many; discover means for the absolute will making itself felt, and for restraining the selfish or the relative, and the trick is turned. In the democracies that experimented with the Rousseau formula, the device of the majorities was set up to ascertain the *volonté general*, which states Rousseau consistently condemned; and he set up something a trifle more obscure and even perhaps ominous.

The state must give back to the individual the rights and liberties of which he has been defrauded. But this is achieved by a curious redefinition of the word liberty. Man must give up his will as an individual and join in the will of the all, the *volonté general*, that is, by willing only those things that all should desire. Any thing that is good only for a few, or a clique, or a party, is *per se* not good for the all. Then what is this general good except the thing we are today, with dismay some, with acclamation others, calling the aim of the totalitarian state? Rousseau, naïvely perhaps, but no less ruthlessly, ignores the very freedom that he began by so passionately cherishing. It is a little hard to see the Rousseau of the *Confessions* in the distilled Rousseau of the *Social Contract*, the Rousseau who here is preaching social uniformity.

Or, to put it in another way, man is moved by two motives, *amour propre* and *amour de soi*. The first is the natural love of self, the quite instinctive and quite proper universal love of self-expression, the natural right to be an individual; the other is the acquired desire to exalt oneself at the expense of one's fellows, by greed, excessive ambition, love of property, and the other evil motives that came with the institution of civil institutions based upon property. (Rousseau is a socialist by instinct and not by logic.) The *amour propre* leaves the individual with but the single motive, to live according to nature, the *volonté general; amour de soi* divides the state into warring factions, parties, cliques as their particular motives criss-cross or ally themselves with others like them, and these it is that divide a state by the conflicting *volontés de tous*. The one preserves the welfare of all the individuals, the other promotes the welfare of only the victorious, and reduces the others to a species of slavery. The will of nature is to promote equally and uniformly the well-being of all, the absolute or totalitarian state. [3]

How then shall this will of the absolute state, the *volonté general*, get itself expressed? To this practical question Rousseau gives only the vaguest of answers. The *volonté de tous*, the complex of the individual wills, expends itself upon particulars, it groups itself into cliques and parties. These differences must be ignored, and in practice they will tend to neutralize each other. But after they have like the Kilkenny cats devoured each other there will a residue remain, the pure *volonté general*. "If when the people, sufficiently informed, deliberate without communication and in complete independence of one another, then from the large number of little differences will come always [a common agreement] as a result of the general will, and the deliberation will always be good."

This is excellent practical advice to a practical politician! But there is a saving reservation. There is always

---

[3] It will be curious, if one wishes, to contrast this theory that Rousseau considers natural, with a later definition of the natural theory of survival, of which there will be something said later. But Rousseau is never more anti-scientific than in his social and ethical postulates.

in the offing the arch-prophet, the Jean Jacques perhaps, to act as the interpreter or diviner of the general will. Rousseau calls him the legislator, the man who can interpret the general will. "Of itself the people always wills the good, but of itself it by no means always sees it. . . . This makes a legislator necessary. . . . The great soul of the legislator is the only miracle that can prove his mission." The leader of the people, the *duce* or the *fuehrer;* and with him Rousseau's argument comes to full circle. Thus people in history to preserve their liberties have chosen their Sauls to be king.

Yet this summary is not quite fair to Rousseau. For what the prophet is seeking in the general will is something essentially moral, something affecting the will, and not economic or political organization. He would educate for the moral factors, or motives in human conduct. When in conflict with the other motives of an economic or political nature these are usually, he would say, submerged, and to allow them free expression nothing short of a complete revolution in human nature and human society is necessary. He at times will even ask whether such a transformation is possible; and it is here, possibly, that he is farthest from the reformers of the state of today and the social and economic revolutionaries. It is not the forgotten man he is interested in, or the "new deal," but the forgotten moral motive and the new education. Rousseau would be as lost in Communism as in Fascism as we know these today.

For it is not the logical constitution that Rousseau devises in the *Social Contract* that made it and still makes it one of the most potent influences of the century. By itself the thought would not have sent Europe into the orgy of humanitarian reform and constitution making; nor was it either quite novel or unattractive to the blasé eight-

eenth century. The secret of Rousseau's power lies in
the absolute nature of his creed, and in the potency of
feeling that was its motive, the profound emotional conviction that the soul of man is by nature good. This is
not an intellectual conviction subject to the premise or
conclusion of any logical syllogism. It is not in the last
analysis even a moral conviction, but is the overflowing of
a heart that cannot help loving the creatures of its imagination. And Rousseau never doubted the utter justice
and validity of his feelings.

It is for this reason that the prophet's ideas on children,
or on men and women, on the state of society, on nature
and man's relations to nature, all became a species of
mystical religion destined to purge the will and set the
world free for the ultimate triumph of good. His vision
of things was all in black and white, truth forever on the
scaffold, fraud forever on the throne. The thing was un-
thinkable, if only one had the ecstatic vision of good and
truth and beauty as the only essentially real, and evil,
fraud, and ugliness as an accident. The restoration of
man then was in effect a crusade, and those engaged a new
soldiery of a new religion, the religion of the man divine.
How splendid to be enrolled in the army of the eternal
verities. The thought and the conflict were intoxicating.

As an emotional motive to reform of the individual,
of society, as a motive to the search for the gates of a
new Garden of Eden for society, Rousseau is in the full
stream of the restless and revolutionary nineteenth century. He began the restless tinkering with the ideals and
the machinery of education, but behind this also is his
and the nineteenth century's trust that by education the
intelligence and will of the citizen can be assured for the
welfare of society. He inspired the nineteenth century

confidence in constitutions for insurance against social evils. He began the unending list of tendency novels which would in their living panorama of society point the way for better living. *Uncle Tom's Cabin,* and many to come earlier and later follow the path of *The New Heloïse,* the novel with a moral pistol in its pocket.

Above all he was the first to betray a loss of faith in the new sciences, of physics and economics, which were shaking man's confidence in his moral prerogative and reducing him to a plaything of natural law. The old faiths were dying, who shall discover for man a new? Rousseau was the first to turn his back on science and in its spite to search in man's own soul for a new emotional science, a science of the unique self-expression of the human heart. Again we turn to the words of the Savoyard Vicar: "Follow nature in preference to the laws of man. Oh, happy young man! She has not yet spoken in your ear; may you live long in this happy state when her voice is the voice of innocence."

These are almost the words of Virgil to Dante as the poets ascend through the portals of the Terrestrial Paradise. But Dante had had his vision purified, his intellect made unerring and his heart fortified by the sojourn in Hell and Purgatory. For Rousseau these earlier disciplines are a painful irrelevance.

III. THE ROMANTIC QUEST

"When aloft, I find myself always alone. No one speaketh with me; the frost of solitude maketh me tremble. What do I seek on the height?"

NEITZSCHE—*Thus Spake Zarathustra*

THOSE who have watched even from a secure distance the social upheavals in the past half a generation in Russia, and the threatened upheavals and land-slips in other regions of Europe, can easily put themselves in imagination back in the last decades of the eighteenth century and the first decades of the nineteenth and quiver again with the sense of social and individual insecurity. Indeed in spirit we are terribly close to the Terror that sent its shudder through all Western Europe in those days of falling dynasties, the ruin of old and established houses and institutions, the flight of the dispossessed, yes, and the dawning of new hopes and confident trust in new deals and novel constitutions, that kept imaginations alert in spite of disasters and wars and the uprooting of old faiths. For it was felt by some that a new humanity was being born of all these pangs; and also by others that this was the end of time, the war of all peoples that was to precede the dissolution of society and the triumph of darkness.

The transformation that has taken place in Russia in

our decades is in a way far less momentous than the changes Europe as a whole saw and felt in the years that separated the death of Rousseau from the end of the first half of the nineteenth century. The Russian Revolution has in the main been social and economic, and the route had long been charted by prophets and teachers, who were none the less significant because their contemporaries called them fantastic dreamers. But in far less than a life time at the beginning of the nineteenth century the transformations in Western Europe were cataclysmic for all age-long habits of life and thought.

Yet the succession of events to a contemporary, who had been born and bred in the *ancien régime*, must have seemed so gradual, at times so imperceptible, that their significance was lost in the growing sense of insecurity and pained surprise. As to the Russian White refugees, as to us indeed who are unwilling to accept the transformations of today, it must have seemed always possible to wake up some bright morning and see the restoration of the good old days and the comforts of traditions one is always loath to abandon.

The Terror of 1793 was preceded by years of jockeying by all parties for position and influence and compromise. Even the Fall of the Bastile was an occasion for French Society to make a parade past the demolished fort-prison, and for the concessionaire to set up his booth for what then took the place of ice cream cones and hot-dogs. [1] It was a holiday and none felt that below its conviviality was the possibility of stark horror. Napoleon Bonaparte was then an obscure lieutenant of artillery who, disgusted at social distinctions in the army, had gone to bookkeeping. But in a very few years the whole feudal edifice in France and later in much of Europe was to be shaken to its fall.

[1] See Chateaubriand, *Memoirs*, Part I, Book 5.

For even in 1789 the National Assembly, quoting Rousseau, planned an unheard of constitution for France.

"Men are born and remain equal in rights. Social distinctions can only be founded upon the general good." "Law is the expression of the general will. Every citizen has a right to participate, personally or through his representative, in its formation. It must be the same for all." "No person shall be accused, arrested, or imprisoned except in the cases and according to the forms prescribed by law." "No one shall be disquieted on account of his opinions, including his religious views, provided that their manifestation does not disturb the public order established by law." "The free communication of ideas and opinions is one of the most precious of the rights of man. Every citizen may, accordingly, speak, write and print with freedom, being responsible, however, for such abuses of this freedom as shall be defined by law." "The rights of man had been misconceived and insulted for centuries and are reëstablished for all humanity in this declaration, which shall serve as an everlasting war cry against oppressors."

Then the long wars, almost incessant wars, from the early nineties to the Battle of Waterloo—wars that spread their battle fields from Moscow to Spain and the West Indies to the Pyramids; wars dominated by the glory and terror of Bonaparte. A generation of battles and treaties and constitutions and tumbled crowns. Then the Peace of Paris and the attempt by Metternich to set back the hands of the clock and restore absolutism. The old institutions seemed to awake from a bad dream and to make discourse as they had done in the good old days. But the paving stones of Paris were torn up for barricades again in 1830, and again in 1848. New constitutions were made. England passed the Reform Bill of 1832, the year when Goethe, the last of the Old Europe died; and Modern Europe seemed to settle down to set its new house in order, and to accommodate itself to the new tradition of democracy.

But all this while other new institutions were being forged to take their place amid the debris of the old order.

These were the years when the new sciences put on their modern dress. Modern chemistry, modern physics, modern biology were all having their formulas set and defined in these days; and more and more the scientific logic was displacing the old logic in men's methods of thought. And the social sciences, economics and history, were at last looked upon as inevitable descriptions of human institutions, as inevitable as the descriptive formulas of physics and chemistry. And all this reign of uniform natural law was as devastating to the tender in conscience then as the psychology of Freudism is today. How can the unique human soul escape the meshes of this all embracing net of science? The thought was terrifying.

And to complete the picture of the rude transformations of those days came the new invention of steam and power machinery to destroy the old social order and to found the new industrial order in factories and crowded cities. The old rural peasantry had been largely freed by the gradual breakdown of the feudal manorial system. But here was a new class, now to be called the proletariat, that the new constitutions seemed somehow to overlook. They are going to have an increasing influence on all thoughtful imaginations. At least they and the smoke and grime and ugliness of their places of work and the dens in which they find shelter are not beautiful.

The old certainties, the old landmarks have disappeared under the flood of the revolution; the new have not yet appeared or are just beginning to take on unpleasant or forbidding shape. The imagination at a time like this cannot accept things as they are, still in formation. Man, society, nature once in relationship have become estranged and are seeking new bonds with each other and new knowledge. The challenge for the poet and novelist is for a new point of view, a new perspective so that the claims of each will be mutually accommodated—science, industry, society, man. There are two possible alternatives. A realistic looking of the new facts in the face, as a preliminary and necessary state of knowledge before any attempt can hope to be successful to control them or to find a pattern in them. Yet strangely, though this would seem to be the first and most necessary step, it is going to be the last to be attempted.

The more easy alternative is the turning of one's back on the whole ugly and unpleasant business, and retiring into one's own inner life, and then sharply drawing the door between the everyday world of outer reality and the inner world of one's dreams and ideals. And this is all the easier, for what can be more profitable than the contrast between the ideal and the real, between the poet's imagination and the ugly world of every day science and business? In this inner world at least the poet can be free and assert his moral humanity. And who can tell, now that science has created a new objective world of doubt, if the inner world of the creative imagination cannot be after all the truer reality? At least it will be more beautiful and better; and if Beauty be cognate with Truth, and Goodness also be cousin to Truth, how can the third member of the trinity, Truth, be absent? [2]

Thus it came about, a thing that will be discussed also later, that there came to be in the nineteenth century a conflict between the world of science and the world of poetry—the thing already noted in Wordsworth. And science and literature were for a time to go each its own way, to the hurt of both. But this is a long story.

All of the effects of the Revolution, as I said, did not come suddenly, nor was their discomfort felt by all in

[2] The German Romantic School discovered a philosophic basis for the answer yes to these questions.

equal proportion. But no one in the first quarter of the century was as sensitive to their presence as the French *émigré*, Count Chateaubriand, or the English son of a Tory baronet, Shelley. Not that they responded in the same way, quite the contrary. But both are peculiarly of their own age, and both show how ardent youth was driven into poetic utterance by the birth of a new world. And both were children of the same father, Rousseau.

Of the two Chateaubriand is the elder and follows closest in his father's footsteps. Where Rousseau pointed with the finger of admiration at the primitive savages, Chateaubriand will lay off his western finery and, in imagination if not wholly in fact, emigrate to their idyllic society. Here at least his soul, wearied and distressed by the blatent new, will be able to feed its imagination and shed tears amid scenes of nature's peace. Humanity losing itself in nature that it may find its natural heritage in the warm deluge of natural emotions, such is one escape from reality, and a fashionable one.

A new humanity, the belief that out of the chaos of revolution a regenerated man, the Promethean man, would emerge triumphant over error, secure in his natural goodness, the ideal of the new democracy: here was another escape from the clutch of ugly reality. The previous century had believed in democracy; many in the beginnings of this century were to offer themselves up on the altar of its devotion.

> "A prince can make a belted knight,
>   A marquis, duke, and a' that;
> But an honest man's aboon his might,
>   Guid faith he mauna fa' that!
>   For a' that, and a' that,
>   Their dignities and a' that,
>   The pith o' sense, and pride o' worth,
>   Are higher rank than a' that."

This is not political democracy and reform, as much as the idealistic conviction that in the average man may be discovered the hero of the future.

Shelley has been called the poet of idealized democracy. His is an emotional conviction. But the note is sounded over and over again, even where one might least expect it. Some of Walter Scott's best characters are his lesser folk. Old-fashioned Tory that he is, fashioned in the mold of the eighteenth century, he believes in a certain fundamental sanctity in mankind. We remember the Highland vassal who demands the privilege of taking his chief's place on the scaffold. Who can forget Jeannie Deans, Edie Ochiltree, and the others in humble life, who are yet true aristocrats? Manzoni, in Italy, a follower of Scott, writes an historical novel and makes the hero and heroine the inconspicuous whom history never mentions. Dickens—Dickens is all average humanity, idealized of course, and sentimentalized as it will be if like Rousseau one writes with one's emotions.

At the same time all the world was watching the experiment in America, and sending over some of its best scholars to tell its story. Goethe introduces the experiment in American democracy into his conversations, and writes the conclusion of Faust under the inspiration of new traditions. De Tocqueville does a close-up portrait of American Democracy that is going to stand unrivalled until the study by James Bryce. And this democracy is going to have its own poet who, to Europe at least, is going to sing its buoyant and vociferous faith.

Yet this idealization of the average man is an escape from, or a closing of the eyes to, the new and growing complexity of life. It is a faith in a happier future, not a struggle with the present. In some, as in Scott and Manzoni, the scenes will be laid in the past, an imaginary past perhaps with Scott, where the present problem cannot intrude. Even Whitman will not deal much with cities, or the problems of the new industry. He prefers "the open road" and the breath of natural freedom. Shelley with the wings of his imagination will take us beyond the bounds of time and space and show us the poet's dream; and yet one not wholly different from Dante's vision.

There is yet another road for escape from the bewilderment and discomfort of fact—the road of philosophy and metaphysics. Plato once tried something that suggests it in the *Republic* where he planned a perfect state, and reluctantly confessed that perhaps humanity was not yet ready for the venture. "In heaven there is laid up a pattern of it, methinks, which he who desires may behold, and beholding, may set his own house in order. But whether such an one exists, or ever will exist in fact, is no matter; for he will live after the manner of that city, having nothing to do with any other." On this pattern that is laid up against the day when man is ready, might be designed a state that would bring happiness to all.

But the new metaphysics is going to try to read the present by an eternal pattern and find the present good. Plato found the present bad, and held up the eternal pattern as a model for improvement. The new is going to try to accept the present *sub specie aeternitatis.* If we could only see the present complex as a full panorama stretching across history as a design worked by immutable law, then, though we might see momentary distress, we would understand that in the fullness of time pain brings progress, and nature justifies even its tragedies. This is splendid—for thoroughgoing minds that won't compromise with Eternal Law and can understand its mystery. But it is going to be a hard road for tender consciences.

Yet the noble effort was made and at least one philosopher poet and one writer of poetic tragedy deserve serious consideration—and both are receiving it in full measure.

The other alternative, to face the facts, though the more obvious effort, was almost in every instance the last to be tried. Realism. There is an excellent reason why the realistic novel should have come to its own in Russia. There were, to be sure, Balzac and Thackeray, to name only two, who had ventured realistic studies, but their manner was yet more that of the romantic. The realist's quest of fact that he might by it understand life utterly, the conviction that only from the fact could a theory of life be discovered, this can only occasionally be seen in their books. Russia opened the doors of the imagination to the flood of human fact, external and internal, man's outer life of action and failure, and man's inner life of emotion and impulse. And Tolstoi and Dostoevsky, as the greatest gifts of Russia to the world, undertake in this welter to discover the meaning of life.

Behind all this romantic quest of man's destiny, whether by flight from the bewilderment of reality or by resolute study of fact, is the certainty that life is worth while for its own sake, and more, that man somehow has a superior destiny that science can't touch or discover. Human nature, human moral law, human life, these are things that the scientist may talk about, but never capture with his formulas or drag into his laboratories. There is the zest of real adventure about the struggles of all of these men that makes them in truth the protagonists of human liberty, or at least of its human significance. Above all there is inspiring them, even the most mordant, an optimistic faith in human destiny.

IV. THE MAN WITHOUT A COUNTRY

CHATEAUBRIAND

"Mon enfant, je voudrais que le père Aubry fût ici: il tirait du fond de son cœur je ne sais quelle paix qui, en les calmant ne semblait cependant point étrangère aux tempêts; c'était la lune dans une nuit orageuse: les nuages errants ne peuvent l'importer dans leur course; pure et inaltérable, elle s'avance tranquille au-dessus d'eux. Hélas, pour moi, tout me trouble et m'entraine!"

CHATEAUBRIAND, René

"Mon chagrin était devenu une occupation qui remplissait tous mes moments." My melancholy became an obsession that occupied my every moment. This curious sentence, curious to us today, but utterly and naïvely appropriate then, is almost a motto for the best in Chateaubriand. He is a figure of naïve and proud *ennui,* and he never lets us forget it. He seems designed for the symbol of world-weariness, always seeking and never able to find the peace and repose for which his spirit longs, but which he with his sophistication knows has never existed, for such as he. We can call it the *mal de siècle,* the *mal romantique,* the illness of the romantic age, but that makes it none the less interesting and instructive.

Some authors are as interesting in their personalities as they are in their works. Such was Goethe, such in all probability was not Shakespeare, such certainly was René, the Vicomte Chateaubriand. The story of his life, as he recounts it in his *Memoirs from Beyond the Tomb,* reveals as interesting a character astray in the world as his personifications of himself in the *Atala* and *René.* Both are equally studies of the man trying to find himself in a world suddenly gone unfamiliar and uncongenial, and, failing the effort, to find some substitute in the world of imagination. This was also Rousseau; but the Genevan was a homeless, footloose vagabond without position and without friends; Chateaubriand is a nobleman of the *ancien régime,* a soldier, traveller, man of affairs, and diplomat, and pet in the best salons of all European capitals. So these two will wear their vagabondage with a difference. Rousseau is intimate, Chateaubriand will always have the grand manner.

The extravagant scope of this nobleman's adventures in life: his retired boyhood on the shores of Brittany, tempest lashed, fog bound, and romantic in story, where France thrusts an exploring arm into the bleak Atlantic. The gloomy castle which the half mythical traditions of the family haunt like wraiths. The somber, austere father, the affectionate mother, and the sister whose figure will never be long absent from the hero's dreams. It was a half sinister nest, wholly in the romantic tradition for his brooding imagination.

"The autumn and winter evenings were different. Supper over, the four of us would leave the table and gather round the chimney. My mother flung herself, with a sigh, upon an old couch covered in imitation Siam; a stand was put before her with a candle. I sat down with Lucile by the fire; the servants cleared the table and withdrew. My father then began a tramp which lasted till he went to bed. He was dressed in a white ratteen gown, or rather a kind of cloak, which I have seen no one wear except him. His half-bald head was covered with a big white cap that stood straight up on end. When he walked away to a distance from the fireplace, the huge hall was so badly lighted by its solitary candle that he was no longer visible; we could only hear him still walking in the darkness: then he would slowly return towards the light and gradually emerge from the dark, like a ghost, with his white gown, his white cap, his long pale face. Lucile and I exchanged a few words in a low voice when he drew nearer to us. He asked, as he passed, 'What were you talking about?' Terror-stricken, we made no reply; he continued his walk. For the rest of the evening, the ear heard nothing save the measured sound of his steps, my mother's sighs, and the murmuring of the wind."

The long reaches of the family park, more like an enchanted wood than a setting for a home, the background for the growing boy's visions of enchanting beauty and love.

"And so I built up a woman out of all the women whom I had seen: she had the figure, the hair, the smile of the stranger who had pressed me to her bosom; I gave her the eyes of one of the young girls of the village, the complexion of another. The portraits of the fine ladies of the time of Francis I, Henry IV, and Louis XIV which adorned the drawing-room supplied me with other features, and I even borrowed graces from the pictures of the Virgin that hung upon the church walls.

"This invisible charmer accompanied me wherever I went; I communed with her as with a real being; she varied in the measure of my folly: Aphrodite unveiled; Diana clad in the dew and the blue of heaven; Thalia with her laughing mask; Hebe bearing the cup of youth; sometimes she became a fairy who laid nature at my feet. I touched and retouched my canvas; I took one attraction from my beauty to replace it with another. I also changed her finery; I borrowed it from every country, every century, every art, every religion. Then, when I had completed a masterpiece, I dispersed my drawings and painted again; my one woman turned into a crowd of women in whom I idolized separately the charms I had adored when united."

Into this background he paints the story of his earliest passions. First the passionate influence of religion, a motive that will have lasting and enormous significance on his whole response to life. It is not, and never will be, a religion of creed or of conscience, but an emotion stirred

to the depths by the mysteries of the rituals and sacraments.

"Raising his hand, he pronounced the Absolution. On this second
occasion, the fulminating hand showered upon my head only the
heavenly dew; I bent my brow to receive it; my feelings partook of
the joy of the angels. I rose and threw myself upon the bosom of my
mother, who was awaiting me at the foot of the altar. I no longer
appeared the same being to my masters and schoolfellows; I walked
with a light step, my head held high, a radiant air, in all the triumph
of repentance.

"I delight in recalling these joys which my soul felt but a little
while before it became filled with the tribulations of the world. Those
who compare these ardors with the transports which I shall presently
depict, who see the same heart experiencing, within a space of three
or four years, all that is sweetest and the most wholesome in innocence
and in religion and also that is most seductive and most baneful in the
passions, will choose one of the two forms of joy; they will see in
which direction to seek happiness and, above all, peace."

Against this background flits his earliest imaginative response to the still greater mystery of death. And what
more natural, against these somber reminders of the tran-
sitoriness of life, the traditions of the past, in a world into
which the present, save in its most irrelevant aspects never
entered, than that his imagination should turn for its real
sustenance to the past. The pettiness of the present, when
even an adventure is a commercialized commonplace; the
glory of the days of old when even the commonplace was
an adventure.

These were the early ingredients that prepared the boy
for what was to follow; and it was to be a life lived in the
midst of a half-century of revolution. In Paris as a soldier
he saw the beginnings of the climax of the Revolution.
He knew its leaders. See his picture of Mirabeau:

"Too early for himself, too late for Court, Mirabeau sold himself
to the Court, and the Court bought him. He staked his reputation

for a pension and an embassy: Cromwell was on the verge of bartering his future for a title and the Order of the Garter. Notwithstanding his haughtiness, Mirabeau did not rate himself high enough. Nowadays when the abundance of cash and places has raised the price of consciences, there is not a street-boy but costs hundreds of thousands of francs and the leading honors of the State to buy. The grave released Mirabeau from his promises, and shielded him from the perils which he would probably not have been able to conquer: his life would have shown his weakness in good; his death left him in possession of his strength in evil.

"At the end of dinner, the discussion turned upon Mirabeau's enemies; I found myself by his side and had not spoken a word. He looked me in the face with his eyes of pride, vice, and genius, and laying his hand upon my shoulder, said:

" 'They will never forgive me my superiority!'

"I still feel the pressure of that hand, as though Satan had touched me with his fiery claw."

Though his heart is aroused, his head remained cool to the watchwords of liberty, equality and fraternity.

"The Revolution would have carried me away, had it not started in crime: I saw the first head carried on the end of a pike, and I drew back. Murder will never to my eyes be an object of admiration or an argument in favor of liberty; I know nothing more servile, more contemptible, more cowardly, more shallow than a Terrorist. Have I not in France seen the whole of this race of Brutus take service with Caesar and his police? The levellers, regenerators, cut-throats had been transformed into lackeys, spies, sycophants, and even less naturally into dukes, counts, and barons: such a mediaevalism! . . ."

A fantastic idea of discovering the Northwest Passage to Asia sends him to the New World, and he catches his first glimpse of the savage. Again we have a motive that will never leave his imagination cold. He meets Washington, later he is to know Bonaparte. And again the coolness of his judgment and the warmth of his admiration and detestation.

"Bonaparte is but lately dead. As I have just knocked at Washington's door, it is natural that the parallel between the founder of the United States and the Emperor of the French should occur to my mind: the more so since, at the time when I am writing these lines, Washington himself is no more.

"Washington does not, like Bonaparte, belong to the race that surpasses human stature. There is nothing astonishing attached to his person; he is not placed upon a vast stage; he is not engaged in a struggle with the ablest captains and the most powerful monarchs of the time; he does not rush from Memphis to Vienna, from Cadiz to Moscow: he defends himself with a handful of citizens in a land not yet famous, within the narrow circle of the domestic hearth. He delivers none of those battles in which the triumphs of Arbela and Pharsalia are renewed; he overturns no thrones to build up others from their ruins."

The young nobleman, still a dilettante, next is to know the bitterness of the lot of the exile, and to hear of the horrors of the Terror, as it struck one by one at friends and family. He serves as a soldier in the ill-starred effort of the Emigrés, like the White Russians of our day, to restore the tottering throne. And this experience brings new disillusionment. Then when the whole agony is over, peace restored and the monarchy re-established under a constitution, he receives his reward, ambassadorships, counsellorships, ribbons and decorations, literary honor, and a long life of travel and attempted repose.

Appropriately then, with pardonable pride, in the Preface to his *Memoirs* he surveys the moving tale of his past and pronounces judgment. Contrast his words of self-commendation with the challenge of Rousseau as he presents his *Confessions*. There is the same confession, the same pride, the same sense of uniqueness, but again with what a difference.

"I have met nearly all the men who in my time have played a part, great or small, in my own country or abroad: from Washington to

Napoleon, from Louis XVIII to Alexander, from Pius VII to Gregory XVI, from Fox, Burke, Pitt, Sheridan, Londonderry, Capo d'Istrias to Malesherbes, Mirabeau, and the rest; from Nelson, Bolivar, Mehemet Pasha of Egypt to Suffren, Bougainville, La Pérouse, Moreau, and so forth. . . .

"I have explored the seas of the Old World and the New, and trod the soil of the four quarters of the globe. After camping in Iroquois shelters and Arab tents, in the wigwams of the Hurons, amid the remains of Athens, Jerusalem, Memphis, Carthage, Grenada, among Greeks, Turks and Moors, in forests and among ruins; after wearing the bearskin of the savage and the silken caftan of the mameluke; after enduring poverty, hunger, thirst and exile, I have sat, as minister and ambassador, in a gold-laced coat, my breast motley with stars and ribbons, at the tables of kings, at the feasts of princes and princesses, only to relapse into indigence and to receive a taste of prison.

"I have been connected with a host of personages famous in the career of arms, the Church, politics, law, science, and art. I have endless materials in my possession: more than four thousand private letters, the diplomatic correspondence of my several embassies, that of my term at the Foreign Office, including documents of an unique character, known to none save myself. I have carried the soldier's musket, the traveller's cudgel, the pilgrim's staff: I have been a seafarer, and my destinies have been as fickle as my sails; a halcyon, and made my nest upon the billows.

"I have meddled with peace and war; I have signed treaties and protocols, and published numerous works the while. I have been initiated into secrets of parties, of Court and of State: I have been a close observer of the rarest miseries, the highest fortunes, the greatest renowns. I have taken part in sieges, congresses, conclaves, in the restoration and overturning of thrones. I have made history, and I could write it. . . ."

Such is Chateaubriand, always the *émigré*, always, even in his father's chateau at Combourg, the exile, the exile when he shakes off the dust of his native land before the Terror. "Je désertais un monde dont j'avais foulé la poussière et compté les étoiles." I abandoned a world where I spurned its dust and numbered its stars. His life is a perpetual search for the stars. He is always the comet without an orbit. Contrast him with Goethe with his homely duties of managing a little theatre or cataloguing the mineral resources of a little state. Contrast him with Dante, for half his life a banned exile, yet who never in imagination set his foot outside the walls of his native Florence, and yet was able to envision the tragedy and comedy of all human nature.

He will be a man without a country; and all of his works a nostalgia. His story will be the wanderings of a Ulysses who has no Ithaca, a search for a home he knows does not exist, and a peace he knows is humanly unattainable. Yet always he will discover the charmed spot that could be home, a romantic Ulysses sipping the beauty of Calypso, Circe, or Nausicaa, finding something wanting, and passing on; the *émigré* gives us one and perhaps the most obvious clue to his personality, the one that makes him most romantically thrilling; the term will give a clue, too, to all his work, whether the *Atala*, the story of the romantic savage, or the *Spirit of Christianity*, his discovery of a romantic religious faith. And as he took pained pleasure in his own accepted character of René, the world-weary wanderer, so he will take the same pained pleasure in the works of his literary imagination.

But he is a wanderer with no settled or attainable purpose. Goethe in his novel *Wilhelm Meister's Apprenticeship* gives us the story of another romantic youth who sets forth on his travels, but who uses his adventures that he may accommodate himself to life. And though the book does here and there breathe a nostalgia, like the lovely lyric, "*Kennst du das Land, wo die Zitronen bluehen*," and cries out with resentment against the weariness of the commonplace, Meister learns at last not only to accept the humdrum of living, but to glow with health in its routine.

"For nothing more exposes us to madness, than distinguishing ourselves from others, and nothing more contributes to maintain our common sense, than living in the universal way with multitudes of men. Alas! how much there is in education, in our social institutions to prepare us and our children for insanity!"

Chateaubriand on the contrary ends where Goethe's romantic hero begins, and the charm of *Atala, René* and even his *Memoirs* is largely due to his resolute refusal to compromise with the commonplace. He will at all costs remain forever aristocratically aloof and melancholic.

Judged by any commonplace standard this man is one of the heroes of history, in his way quite as significant as Leonardo, a giant in an age of giants, and worthy quite, as he prided himself in doing, to be set beside the figure of even Napoleon Bonaparte. As we watch him from his solitary and imaginative boyhood weave his career so easily, soldier and courtier, dandy, explorer, exile, school teacher and translator, diplomatist, friend of kings and trusted counsellor, supreme writer almost, one is astonished at his manifold facilities. He touches the life of his time at every angle, real and imaginary, sordid and romantic. There seems to be nothing lacking; and though in his last years his fortunes were at times clouded, he seems one, who of all his contemporaries should have been blessed with supreme content.

In all this, too, there is seen his proud, indomitable will that sustained him in the loneliness of exile, and made him turn his experience into high romance, that left him unsatisfied when victorious he received the scorned flattery of his contemporaries. He is always seeking a rôle, like an actor, that will be a more adequate expression of his personality; and finding none quite the perfect rôle to express his resentment against an uncongenial world, he spurns it and prefers the primitive savage. It is the misery in Europe that afflicts him. "Unfortunate Indians! whom I have seen wandering in the deserts of the New World, with the ashes of your ancestors! you who have afforded me hospitality, notwithstanding your wretchedness! I cannot recompense you at the present time, for I am wandering, as well as you, at the mercy of men; and, less happy in my exile, I have not brought with me the bones of my fathers." But, like Rousseau, it is not the misery of the active reformer bent on assuaging suffering, but a sentimental misery, all the reflection of his own impatient uneasiness.

But nothing is more striking at this point than his utter unlikeness to his spiritual forebear Rousseau. The prophet like Wordsworth, like Rousseau, is looking for love in huts where poor men lie and the peace that is among the lonely hills. Such bewilderment in the world and a conviction of its essential falseness look for compensation away from its turmoil. And there among the truths of nature and of natural men it discovers a magic healing, though perhaps only a momentary one. Chateaubriand, on the other hand, seeks for peace through accomplishment, through what his imagination would recognize as the supreme experience; but because all experience is mortal and finite, and the thirst of his soul infinite, this peace may never be hoped for this side of the grave. It is this ever present lack that brings *chagrin* and *ennui*, until like René he breaks forth, *"Mon chagrin était devenu une occupation qui remplissait tous mes moments."* A curious perversion,—is it not?—of the curse of Cain, who for another reason became also an exile and wanderer, bitter at life.

Irony, the irony of a romantic Prometheus, a Faust; a titantic personality aware of his giant proportions and challenging life to present it the cup that it cannot quaff. Goethe by the tragi-comedy of ever renewed experience led his Faust to know his human limitations, and to clip his wings to the attainable. Chateaubriand's wings will expand with each new flight, and his gesture of refusal of human destiny will become more imperious. For against his spiritual pride is set the narrow range that life offers of the attainable. Goliath seeks a foeman worthy of his courage and stature, and life sends forth the puny youth, David, armed with a sling and a stone. And David was ironically victorious. So life's irony will appear to this Goliath of the early nineteenth century, in spite of the long catalogue of his accomplishments. Even his victories could not minister to his pride, and his defeats at the hands of his David—what bitter cause for *chagrin* and *ennui!*

Thus the *chagrin* in the best known and the most typical of his novels *Atala* and *René* is due to the impossibility of fulfillment in this life for the hero of his soul's infinite cravings. The longing for the impossible; for the moment any longing becomes realized or possible it loses its romantic bloom, and the stature of the hero is reduced to mere common humanity. It is this fear of the banal that pursues him like a spectre all his life; it drives him into each of his activities—as a youth to search out the Northwest Passage, as a man to pit himself in act and imagination against Napoleon, as a courtier to shine in the councils of diplomats, as a traveler to plumb the depths of unknown regions, and as a poet to drink the ecstasy of a religion of imagined asceticism, or of bizarre and forbidden sin that will sting the imagination with the luxury of sorrow.

It is for this ecstatic and ascetic thrill that Chateaubriand the novelist turns his back on life which can minister only to banal and commonplace minds. With *Atala* and *René* he betakes himself to the wilderness of the New World and the simpler and more passionate souls that he finds in its solitude. The very grandeur of the scene feeds his mind with noble, unrealizable thoughts.

"In the meantime, the darkness increases: the tops of the trees are enveloped in thick mists. Suddenly the black cloud bursts, and streams of lightning fill the waste with fire. An impetuous wind breaks from its prison, mingling clouds with clouds, and forming one vast chaos. The sky opens to view at every flash, and through the crevices of the clouds are seen new heavens and burning fields of ether. The whole mass of the forest bends. What a frightful and magnificent spectacle! The lightning sets fire to the woods in divers places; the devouring element spreads, and rises in volumes of flame. Columns of fire and smoke besiege the clouds, which disgorge torrents of sulphur upon the vast conflagration.

"The roaring of the storm and of the fire, the noise of the winds, the groaning of the trees, the cries of imaginary beings, the howling of beasts, the dashing of the floods, the hissing of thunderbolts in the quenching waters; all these noises, multiplied by the echoes of the sky and the mountains, were enough to deafen the whole wilderness." [1]

Nature lifting man above the petty and conventional routine of the jarring commonplaceness of distraught Europe, in those days of the return after the Revolution. Here in these vast solitudes should brood a peace the harassed man of human affairs can never know, the peace of the majesty of nature.

Nor will human tragedy, the conflict of human passion in regions like this, be other than equally titantic. *Atala* is the story of the Indian convert to Christianity, Chactas, told to René, the world-weary, who has fled his country and civilization as a curse, and is searching for "an unknown happiness, whose phantom he pursues." And there in the forest he meets Chactas, an Indian now old and at

---

[1] It is a pity to give this and the other things like this in a crude translation. The original is poetic prose.

peace with life, from whose lips he learns the ecstasy of full renunciation. It is a story of primitive passion of primitive youth the Indian tells, that he may from his own suffering distil a moral for the restless European.

In his youth Chactas had wandered far from the Louisiana tribal haunts and been taken captive by the Seminoles of Florida.[2] There he is to be slain, but escapes by the aid of the ward of the tribe, a beautiful Indian maiden, Atala. Together they flee and when in safety confess their love. But she recoils with horror, for her mother when dying had devoted her, when yet a baby, to a life of religious celibacy. They come to the mission of a Catholic priest, who could absolve her of the vow; but the story is not one of the accomplishment of even perfect love, but of the greater ecstasy of its renunciation. And there in a cave-bower she dies; and there the Indian and the missionary dig her grave; and there the primitive savage learns that it is not the ecstasy of fulfillment that the heart craves, but the larger luxury of an infinite sorrow, whose reward alone can be infinite peace.

It is a good story, and poetically told. The wonder is that it has never become the theme of a romantic opera. For it is not the realistic details, nor the interest in character or situation, that gives this narrative its compelling charm; it is a poem in prose, with the rhythms and movements of music and above all the poignancy of emotion throughout, from the overwhelming grandeur of the forests to the final parting. Perhaps Chateaubriand's words can best convey its mood. "The heart is an instrument not quite perfect, a lyre with missing strings, and on which

[2] Chateaubriand is as careless of geography here as he is in the accounts of his travels in America in the *Memoirs*. What are time and space, anyway, among romantic friends?

we are asked to strike the notes of joy with chords consecrated to tears."

René is the sequel to *Atala*. For the European has renounced his home and buried himself in the wilderness of Louisiana. Again the aged Chactas and the restless René meet, and this time it is the younger man who tells his story. The desolate René who had tasted the life of Europe and discovered its poison. "At once everything was lost; friendship, the world, solitude. I have tasted all and all taste of death." The misery of Europe: "We of Europe, never at rest, must devise our own solitude. The more the heart is deafened by tumult, the more we hunger for peace and silence." The misery of the young man: "And after all what is it that I have learned from this trouble? Nothing of security among the ancients, nothing of beauty among the moderns. The past and the present are two incomplete statues: the one is half hidden and mutilated by the debris of the ages, the other has not yet received the perfection of the future. . . .

"A young man full of passion, seated on the lip of a volcano, and weeping over human mortality whose dwellings he scarcely sees below his feet, cannot fail to be, O venerable man, an object of your pity; but, whatever you may think of René, this image offers you a hint of his character and of his life; it is in this manner that all my life long I have had before my eyes a panorama at once immense and intangible with an abyss yawning at my side." This is all that life could offer.

No, not all. It had offered also the love of the impossible, the forbidden, the unspeakable, the fatal passion of brother for sister, and sister for brother. With Chactas, love had been made unattainable by the vows of religion, with René, by the horror of incest. And because it is the more hideously impossible, its thrill is the more hideously ecstatic. So, torn with passion, weary with the weight of the world and society and its lesser codes, René fled Europe, a region that seemed to celebrate only the triumph of death.

"Oh, power of nature and feebleness of man! a slender root fiber of a weed will often pierce the hardest marble of tombs from whence the dead, once so potent, shall never arise!

"Often a single column will rear itself lonely against the desert, as a superb thought rises, at times, within a mind overwhelmed by time and melancholy.

"I have meditated these memorials during all the fortunes and all the hours of my quest. When the same sun, which has seen the laying of the foundations of these cities, now sets in majesty, before my eyes, over their ruins; when the moon, rising in a serene sky, between two half-overthrown funeral urns, etches for me the spectral tombs. Often by the rays of that star that inspires revery, I have fancied I saw their ghosts seated all pensive at my side."

Here are two books on the luxury of sorrow, almost a piece of romantic sadism one might say, a glorification of suffering for its ecstasy. A picture of forbidden love for the exquisite pain of renunciation. Dante's lovers who had been unwise, now in torment, had the memory of happier occasions, though the memory brings its added sting. Dante can sympathize, but he must also condemn. Chateaubriand's lovers are of a different breed; and their pained renunciation, which brought its own emotional reward, would to Dante be a strange perversion of orthodox repentance. It is almost mortification of the flesh in order that the imagination may be loosed for a yet more abandoned rôle with the forbidden. Were this all that there is in Chateaubriand, though popular for an age, he would scarcely reward study today.

Nor are the characters though charged with pathetic or even tragic emotions, in any sense felt to be real. René is Chateaubriand himself, not the real Chateaubriand, but the personification of Chateaubriand the solitary, the misanthrope, the unfortunate. It is not a pose quite, but a concentration of one motive with all others carefully excluded as irrelevant. He is born out of the acute disharmony felt as an exile in London, where he learned to live in a dream world and to seek compensation for the agony of the almost menial rôle he must assume to make his daily bread. Pride is the only virtue left—to Dante a vice—but "pride," in René's own words, "is the virtue of suffering!"

So *Atala* is a companion picture of *René*. How much in her there is of Charlotte Ives, the young English girl whom he fell in love with, like St. Pierre with Lucie, we may never know. Like René she too must learn to renounce the love that is forbidden. She is the ideal of the purity of feminine beauty, unattainable, not to be contaminated by any gross embrace. Her figure may be seen in any of the feminine saints of mediaeval legend, resolution in her vow, but in all else service and lowly humility, and glowing always with the aura of saintly loveliness. But her radiance is of the other world, for this world and its followers there is the ominous warning *noli me tangere*.

These novels took France and Europe by storm. The former triumph of *Paul and Virginia* was more than duplicated, for here was also something novel. Here was tremendous passion, yet softly, romantically, poetically displayed as by music, and kept under poetic and religious control. Here was love of the forest and nature and the new world, done in a prose for which French literature, or any other for that matter, at that date, had no example. Here was a love of the primitive, the exotic primitive, the romantic savage, that even to this day has not lost its charm. But here was also a reverence and joy in the emotional power of religious faith, in a day when Roman

Catholicism was again asserting its worth, after being banished by the Revolution, that brought comfort to many a believing heart. The Catholic faith and its rituals, as an emotional creed, no longer speaking the jargon of logic or theology, but making its appeal to the human heart through the poetry of its liturgies and the magic of its asceticism. Chateaubriand sought to make the mysteries of religion as much a thing of poetic beauty as did the ancient Greeks the myths of the Olympians.

This last will explain much of the power of his *Génie du Christianisme*, the *Spirit of Christianity*. Perhaps of all his books, except the *Memoirs*, this is most characteristically Chateaubriand's masterpiece. It is as though he took his place before the altar of some mighty cathedral, and, accompanied by the chant of choristers and the roll of the organ, recounted the splendor of his mystical faith. Around him, as silent witnesses, are the effigies of saints and martyrs. Above is the last agony of the Christ immortalized as the ecstasy of devotion. The Virgin Mother, the *mater dolorosa*, the symbol of love that ever endures. All these are the themes of the new emotional religious rhapsody in which he gives form to the spirit of Christianity.

"As we were passing between two lofty walls in a lonely street, all at once the sound of an organ struck our ear, and the words of that triumphal hymn, *Laudate Dominum omnes gentes*, issued from a neighboring church; it happened to be the octave of Corpus Christi. It is impossible to express the emotion excited in us by these religious strains; it seemed as if we heard a voice from heaven saying, 'O thou of little faith, why mournest thou as those without hope? Thinkest thou that I change my mind like men? that I forsake because I punish? Instead of arraigning my decrees, follow the example of these faithful servants, who bless my chastening hand even under the ruins beneath which I crush them.'

"We entered the church just at the moment when the priest was pronouncing the benediction. Old men, poor women, and children were on their knees. We knelt down among them; our tears flowed, and from the bottom of our heart we said, 'Forgive us, O Lord, if we murmured on beholding the desolation of thy temple; forgive our overwhelmed reason! Man himself is but a decayed edifice, a wreck of sin and death; his lukewarm love, his wavering faith, his limited charity, his imperfect sentiments, his insufficient thought, his broken heart,—in short, all things about him,—are but ruins!' "

There are no dogmas here, no philosophical bases for intellectual creeds, no defense of articles of faith, no moral tests for orthodoxy of conduct. Dante in his long poem on the church, the *Divine Comedy,* lists in detail, as he performs his arduous pilgrimage through Hell and Purgatory, the vices that must be purged and the virtues that must be acquired; and in his triumphant flight through Heaven, the stages of deeper and deeper insight into the meaning of faith and hope and love and the moral virtues that equip the transformed Christian's soul. But all this is beside the mark to the emotional creed of Chateaubriand. His Christianity has no bearing, directly, upon life and conduct. It is the mystical fervor, the warm glow, that accompanies the imaginative vision of its triumphant spirits. The joy of renunciation, the passionate clinging to pain and sorrow, the ecstasy even of annihilation. It is these that the liturgies of the church celebrate, it is these last-suppers, these baptisms for a life of voluntary privation, that are its sacraments. In them the world-weary, the disillusioned with life, can for a moment forget their *"chagrin."* The book in a way is almost a eulogy of death. Here his romantic pride in suffering translates itself into a religion.

Thus in romance and romantic religion Chateaubriand provides himself and his kind with a city of refuge for the perplexed and bruised by life—a new life in a new dimension dominated by the ethereal ideals and the unattainable visions of poetry. It is a world that has no relation with conduct or with any practical considerations whatsoever. Aesthetic values alone remain, and these are to be measured only by the tensity of the accompanying thrill; and because the thrill of pain is more keen than the thrill of pleasure, pain seems to become more to be sought after than joy, or better pain and joy meet in one ecstatic embrace.

In its way this grand gesture of refusal of life was the natural reaction against the bewildering upheaval of the age when the new Europe was being made, and against the loss of security that terrified all thinking people. But the result is going to have far-reaching consequences. For the first time in the tradition of great literature, a conscious break with the life of the present is going to drive literature to cultivate the region of the pure imagination; and poetry and life are going to be openly felt to have little between them in common. The final result is going to be wholesome for neither. By some, literature will no longer be felt to have any significance for conduct, and its appreciation only a question of aesthetic taste. Life on the other hand will begin to look with suspicion on all ideas of beauty, and insist more and more on the remorselessness of the laws of science, and on the poet as a fascinating but idle entertainer.

And there is a slight measure of truth in the judgment of the practical world in the case of this weaver of imaginative pictures. There is never any intellectual bridle for any of his flights of the imagination, even the greatest. Though he can at times be quite objective and criticize with reasoned judgment, as he frequently does in the *Memoirs*, these are the moments when he is scholar, statesman, critic, a very different being from Chateaubriand the writer. There are no better criticisms of his contemporaries, strong and weak, than in his *Memoirs*. His comparison of Washington and Napoleon, written when the body of Napoleon was being conveyed to the Invalides, is a classic in character study. His discussions on the new American republic are as fine as any by the foremost historians of statecraft.

"At the same time, the United States must not be searched for that which distinguishes man above the other beings of creation, for that which constitutes his certificate of immortality and the ornament of his days: literature is unknown in the new republic, although called for by a multitude of institutions. The American has replaced intellectual by positive operations. Do not impute to him as an inferiority his mediocrity in the arts, for it is not in that direction that he has turned his attention. Cast through various causes upon a desert soil, he made agriculture and commerce the first objects of his cares: before thinking, one must live; before planting trees, one must fell them, in order to till the ground."

But all this is the work of a quite different man from the creator of *Atala* and *René* or the *Spirit of Christianity*.

He was inspired to these latter by the immediate mood of the present. *Atala* grew, not out of North America, but out of the bitter excesses of the French Revolution and his years of making a living in London. His *Spirit of Christianity* came as a direct gift of the emotions aroused in him by the death of his mother. His was the hyperaesthetic nature of a Rousseau, a nature whose overflowings are nearly a convincing proof of revelation, when one has not only the genius to feel deeply, but also the genius to give one's emotions full imaginative form. But these are also the things the practical man fears.

He came of an age that felt itself tied to no dogma or creed, or that had no dogma or creed of its own to offer in the place of those that had gone with the Revolution. In this at least he resembles many of the later generation of our post-war days. Hence the revolt, hence the impatience, hence the ceaseless search somewhere for a substitute, some impossible happiness. He cannot take the advice of Chactas, which is that of Rousseau and of Wordsworth: "In truth you must give up this your life of extravagance that is full only of sadness, happiness can be found only on the path of the lowly." Least of all could he in his religion go back to Dante's *"e'n la sua volontate è nostra pace,"* in His will is our peace. Both ways were to him closed by the events of his own lifetime. It was only in the responses of his own heart, and in its emotional stirrings, that he could find something that he could recognize as his own. So his native country becomes the world of his own building. There he can and will owe responsibility to no one. There at least he will be lord and master and feed his own lordly pride.

In thus revolting from unpleasant reality and setting up the imaginary world as the only world free to genius, Chateaubriand is going to have many who will be like him. He shows one aspect, and a large one, of the whole Romantic movement of the early nineteenth century. The German will go so far as to discover for it a complete metaphysical creed, and we will have the romance of *Heinrich von Ofterdingen* by Novalis (Friedrich von Hardenberg) who will devote his life to the search for the Blue Flower, the symbol of aesthetic perfection, and Schlegel's *Lucinda*, which will look for the same goal in quite another direction. Or in France we shall have the reveries in the presence of Nature in Sénancour's *Obermann*, or the eternal restlessness in Benjamin Constant's *Adolphe*. These four books are interesting to put together, *Obermann* and *Heinrich*, and *Lucinda* and

Adolphe, to glance at the essential and illuminating difference between the characters of the French and the German, when both find themselves in a revolt against the established order.

V. WHEN WE DEAD AWAKE

SHELLEY

"Man who man would be, must rule the empire of himself; in it must be supreme, establishing his throne on vanquished will, quelling the anarchy of hopes and fears, being himself alone."

On Political Greatness

"The world's great age begins anew,
The golden years return, . . .
The world is weary of the past
O might it die or rest at last!"

Chorus from Hellas

"Rule the empire of himself"—one of the young Percy Bysshe Shelley's earliest acts was to set a haystack on fire, that "he might have a little Hell of his own;" and all his life he was an incendiary of haystacks, to the consternation of his good old Tory father, Sir Timothy Shelley, Baronet, his conservative neighbors and all his friends. He was the "mad Shelley" at school and college, writing the pamphlet on "The Necessity of Atheism," and circulating it among the heads of the university, when all students were supposed to subscribe to the Thirty-Nine Articles of the church dogma; and for his refusal to recant or apologize, being denied the virtues of further academic discipline. The "world's great age" began anew with him with a kaleidoscope of bewildering conflicts with all law and order. And it is the joy of recent

69

biographers to psychoanalyze this precocious youth to discover his particular tangle of complexes.

But this boy and young man, whatever of curious interest the new psychology may discover, is simply the new generation chronically in revolt, a revolt in him intensified by his own peculiar personality, and blazing all the brighter because it has for its background the years of the Revolution with its intoxicating creed, and its dismal anticlimax after Napoleon and Waterloo. The very conflicts and terrors that drove Chateaubriand into the restless search for imaginary New Worlds and romantic savages, drove Shelley into a very real conflict with things as they are for the ultimate triumph of the good and the true. It is as the confident warrior and optimistic crusader for a Cause that Shelley is significant today. He has been called an English Don Quixote, and perhaps the title is the best compliment to him and to the one-time idealist of La Mancha. For after all Don Quixote was a hero, though only of lost causes and imaginary beauty, which he thought were real. And his escapades were no less an honor to his knighthood, though grotesque to most eyes, than were those of Shelley.

For some of Shelley's poems, like his acts in real life, are grotesque escapades. Set beside his sudden marriage to Harriet Westbrook or to Mary Godwin or his attachment to Miss Hitchener, the poem *The Sensitive Plant* or *Epipsychidion*. Or against his departure for Dublin with a portmanteau full of tracts dedicated to "tolerance, sobriety, wisdom and kindliness," to hasten the emancipation of Catholic Ireland, set his *Revolt of Islam* and its allegory of man's fall and regeneration. A confirmed romantic fantastic? Precisely. For these poems are as full of the romantic love of grotesque horror and an imagination quite out of touch with any semblance of reality, as his acts are irreconcilable with any of the canons of common sense. These may be like the Don's adoration of the Donna Dulcinea and the duel with Death or the lion; but there is a something more in both Shelley and the Spanish knight-errant that escapes through the meshes of common sense; and this elusive remainder is precious.

Shelley is youth in revolt and youth also fascinated by the new world, the golden age whose aurora had lightened the whole horizon of Europe, after Rousseau preached the thrilling faith of liberty, equality, fraternity, and the French Revolution tried to build of them a constitution. After that the world could never be the same again; "the world is weary of the past, O might it die or rest at last." And Shelley will hasten its delayed demise. Against the dying past he sees the new world with all its idealized beauty, with past and decayed institutions in a flux, and a new science to assist man to create it anew. "Bliss was it in that dawn to be alive, but to be young was very heaven." And Shelley died when he was yet close to celestial regions.

Rousseau was in much his spiritual god-father, and left in his cradle many of the ideas charged with the new heady wine. The idea that man was by nature good—that flat contradiction of the old orthodox theory of human depravity—philosophically belongs to the followers of John Locke, to whom the mind of the child is a *tabula rasa,* a blank sheet of paper for experience to write upon what it will. But this faith with the Genevan became the article of a fighting creed. This idea Shelley will hold to passionately while life lasts. It will make of him a militant missionary bishop *in omnibus partibus infidelium.* But unlike his great predecessor, he will not urge a return to the primitive, to the simple life, and the elemental emotions. No, he is a child of his age and he has no will to live among the shepherds of Westmoreland, or the peasants in the Hermitage, or the savages of North America, or among the great works of nature. He is first and foremost a poet, convinced as few before him of the efficacy of poetry. And it will be to the poet that he will address his call: for through poetry alone can the new world be created for a happy and harmonious humanity. "Poetry ever communicates all the pleasure which men are capable of receiving: it is ever still the light of life." Shelley will be a man among men, but man the poet, dedicated to the great cause.

Too much has been made of Shelley the mystic, Shelley the recluse, Shelley the hero of the fantastic *Alastor*, Shelley of the *Adonais*,

> "Midst others of less note, came one frail Form,
> A phantom among men, companionless
> As the last cloud of an expiring storm
> Whose thunder is its knell; he, as I guess,
> Had gazed on Nature's naked loveliness,
> Actaeon-like, and now he fled astray
> With feeble steps o'er the world's wilderness,
> And his own thoughts, along that rugged way,
> Pursued, like raging hounds, their father and their prey."

Shelley, the exile from his native land, had his moments of dejection when he felt his limbs too frail for the poet's responsibility. And what more natural? But he, too, had among his friends some of the finest spirits of his age. He, who in his youth could stand before university dons and not quail, all his life fought single-handed for his faith. The closing strophe of the *Ode to the West Wind* is much nearer the Shelley we should know today.

> "Make me thy lyre, even as the forest is:
> What if my leaves are falling like its own!
> The tumult of thy mighty harmonies

Will take from both a deep, autumnal tone,
Sweet though in sadness. Be thou, spirit fierce,
My spirit! Be thou me, impetuous one!

Drive my dead thought over the universe
Like withered leaves to quicken a new birth!
And, by the incantation of this verse,

Scatter, as from an unextinguished hearth
Ashes and sparks, my words among mankind!
Be through my lips to unawakened earth

The trumpet of a prophecy! O, wind,
If Winter comes, can Spring be far behind?"

And he has left us the allegory of his life in the *Revolt of Islam,* fantastic perhaps in its allegorical machinery, but none the less true in its aggressive poetry.

The need for the poet was very great. For he alone of all men could turn to true human use the treasures of science. Such to this poet is the mission of all great poetry. Rousseau had condemned science and fled its insidious snare that captures and enslaves mankind. Chateaubriand and the Romantic School of his pattern had ignored it as a part of the moral ugliness of reality, and had built them cities of refuge in the poet's imagination. Shelley boldly seeks a synthesis of these two regions of man's activity, for both are human and hence if rightly employed must be good. Of all of this generation this English youth in this faith stands closest to Goethe.

Shelley is fascinated by the new regions that science was opening up for the human imagination. To be sure there was none of the cold, impersonal scientist in this ardent spirit. Its hypotheses, its magical powers, glowed with much of the mystical significance they possessed for the dealer in alchemy, and there was something spiritual about their potency, reminding us of the scene in Faust's study as he summons the Earth Spirit or utters his magic formulas. Science to Shelley is the key that shall unlock all secrets and unite man more closely with nature.

> "Mother of this unfathomable world!
> Favour my solemn song, for I have loved
> Thee ever, and thee only; I have watched
> Thy shadow, and the darkness of thy steps,
> And my heart ever gazes on the depth
> Of thy deep mysteries."

And he had, like Goethe, from his scientific studies caught something of the significance of evolution. Above all, like Dante, he sees no essential difference between the "laws" of nature and those of the human heart. For him too love is the motive "that moves the sun and every star." It is the spirit of animation, the *élan vital* of all life, it is electricity, gravitation, the ultimate secret of all nature. Above all it is vital, illuminating, the essence of reason itself, the neo-Platonic logos; but by man's disingenuity or depravity also capable of being thwarted and made impotent—such is the theme, as we shall see, of the *Prometheus Unbound*. It is only as the true poet thus understands the true significance of this mystic bond that unites man and nature that he will have the power to wed men's lives to noble thoughts, and thus usher in the new day. Science studies it patiently in the laboratory, poetry makes it the motive for life.

It is characteristic of Shelley that, like Rousseau, he had "this passion for reforming the world," a sincere moral passion for regeneration, like Dante's desire to save those who were in the pathway of sin and set them on the road to salvation. He had the same bottomless fund of benevolence, and was fascinated by the idea of direct action.

Hence his desire to convert his university heads to the necessity of atheism, for he had a profound contempt for the theological idea of Jehovah. Hence his vagaries like the mission to Ireland. Hence his readiness to flout every social convention which barred the way to the free dictates of his swelling heart. Hence the "mad Shelley." For on the one side is the burning desire to act, and on the other the web of social inhibition in which he is forever finding himself entangled. He is never permitted to act freely, because he is forever unable to see the grotesque limitations of stubborn fact. Hence Shelley the Don Quixote of the nineteenth century. And it is precisely here that he is at the farthest remove from Goethe. It is because of this paradox, Shelley the poet bent on becoming also Shelley the man of action, that there grew up in the nineteenth century the myth of the futile Shelley, the Shelley of "marvelous gentleness, of feminine refinement,—and the pernicious nonsense which we have found him talking," of the "beautiful and ineffectual angel, beating in the void his luminous wings."

This is the criticism that would have pained him most, and is in essence most unfair to his poetic creed. What he has to say of poetry may after all, even in our own disillusioned day, be not such pernicious nonsense after all. For though Shelley's ideas on science may be mystical and crude beyond words, and his hope of a regeneration of the world be equally mystical and to us in our state of mind hopeless, there are some of his ideas on the conditions of moral progress that we may very well take to heart.

For much of Shelley's apparent futility is the futility of every one who finds himself in revolt against any established order; and it must be remembered that he was coming to maturity in those days of conservative reaction after the battle of Waterloo, when the very thought of change in the order sent shivers down men's spines, and they dreamed of barricades in the streets and heard the crash of the guillotine. Yet here was the boy writing such nonsense as this, "I swear, and as I break my oath may Infinity, Eternity blast me, here I swear that I will never forgive intolerance." Or again in the same early years before he was twenty, "the sublime interests of poetry, lofty and exalted achievements, the proselytism of the world, the equalization of its inhabitants were to me the soul of my soul." And the futile thing is he meant it. Don Quixote to Sancho was never more knight-errantly.

But is Shelley's idea of the poet after all quite as fantastic as his gestures in these letters? Fortunately for the history of literary criticism in the nineteenth century, and for his own apology, he wrote his *Defense of Poetry*. There in prose he sets down the mission of the ideal poet.[1] He is "the happiest, the best, the wisest of mankind," and poetry "the record of the best and happiest moments of the happiest and best minds."

"The production and assurance of pleasure in this highest sense is true utility. Those who produce and preserve this pleasure are poets or poetical philosophers.

"The exertions of Locke, Hume, Gibbon, Voltaire, Rousseau, and their disciples, in favour of oppressed and deluded humanity, are entitled to the gratitude of mankind. Yet it is easy to calculate the degree of moral and intellectual improvement which the world would have exhibited, had they never lived. A little more nonsense would have been talked for a century or two; and perhaps a few more men, women, and children, burnt as heretics. We might not at this moment have been congratulating each other on the abolition of the Inquisition

---

[1] He knows how he falls short, for even in an early letter he remarks: "I am formed . . . to apprehend minute and remote distinctions of feeling, whether relative to external nature or the living beings which surround us. . . . Yet, after all, I cannot but be conscious in much of what I write, of an absence of that tranquility which is the attribute and accompaniment of power."

in Spain. But it exceeds all imagination to conceive what would have been the moral condition of the world if neither Dante, Petrarch, Boccaccio, Chaucer, Shakespeare, Calderon, Lord Bacon, nor Milton, had ever existed; if Raphael and Michael Angelo had never been born; if the Hebrew poetry had never been translated; if a revival of the study of Greek literature had never taken place; if no monuments of ancient sculpture had been handed down to us; and if the poetry of the religion of the ancient world had been extinguished together with its belief. The human mind could never, except by the intervention of these excitements, have been awakened to the invention of the grosser sciences, and that application of analytical reasoning to the aberrations of society, which it is now attempted to exalt over the direct expression of the inventive and creative faculty itself."

This is superb. All human progress is due to art and poetry, these are the incentives to inventive minds; and without them there can be no science and none of the nobler institutions of man. There is something in their potency to keep the mind alert, so he would seem to say, and only through them man comes to know himself and the world about him; or, to put it in another way, they perpetually renew interest in life.

But he has something yet more to say, and which in this our day would seem to have a double significance:

"We have more moral, political and historical wisdom, than we know how to reduce into practice; we have more scientific and economical knowledge than can be accommodated to the just distribution of the produce which it multiplies. . . . We want the creative faculty to imagine that which we know; we want the generous impulse to act that which we imagine; we want the poetry of life: our calculations have outrun conception; we have eaten more than we can digest. The cultivation of those sciences which have enlarged the limits of the empire of man over the external world, has, for want of the poetical faculty, proportionately circumscribed those of the internal world; and man, having enslaved the elements, remains himself a slave. To what but a cultivation of the mechanical arts in a degree disproportioned to the presence of the creative faculty, which is the basis of all knowledge, is to be attributed the abuse of all invention for abridging and combining labour, to the exasperation of the inequality of mankind? From what other cause has it arisen that the discoveries which should have lightened, have added a weight to the curse imposed on Adam? Poetry and the principle of Self, of which money is the visible incarnation, are the God and Mammon of the world.

". . . The cultivation of poetry is never more to be desired than at periods when from an excess of the selfish and calculating principle, the accumulation of the materials of external life exceed the quantity of the power of assimilating them to the internal laws of human nature. The body has then become too unwieldy for that which animates it."

Here Shelley gives us the heart of his poetic faith. Scientific invention, the mechanization of life, may go so far as to reduce humanity to the bondage Rousseau deplores. But where Rousseau would deny progress and turn his back, as he did, on the arts and sciences as things essentially evil, Shelley would transform them into agencies for freedom and further progress by the illuminating and humanizing power of poetry. It will be interesting, I think, to see how Shelley attempted to realize in his own poetry his ideal of the function of the poet.

The theme of the *Revolt of Islam* is in part the allegory of the life of the poet and its temporary failure. "It is a succession of pictures illustrating the growth and progress of individual mind aspiring after excellence, and devoted to the love of mankind." Thus it illustrates the virtues and ideals in his poetic creed: "public hope," "moral dignity and freedom," "true philanthropy," the hatred of religious and political fraud, kindness and pity for vice and the faithlessness of tyrants, and, above all, "the transient nature of ignorance and error, the eternity of genius and virtue." As it tells of the first glorious success of the youth Laon's appeal to the oppressed and then his terrible disappointment, the poem becomes an allegory also of the final failure of the recent Revolution. It is an exhibition

of human character at its noblest and best, and at the same
time an arraignment of all tyrannies that restrain, combat, and even for a time defeat humanity.

The poem begins with the vision of the conflict between
the Eagle and the Snake, the powers of Evil and Good,
the allegory of history, with Evil triumphant though we
are promised that its reign cannot be eternal.

> "Thus evil triumphed, and the Spirit of evil,
> One Power of many shapes which none may know,
> One Shape of many names; the Fiend did revel
> In victory, reigning o'er a world of woe,
> For the new race of man went to and fro,
> Famished and homeless, loathed and loathing, wild,
> And hating good . . ."

Such is the introductory canto, in the fantastic manner of
the romantic extravagance of the age with its love of
straining symbolism. This is the text, the comment follows
in the story of Laon, the poetic youth, and Cythna, the
poet's Beatrice, the crown of his achievement, but also
his ally in the task of softening and reforming the world.
For in this task must join the aggressiveness of man and
the patience of woman.

> "Can man be free if woman be a slave?
> Chain one who lives, and breathes this boundless air,
> To the corruption of a closed grave!"

Now it is the story of these two, yet children, and of
their naïve love. They are rudely separated by savage
warriors, each to undergo the pains of slavery as a discipline for the task to which they devote themselves. Laon
is rescued by a hermit, who by the power of his holiness
gains access to where the boy is chained, breaks his fetters, takes him to his hermitage, and there gives the moral
lessons necessary to discipline both courage and intelligence

for the poet's mission. In the meanwhile he hears tales
of Cythna, whose power of patient love is moving the
respect and adoration of all.

> "Thus she doth equal laws and justice teach
>   To woman, outraged and polluted long;
>   Gathering the sweetest fruit in human reach
>   For those fair hands now free, while armèd wrong
>   Trembles before her look, though it be strong;
>   Thousands thus dwell beside her, virgins bright
>   And matrons with their babes, a stately throng!
>   Lovers renew the vows which they did plight
> In early faith, and hearts long parted now unite."

Laon now goes forth, resting his cause on the sweetness
of persuasion, "great is the strength of words." The revolution is instantaneous; soldiers, workers, all flock to the
new leader.

> "Lifting the thunder of their acclamation
>   Towards the City, then the multitude,
>   And I among them, went in joy—a nation
>   Made free by love, a mighty brotherhood
>   Linkt by a jealous interchange of good;
>   A glorious pageant, more magnificent
>   Than kingly slaves arrayed in gold and blood,
>   When they return from carnage, and are sent
> In triumph bright beneath the populous battlement."

A new age has risen like magic and the song of triumph
is one of peace.

> "Revenge and Selfishness are desolate—
>   A hundred nations swear that there shall be
> Pity and Peace and Love among the good and free!

> "Our toil from thought all glorious forms shall cull
>   To make this Earth, our home, more beautiful;
>   And science, and her sister Poesy,
> Shall clothe in light the fields and cities of the free!"

But the victory of the people is short lived, for the tyrant, in the unsuspecting love for all, has been spared, with the hope that his heart will melt in the new found cult of unselfish love. The allegory here is plain, the French Revolution, the Terror, the Empire, the return of the old regime. And the joyous hordes of mankind are overwhelmed by the trained soldiers of the tyrant. Laon escapes to the wilderness, that with Cythna he may ponder the fate of mankind and the more arduous task that it will be to reform humanity. Finally as a climax Cythna, the symbol of sweetness and love, poetry, is brought to the stake and sacrificed to the god of hate and tyranny.

Here are the poet's less mature and yet significant reflections on the lesson of all sudden revolutions. Man is essentially good, as Laon discovered when he went forth with his sudden gospel, and may momentarily be aroused to deeds worthy of his best nature. But Evil is stubborn and deeply ingrained, and the forces of superstition and tyranny are cruel and sleepless and crafty, and they know the meaning of power. Can we hope for anything other than a great final disaster from the efforts at sudden regeneration? It makes martyrs of the choice spirits, but not of them alone, it involves also their followers in the common ruin. Flamboyant and at times even grotesque, but I find it difficult to discover "pernicious nonsense" in the *Revolt of Islam.* It may at times be hectic and shrill poetry, but it may also be the necessary training for a much greater poem.

When he was only nineteen, this was in 1812, Shelley wrote to William Godwin, that half philosopher, half charlatan, whose writings, especially the *Political Justice,* had had so profound an influence on the poet's youthful thought: "I am now earnestly pursuing studious habits. I am writing *An Enquiry into the Causes of the Failure of the French Revolution to Benefit Mankind.* My plan is that of resolving to lose no opportunity to disseminate truth and happiness." Such a letter from a youth of nineteen doubtless would bring to most teachers a half-pitying, half-cynical smile. But in reality is not the poet attempting to do in the *Revolt of Islam* precisely what he describes in the *Defense of Poetry* as the duty of the interpreter of the facts of the science of history? For to Shelley history is the interplay of moral and imaginative forces, love and hate, greed, ambition, benevolence, and sacrifice. And thus in his allegory of the French Revolution, as in part of Hardy's *Dynasts*, the characters are personifications of moral qualities, but all either black or radiantly white. The cosmic significance of the martyrdom is supposed to be caught in the heightened tone of the poetry and its lurid colors. Doubtless he saw that in the poem there was an absence "of that tranquility which is the attribute and accompaniment of power." Perhaps for this reason, some years later, he returned to the theme, but this time with a purged imagination and an even more philosophical purpose. It is thus that he gave us the *Prometheus Unbound.*

The story of the dethroned and overwhelmed god is as old as mythology itself. Christian legend has the story of Satan and the rebellion in Heaven, and Milton's poem of *Paradise Lost* is in part the allegory of this cosmic rebellion. Aeschylus in his *Prometheus Bound* has left us the most significant part of the story dramatised by him in three plays. Shelley in taking the story of Prometheus takes for his hero a character who was a favorite in the imagination of the romantic beginnings of the nineteenth century. As a symbol of the rebel against organized power, or convention, or tyranny, he is the favorite of the lovers of titanic personality striving for freedom. He is to be put beside the Fausts, the Don Juans and the other majestic defiers of things as they are. But his story is the more thrilling, for he was a god, his rebellion cosmic, and his sufferings and protest sublime.

As a hero Prometheus was the more congenial to an age that understood Rousseau's *Social Contract* and Godwin's *Political Justice,* because he could so easily be made to symbolize human benevolence, and his great and triumphant opponent, Jupiter, lawless tyranny. Prometheus, the new and benevolent creed of liberty, equality, and fraternity, and sweetness and light; Jupiter the *ancien régime* of irresponsible power and blind ignorance. The old Greek myth so easily allowed this antithesis; for Prometheus, one of the Titans, who had assisted Jupiter or Zeus to his throne in Heaven, had disobeyed. He had contrary to express command brought the blessings of culture to degraded and impotent humanity in the form of fire and the arts, and above all given the bliss of hope. For this he was riveted to the crag Caucasus, there to suffer the rigors of the ice and tempest, until he would in the course of aeons discover to Jupiter a secret that might involve the throne of heaven in ruin. For the Titan foresaw that in the ages to come the divine king would desire a union with Thetis, a goddess of the sea, who was destined to bear a son mightier than his father. This secret Prometheus refused to reveal and there followed the unspeakable torment.

Such is the story that Aeschylus sought to humanize in his plays, and at the same time to preserve the moral grandeur of Prometheus and the divine excellence as well as justice of Zeus. For the great poet was too devout a worshipper of the Olympian King to allow for a moment his trust in heaven's justice to falter; yet at the same time he cannot falter in his admiration also for the god who brought blessings innumerable to man.[2]

Shelley has no such theological convictions of Jupiter's uprightness, and he can correspondingly find no fault with the Titan's defiance of omnipotent power. To him Prometheus is the symbol of righteous rebellion, prompted by the sweetest of motives, and punished by the most grisly of tyrannies. "Prometheus is, as it were, the type of the highest perfection of moral and intellectual nature, impelled by the purest and the truest motives to the best and noblest ends."

Prometheus Unbound is a lyrical drama, much nearer to grand opera than to any imaginable acting play. There is no action, only long lyrical dialogues and exquisite songs and hymns. The characters are even less persons than those in the *Revolt of Islam*. They are allegorical figures, musical statues representing the moral conflict which is the poem, symbols of the varied aspects of humanity in its process toward harmony and perfection. In its way the poem challenges comparison with Dante's *Divine Comedy* and the progress from Hell through Purgatory to the glories of Heaven. Man is its theme, man from the false way discovering, through purification and right knowledge, its final goal of Peace. Or again it is the spiritual drama of human evolution from the days of naïve innocence, through evil and falsehood, to the final acquirement of moral and physical perfection. Man's naïve and beautiful beginnings—this is Rousseau and natural goodness; man's actual evil present—this again is Rousseau's man in chains; man triumphant through a reconciliation of his dual nature by the aid of perfected science

---

[2] See *The Golden Thread,* chapter on Aeschylus, for the interesting manner in which the poet makes the play a study in human institutions.

and poetry; this is Shelley the prophet of optimism. Such is the moral of the poem.

There are three characters, and then a number of abstractions whose significance as the play proceeds becomes reasonably clear. Prometheus and Jupiter are man now hopelessly divided and fiercely antagonistic: Prometheus, man's better nature, his active benevolence and his yet undisciplined reason; Jupiter, man the tyrant, using the forces of ignorance, superstition, and terror to keep man's better nature subjugated. Asia, man's true consort, the highest in the imaginative life of man, poetry, beauty, love, has been torn from his side, and is in retreat among the beauties of remote nature. She is Shelley's allegory of the poet of beauty who retires from the evil of life, and leaves man's suffering uncheered. In the beginnings of innocence Prometheus and Asia, like Adam and Eve, dwelt in the garden of naïve bliss. Man's dual nature had not been revealed by science or knowledge, which gives new and dangerous powers. But with knowledge came Jupiter and the reign of envy, hate, and superstition, and man is chained by the things he himself had made.

It is here that the poem opens. Suffering had taught Prometheus knowledge, and with it patience and fortitude. He now is chastened and dead to hate, and he calls for the curse, that in his agony he had once pronounced against his tormentor, that he may unsay it. It is repronounced by the phantasm of Jupiter:

> "Fiend, I defy thee! with a calm, fixed mind,
>   All that thou canst inflict I bid thee do;
> Foul tyrant both of Gods and Human-kind,
>   One only being shalt thou not subdue.
>
> Rain then thy plagues upon me here,
> Ghastly disease, and frenzying fear;
> And let alternate frost and fire

> Eat into me, and be thine ire
> Lightning, and cutting hail, and legioned forms
> Of furies, driving by upon the sounding storms."

During his long imprisonment all Nature is mute and dead, and before him rise the specters of evil, the Furies, to torment him with the pageant of evil and terror with which all life and nature abound. Nature itself has shared in man's downfall. And Mercury comes to bear the command of Jupiter to submit utterly. But the Titan has the comfort of Ione and Panthea, faith and hope, that have never forsaken him. And finally a chorus of spirits,

> "From unremembered ages we
> Gentle guides and guardians be
> Of heaven-oppressed mortality,"

the stray ideals of humanity, recount the hope that though frustrate can never die.

> "Wisdom, Justice, Love, and Peace,
> When they struggle to increase,
> Are to us as soft winds be
> To shepherd boys, the prophecy
> Which begins and ends in thee."

But the curse has been unsaid, man's natural benevolence reëstablished, but with the discipline now of suffering and fortitude. The ultimate victory is half achieved. Now it is that man's imagination and his reason must in turn have their discipline; and here it is that the action passes to Asia. She catches the vision of her now transformed mate:

> "Methought among the lawns together
> We wandered, underneath the young gray dawn,
> And multitudes of dense white fleecy clouds
> Were wandering in thick flocks along the mountains
> Shepherded by the slow, unwilling wind";

and there comes the cry of "Follow, follow." It is the lonely echo of the call upon the imagination and reason to take up their search of the necessary discipline.

The next scene (Act II, Scene 3) is the allegory of the mystic education in the true philosophy of man and nature. Asia, with Faith and Hope in her train, for Prometheus now needs them no longer, guided by the Fawns and Spirits, man's better spiritual impulses, comes to a place of retirement from the light of common day. Here she learns the laws which both man and nature obey, the true science. It is a preparation for the next scene where from the lofty pinnacle, as the high regions of Dante's Heaven, one can look upon the whole world as one superb plan, the clear spectacle without which the highest philosophy would be impossible.

From this she must descend to the hidden secrets of life and of creative power, the realm of Demogorgon.

> "Through the veil and the bar
> Of things which seem and are
> Even to the steps of the remotest throne,
> Down, down!
>
> "Where the air is no prism,
> And the moon and stars are not,
> And the cavern-crags wear not
> The radiance of Heaven,
> Nor the gloom to Earth given,
> Where there is one pervading, one alone,
> Down, down!"

There Asia reads to the Spirit the history of Mankind, his powers and his ills. There she learns that "All spirits are enslaved which serve things evil"; that all things are subject to Fate, Time, Occasion, Chance and Change, except eternal Love. There the Spirits of the Hours are unloosed, and one more ghastly than the rest speeds to the overthrowal of the Tyrant. The scene ends with the transfiguration of Asia ready now for the union with the released god.

The third act is the overwhelming of Jupiter by Demogorgon and the freeing of Prometheus, according to the legend, by Hercules. It is a rhapsody of rejuvenated and perfected man. Nature and all the arts and sciences join in exuberance of new life. All ugliness has disappeared, for man has come to his own.

> "I wandering went
> Among the haunts and dwellings of mankind,
> And first was disappointed not to see
> Such mighty change as I had felt within
> Expressed in outward things; but soon I looked
> And behold, thrones were kingless, and men walked
> One with the other even as spirits do,
> None fawned, none trampled; hate, disdain, or fear,
> Self-love or self-contempt, on human brows,
> No more inscribed, as o'er the gate of hell,
> All hope abandon ye who enter here."

The last act is a postlude, a pean of joy sung by all nature. The imagery rises almost to fantastic heights. It is a burst of pure music. The earth and moon are wedded. In this happy union of all nature comes the last appeal to man, the cause and also the inheritor of all this beauty and joy: man triumphant.

> "All things confess his strength. Through the cold mass
> Of marble and of colour his dreams pass;
> Bright threads whence mothers weave the robes their children wear;
> Language is a perpetual Orphic song,
> Which rules with Daedal harmony a throng
> Of thoughts and forms, which else senseless and shapeless were.
> The lightning is his slave; heaven's utmost deep
> Gives up her stars, and like a flock of sheep
> They pass before his eye, are numbered, and roll on!

The tempest is his steed, he strides the air;
And the abyss shouts from her depth laid bare,
Heaven, hast thou secrets? Man unveils me; I have none."

Such is Shelley's profound optimism, such is Shelley's vision of man's relation to himself and of his place in nature. Never again in the century are we to have this profound trust in human nature and human destiny. Never again this resolute denial of the ultimate reality of evil. For this reason Shelley does seem remote to us today. But his is not wholly an unschooled, boyish, and easy optimism; nor is his faith in human nature without some evidence. Nor, as certainly, is this philosophy of life quite to be labeled as "pernicious nonsense."

For, undisciplined as Shelley appears superficially in his own life, he is again, like Goethe, the poet of the twofold discipline. And Prometheus is his symbol of human nature in the process of arriving at full imaginative and intellectual maturity, and the way to this lies through purgatorial fires. It is a long and arduous schooling in suffering, at the hands of his own evil tendencies, for evil is man made and can be unmade only when man is conscious of its perfectly human character. Again one must read the long confession of sin that Asia makes before the throne of Demogorgon.

"But who rains down
Evil, the immedicable plague, which, while
Man looks on his creation like a God
And sees that it is glorious, drives him on
The wreck of his own will, the scorn of earth,
The outcast, the abandoned, the alone?"

The clearness of mind that will answer this question of questions—whence comes evil into the fair world man has made?—will come only when man's intellectual training

is made perfect, when his intellectual nature and his moral
are in full accord. But this is the state of harmony that
Plato also foresaw when he described the training of his
philosopher kings in the *Republic*. Only Shelley sees in
the distant future the golden day when all humanity will
be philosopher kings of their own souls. On that glorious
day thrones will be tenantless, and laws will be the spontaneous language of each individual soul. Here again we
have a vision that recalls the triumphant human soul in
the last cantos of Dante's *Purgatory*. The discipline of
intellect and will has been finally achieved, as far as it can
go short of Heaven. Now Virgil the philosopher king
turns to Dante, the rejuvenated human soul, and crowns
him lord of himself.

> "Hither with wit I brought thee, and with art.
>   Henceforth take thine own pleasure for thy guide;
>   From the steep ways thou'rt free, and from the strait.
> Await no more my words, nor sign from me,
>   For free, upright, and sound thy judgment is;
>   'Twere wrong to disobey its will, and hence
> Over thyself I crown and mitre thee."

Now man is in accord with Nature's law. There can be
no falling away. This is the "far-off divine event," the
goal of evolution, the rightful heritage of man, a far more
glorious destiny than the original golden age of thought-
less innocence.

In man's training for this goal poetry and science unite,
each ministering to its separate power. The poet is the
moral guide to mankind, the scientist, the intellectual. But
science and poetry do not proceed on quite separate paths.
For the poet must receive the gifts of science and transform them into the living tissue of his poetry, and thus
make of them the food of life. There is a turn more or
less of the attitude of the mystic here, and a suggestion

that poetry is a species of scientific metaphysics, almost the suggestion that it will supply the magic formulas that will make man's communion with nature something of a sacrament, where the facts of science become transmuted into a mystic bread and wine to feed men's souls. The orthodox scientist today staggers uncomprehendingly, but there is also today a school of metaphysical scientists in good standing who seem to be approaching the confirmation of faith of Shelley, the poet of this new Platonism.

Shelley was the poet of revolt, but it was not a revolt that carried him into an imaginary wilderness to live apart from the routine of life he found uncongenial to his imaginative needs, like Chateaubriand. Much less did he, like some of the romantics, go into some imaginary past where men could be heroes and women queens of love and beauty. Rather he pushed his quest into the imagined realms of a glorious future, where through conquest of himself man could be self-sufficient and yet modest in his triumph, where governments would be unnecessary, for there would be none to govern, where the triumph of anarchy would be a spiritual and social peace. And he makes his stirring appeal to the best in human nature, fortitude and hope.

> "To suffer woes which Hope thinks infinite;
> To forgive wrongs darker than death or night;
>   To defy Power, which seems omnipotent;
> To love, and bear; to hope till Hope creates
> From its own wreck the things it contemplates;
>   Neither to change, nor falter, nor repent;
> This, like thy glory, Titan, is to be
> Good, great and joyous, beautiful and free;
> This is alone Life, Joy, Empire, and Victory."

VI. BLESSED ARE THE MEEK

MANZONI

"We ought to thank God, and be content; do whatever we can, work industriously, help one another, and then be content, because it is no disgrace to suffer and be poor; the disgrace is to do evil."

I Promessi Sposi

"THANK God, and be content," be good and you will be happy, or at the least have a clear conscience, how often this word was conveyed in the persuasive chapters of a story once so diligently cultivated, and now so unfamiliar as to seem to belong to another planet or geological epoch. Yet there are names carrying great respect that cultivated generously this same golden text in their novels and poems, and were hugely popular. Goldsmith did it in the *Vicar of Wakefield,* Dickens makes of it a philosophy of life for the unfortunate, and Goethe's exquisite idyl, *Hermann and Dorothea* carries it like a star on its forehead. It may be a naïve faith fit only for unthinking childhood, but it has carried conviction in times even more perilous than these, and has inspired even great literature.

Even today we can't escape its compelling charm, though we shake our heads in pained doubt. It seems like the silver lining of the cloud that childhood would seize but mature age denies. It has the same philosophy as the frequent injunction of my greatly loved aunt, to endeavor even in the worst predicament to look for something that Saint Paul would have found an occasion for giving thanks. Or it may be like Mark Tapley, in *Martin Chuzzlewit*, whose enthusiasm for cheerfulness no hardship could conquer. But we in disillusionment ask today, can such faith have even a tincture of truth? Is there a providence in human affairs? Where is the divinity that shapes our ends in spite of ignorant fumblings or calculated malice? It was precisely questions like these in the first third of the nineteenth century that sent Manzoni to the study of history for the theme of his tragedies and above all of his historical novel, *I Promessi Sposi, The Betrothed*.

It is a commonplace of literary history and criticism to describe one of the phases of the Romantic movement as a revival of interest in the past. Walter Scott is produced as the great paragon of this return. To turn to the past, and in imagination to explore its adventures as a compensation for the matter-of-factness of the present and its ugly and forbidding complexity. There at least the imagination is free of the restrictions of the intransigent present, and may roam at will over its figures and events and create anew a world which shall be more to its liking. Ivanhoe, Quentin Durward, Rob Roy and Die Vernon are not constrained in their actions by the machines of the new industrial age, know nothing of the *Origin of Species* or the *Reform Bill*, or of the 14th of July and the Bastile, or of the policies of Prince Metternich, and have never read Adam Smith's *Wealth of Nations*. In their days men could be men, and life offered free opportunity for large adventure and outlet for the joy of living.

There is a measure of truth in this dangerous generalization. For some did retire to the past as Chateaubriand

retired to the land of the primitive savage and Wordsworth to the hills and shepherds of Westmoreland. Or
as we, after a winter of business, turn for a two weeks to
the simplicity of stream and mountain to forget and recreate. But there is also a wiser motive and more instructive; and even Scott, careless as he is of historical detail,
gets from his history something far more valuable and
real than a vacation for his imagination. If for the present I call that gain an historical perspective for the purpose of a better understanding of that essential thing human nature, I think I shall not be far wrong. From the
distance in time the irrelevancies tend to disappear and
the pattern of the landscape, as in a map, falls into clearer
outline. Against the moving events of times past one can
watch the human panorama, and in its story catch, perhaps, a vision of the meaning of history and the value
of human action. The pattern is simpler, because it has
been purged of lesser detail; and from it the reader of
its story can discover wisdom and a philosophy of life.
Such, I take it, was Walter Scott, and such, almost without peer, was the Italian Alessandro Manzoni.

Manzoni looked at life steadily, across the centuries
and in his novel, *The Betrothed,* set down in detail what
he saw. But not in the manner of a modern realist. The
modern is interested in the exhibition of human nature,
in its psychology, in its intimate behavior. Passion, love,
hate, the conflicts of motive, the story of the relation of
motive and action, the discovery, that is to say, of personality, all this is the theme of modern realism. Or it
may go farther and strive to trace, as in Tolstoy, the
search of the personality for a motive for life, and thus
be the story of bewilderment and faith, of disillusion and
enthusiasm. In all these the heights and depths, the lights
and shadows of human nature, or its background, will be

described with scientific accuracy. But there is none of this in Manzoni. He gives no palpitating love story, nor, though there are adventures and hair-breadth escapes, does he ever leave us in alarmed suspense. From all these points of view Manzoni is decidedly disappointing. For in such adventures he is quite uninterested. He is neither a raconteur, like Scott or Dumas, nor a psychologist like Dostoevsky, nor an exploiter of poignant melodrama like Hugo, nor a scientist like Zola. He is a moralist, seeking in history for a moral pattern, and yet an artist, but one who never allows his story to be other than true to the formula he discovers. He clips off all excess when the story begins to be interesting for its own sake. For his like we must turn back to the narratives of the Bible, with their direct simplicity, and moral convincingness.

For again, like Scott, Manzoni belonged both to the eighteenth and the nineteenth centuries. As the great Italian critic Croce remarks, he had at once the scientific interest in history and human life of the encyclopedists, the irony of Voltaire, and the faith in Christian morals of the Catholic reaction of the early nineteenth century— the reaction whose romantic exaggeration one can see in Chateaubriand's *Spirit of Christianity*. Just so Scott was an eighteenth century Tory gentleman with the glowing nineteenth century trust in good, loyal, and honest, hardworking people of every rank. Like Scott again he had an ideal; with the British Tory it was that of downright heroic manhood, with the Italian patriot, that of the moral worth of the Christian virtues. He will therefore have the historical sense that can recreate the past vividly and accurately and ironically, and at the same time illuminate it in the moral spectrum of human nature.

It was no less an authority than Walter Scott again

that proclaimed this his one novel, *The Betrothed*, to be the greatest novel ever written. If the author of *Waverly* thought so highly of a work for which his own *Waverly* furnished so much of an inspiration, it will surely be worth our while to glance for a moment at its significance in the story of this our past century.

The end of the eighteenth century had been a bleak region for tender religious consciences. Scientific deism is a thin, very thin, substitute for the certainties of faith that one discovers in the poems of a Dante or a Milton. Rousseau had tried the substitute of pure emotional faith in the God of the Savoyard Vicar. But this was vague and uncontrollable, and except for a very genuine human benevolence had little to offer as a code for conduct. Shelley had branded superstition and theology with the anathema of the curse of Prometheus, as a weapon of tyranny to reduce humanity to helpless ignorance and misery. To be sure there were popular reactions, like the creed of Methodism. There was besides the purely aesthetic defense by Chateaubriand of the mysteries and sacraments of the Catholic faith. Then after 1815 came the revival of interest in religion, not so much as a theological or philosophical creed, as a living faith and a motive for life and conduct. We see it in France and Italy, with poets and novelists sincerely devoting themselves to its ministry. It is the motive for that glow of conviction in England that came with the Oxford Movement, with its Christian poet, John Keble. But one sees it also in its more romantic aspect in the altar-piece like work of Rossetti. In Manzoni in Italy it is the result of a sincere conviction, a conviction that there is a God in history, the God of the Catholic Christian faith; and that in the comedies and tragedies of the story of history his will is made evident and vindicated in the human conscience.

More than this, along with this ever present and vital motive of religion, with Manzoni there is also the romantic nineteenth century conviction of the soundness of human nature, especially among the lowly. His peasant folk join the shepherds of Westmoreland of Wordsworth, the primitive savages of Chateaubriand, the peasants at the Hermitage of Rousseau, as those among whom ideals of justice and human dignity and unselfish love and devotion may yet be found, even though the great ones of the world have lost the way. There is this double optimism in this novel of Lombard Italian life, written by a Lombard Italian himself, whose boyhood home was the village of the opening scenes of *The Betrothed*.

For his background he takes Italy of the years of 1628 and 1629, a time of the lowest ebb of Italian culture, a time of selfish decadence among the nobility, and extreme poverty and wretchedness among the peasants, a time of general lawlessness and oppression. Each noble's home was surrounded and maintained by hired *bravos*, ruffians all and escaped criminals most, who sold their swords to the highest bidder and became willing instruments of tryanny. The futility of laws and proclamations is told us at the outset of the novel by the list of edicts that year after year had been aimed at these agents of terror. Yet they flourished, and enabled their master to assert himself with perfect impunity, though *podestàs*, magistrates, or governors of cities, or even viceroys, might declare them public enemies to be punished by exile. Such were some of the nobles, and such their lives of open violence.

The church was not much better. The clergy was terrorized or flouted, or cajoled into acquiescence. Should a cleric prove intractable there was always an "influence," an uncle in a high place, who could through some higher church officer move the offender to some less embarrassing position. The peasantry, unprotected by the church, pillaged by the tyrant, lived in unending toil and distress. It was a world ruled by force, violence, corruption, servility, in castles and convents, with desolation among the poor. The only evidence of morals or of intellect that can be discovered is in the proclamations unread, and in the speeches and writings unheeded. It was this unpromising age that Manzoni selects to explore for the moral factor in human history.

It was a time too of tragedy in the footsteps of tragedy. The year 1628 had been one of famine. Then as now the people blamed "special interests" and profiteers. In Milan there were riots and lootings of bakeries. But as the year grew older the suffering became universal.

> "But so constituted are we mortals in general, that we rebel indignantly and violently against medium evils, and bow in silence under extreme ones; we bear, not with resignation, but stupefaction, the weight of what at first we had called insupportable.
>
> "The nobility were seen walking in becoming and modest, or even dirty and shabby, clothing; some, because the common causes of misery had affected their fortunes to this degree, or given a finishing hand to fortunes already much dilapidated; others, either from fear of provoking public desperation by display, or from a feeling of shame at thus insulting public calamity. . . ."

Remedial measures, then as now, proved ineffective. "So true it is that even in the scarcest times, public money may always be found to be employed foolishly."

Famine is followed by the invasion of German armies —it is the time of the Thirty Years' War and the great Wallenstein.

> "A great part of the inhabitants retired to the mountains, taking with them their most valuable effects, and driving their cattle before them; others stayed behind, either to tend upon some sick person, or

to defend their houses from the flames, or to keep an eye upon precious things which they had concealed under-ground; some because they had nothing to lose; and a few villains, also, to make acquisitions. When the first detachment arrived at the village where they were to halt, they quickly spread themselves through this and the neighbouring ones, and plundered them directly; all that could be eaten or carried off, disappeared: not to speak of the destruction of the rest, of the fields laid waste, of the houses given to the flames, the blows, the wounds, the rapes, committed. All the expedients, all the defences employed to save property, often proved useless, sometimes even more injurious to the owners. The soldiers, far more practised in the stratagems of this kind of war, too, rummaged every corner of the dwellings; tore down walls; easily discovered in the gardens the newly-disturbed soil; penetrated even to the hills, to carry off the cattle; went into caves, under the guidance of some villain, as we have said, in search of any wealthy inhabitant who might be concealed there; despoiled his person, dragged him to his house, and, by dint of threats and blows, compelled him to point out his hidden treasure.

"At length, however, they took their departure, and the distant sound of drums or trumpets gradually died away on the ear: this was followed by a few hours of death-like calm: and then a new hateful clashing of arms, a new hateful rumbling, announced another squadron. These, no longer finding anything to plunder, applied themselves with the more fury to make destruction and havoc of the rest, burning furniture, door-posts, beams, casks, wine-vats, and sometimes even the houses; they seized and ill-used the inhabitants with double ferocity;— and so on, from worse to worse, for twenty days; for into this number of detachments the army was divided."

That winter, with an impoverished city and a country-side laid waste, came, as the crowning disaster, the plague. Again Manzoni, with his care for historical accuracy writes as an eyewitness.

"It was a party of sick on their way to the Lazaretto; some driven thither by force, vainly offering resistance, vainly crying that they would rather die upon their beds, and replying with impotent imprecations to the oaths and commands of the *monatti* who were conducting them; others who walked on in silence, without any apparent grief and without hope, like insensible beings; women with infants clinging to their bosoms; children, terrified by the cries, the mandates, and the crowd, more than by the confused idea of death, with loud cries demanding their mother and her trusted embrace, and imploring that they might remain at their well-known homes. Alas! perhaps their mother, whom they supposed they had left asleep upon her bed, had there thrown herself down senseless, subdued in a moment by the disease, to be carried away on a cart to the Lazaretto,—or the grave, if perchance the car should arrive a little later. Perhaps—oh misfortune deserving of still more bitter tears—the mother, entirely taken up by her own sufferings, had forgotten everything, even her own children, and had no longer any wish but to die in quiet."

Such is the historical background for the novel—an Italy, physically, morally, and politically in decadence, stricken in succession with the greatest calamities that can fall upon a people. Against this curtain of horror will be played the comedy and tragedy of the lives of individuals, the prey in part of the forces that are weaving the national destiny, the agents in part of their own fate. From this illuminating scene the author will draw the lesson of a directing and judging moral conscience, the ideal that gives moral value to the destiny of mankind. It was a large undertaking.

If one is looking for a historical novel in the manner of a Victor Hugo, tense always in dramatic contrasts, breathing always the intoxicating gasses of melodrama, with characters hideous in grotesqueness or sinister in horror, and fluttering always like the fated moth around the candle of imminent annihilation, one is going to be terribly disappointed. There is here no Hunchback of Notre Dame or Jean Valjean. There are no overblown situations or inflated characters; and no long passages of intolerable suspense. The story moves with the leisurely pace of a summer afternoon, and the characters on their faces or in their attitudes carry none of the marks of a singular destiny. They are utterly and unforgettably commonplace. One would pass them even on a lonely road without comment, and in their villages they would not even be noticed. They are commonplace Italy, responding in the commonplace manner to the urge for life, but lifted for the moment by the stress of an unexpected history out of the ordinary routine, bewildered by the unknown, purged or destroyed by events, and then, when the storm has lifted, dropping back into commonplace and expected routine. That is all there is of drama in the story of *The Betrothed*. Again it is Goldsmith's *Vicar of Wakefield* of which we think, and not Scott, or of Goethe's *Hermann and Dorothea*. It is a novel in which the characters and situations themselves are commonplace beyond belief, but only the history is strange and dramatic. How will these known act in the presence thus of the unknown? The answer is the historical novel of Manzoni.

For chief characters we have peasants, for stage we have a little Lombard village, Lecco, not many miles from Milan. And now their simple annals. Renzo and Lucia —let us here leave off all surnames—are betrothed and about to be married. But on the eve of the ceremony Don Rodrigo, through his bravos, announces dire punishment to Don Abbondio, the curate of the village, if he performs the ceremony. Rodrigo is the villain, an unscrupulous nobleman, who has looked on Lucia and found her to his wandering fancy.

When the coward priest tells the astounded family that the event cannot take place and the secret is guessed, there is consternation. Renzo tries the law, Doctor Azzecca Garbugli (the name is ominous), but he throws up his hands in horror when the nobleman's name is mentioned. The law is not only helpless but corrupt. The

magistrate, the *podestà,* is a crony at the table of the aristocrat; no aid from him. At last they turn to Father Cristoforo, a Capuchin friar, who in the goodness of his heart does what he can. Cristoforo is one of the few bright angels of the story, sweet and affectionate and, within his poor means, resourceful. The situation is desperate; for Rodrigo has set his bravos in motion to capture the girl—there is a wager he wishes to win from his cousin. A ruse, by which Renzo plans for a swift, informal wedding before Abbondio, fails through the curate's comic cowardice; and now only the Capuchin stands between them and desolation.

Lucia is no heroine of the accepted romantic breed; still less is Renzo a hero. There is no knight in shining armor to act as their guardian—only a poor sandalled friar. Lucia is sent off to a nunnery with her mother Agnese to be under the protection of Gertrude, a young noblewoman forced against her will to take the veil. Renzo makes off to Milan to present himself to an acquaintance of the Friar, whom he never finds; and thus we have the first check given to Rodrigo's malicious designs. So far we have history play with their fortunes only through the agency of the common corruption and decadence of the times.

Now gradually the other novel factors enter. Renzo arrives in Milan just at the moment when the bread riots are at their height, and is present and unconsciously shares in the plunder of a bakeshop. In his youthful enthusiasm he even makes a patriotic speech, and describes in outline a "new deal" by which all would be benefited. An evident stranger, loose of tongue, he is taken up next morning, and would without shrift have been hanged had not the crowd rescued him. He gets away; now his native cunning is aroused, and a "free bird" determined to be free, he makes off for his cousin's village near Bergamo, where, with a price on his head as an escaped convict, he goes into hiding.

Rodrigo has not given up his quest. He learns of Lucia's whereabouts, and with the aid of a powerful tyrant, an outlaw flaunting openly his defiance, the mysterious Unnamed—a historical figure—he sets about getting her into his power. The nun has been corrupted by the address of a dissolute young neighbor; and by his aid Lucia is captured and taken to the castle of the Unnamed to be given up to Rodrigo. Evil seems to have triumphed.

But the beauty of innocence has its own protection, and by a miracle, first Nibbio, the Kite, a bravo, is converted to pity, then the Unnamed himself. During the horror of the German invasion she, and many innocents like her, are saved from the ravages of the lawless army. It is at this point of the story, for the complete transformation of the mysterious nobleman's character, that we are made acquainted with another of the radiant angelic figures of the story, the Cardinal Bishop Borromeo. His creed is that of active Christianity. "Love them," he says to the penitent and yet cowardly Abbondio, "because they have suffered, because they still suffer, because they are yours, because they are weak, because they have need of pardon, to obtain which, think of what efficacy their prayers may be." Iniquity is not, to him, all powerful, it "depends not only on its own strength, but often also on the fears and credulity of others."

All now is ready for the final union of the couple, if Renzo can be found and cleared of the charge that hangs over his name. But the third of the catastrophes of that year's history falls heavily. Lucia is living in a good Milanese family. She falls a victim to the plague, and in a city driven to utter distraction, she is carried to the

Lazaretto, to die or to be cured unaided. There Father Cristoforo, too, has gone to minister to the sufferers. Renzo, too, falls a victim, convalesces, and goes off now in a forlorn world to seek his bride. He narrowly escapes death again in Milan, charged fantastically this time with being a "poisoner," one of the fancied spreaders of infection. But finally he meets Lucia herself just recovering; and all that separates them is the vow of virginity she took before the Madonna on the day of her great agony. But Father Cristoforo is generous and absolves her of its obligation. Finally all are reunited.

The plague has been properly discriminating. Rodrigo is put out of the way, lest his still unconverted fancy disturb the long delayed wedding. Abbondio cannot quite make up his mind, even after these harrowing experiences, to do his priestly duty. The spectre of the bravos who beset his path at the beginning loom larger than famine, war, and pestilence. But when at last assured of Rodrigo's death, his words are a vindication of God's way with the world.

"... If the plague did things in this way always and everywhere, it would really be a sin to speak ill of it; we might almost wish for one every generation; and be content that people should be in league to produce a malady. ..."

The story closes with another touch of the same delicate irony. These have been commonplace heroes and heroines. Renzo's fidelity demands at least a princess, so the villagers where he had taken up his new abode fancied. Lucia's adventures with bravos, Rodrigos, and unnamed viscounts, demanded extraordinary charm and beauty. So, too, the careless reader. But when Renzo brings her proudly to his new home, she is only a village maiden, like any other peasant girl, no better, no more beautiful; and the villagers turn away in disgusted disappointment. Does the careless reader, too, have the same disappointment over a moving tale of faithful devotion, of tyranny frustrated of its prey, of famine, war, and plague endured with fortitude, only to discover that the hero and heroine have none of the heroic mould celebrated by orthodox romance? Manzoni leaves this pertinent question for the patient reader to answer. For he must be a patient reader, even in this day of eight volume novels.

It is not the orthodox historical novel. These characters do not in any sense aid to make history, as do those of Walter Scott or Dumas. They are made by history. They do not strut through its pages or even ruffle themselves with its borrowed plumes. They are always unconscious of their own significance. They even seek at all times to hide themselves in their peasant inconspicuousness. Yet to the author they are big with significance, for of such materials is history made. Pawns they may be, but without pawns there can be no history, for they are the ones who bear its burden, who suffer in silence, or in the same silence triumph. In spite of kings and generals, romantic soldiers and princesses radiant with beauty, these are history. They are the people, the country, the stuff of which human nature is made; and to it mankind must look for its ultimate vindication. The people are history.

Manzoni has the democratic faith in the value of the common man and common woman, and in their sound moral natures. It is this faith, in common humanity and in the moral worth of their ideals, that is half of his double creed; and he turns to history to discover its vindication. But in this conflict of the moral and the his-

torical there is a curious bringing together of the ideal
and the real. Unlike Walter Scott, who is accurate only
in the broad, general outlines of history, and who is aristocratically indifferent to its finer shading and color, Manzoni is scrupulously exact in its documentation. He knows
his background from the little village of Lecco to the
streets, churches, and palaces of Milan. His panorama
of the events from street riots to a city desolated by
pestilence, to a countryside forsaken of its inhabitants
fleeing in terror before advancing armies, is as accurate
as a photograph. His pictures of people and the way they
lived, princes and peasants, and their thoughts and ideals,
again are as accurate as though he had himself been an
actor in the drama. He never exaggerates for effect of
light and shadow, as does Victor Hugo. He does not
beat the drums and strike terror into his reader, nor see
history as a sinister and devouring monster, as again the
French romantic. All is cool and impersonal as a lecture
that is concerned only with truth, and it carries only interested conviction, not the gloom of overpowering destiny. Such is Manzoni the realist. The history of the
time was an evil thing, and sinister, it needs no romantic trappings to show its deadliness.

But when it comes to the characters, then the author's
point of view and purpose undergo a complete transformation. The central character, the one whose existence puts
the whole story into gear, is Lucia; and she is only simple
and attractive rural innocence. She is a heroine by no
possible stretch of the most elastic imagination. She is
good, childlike, pure, *so hold und schön und rein,* a village flower, with a child's sweet, naïve religion; and the
child's horror of sin. She is even less complex than
Rousseau's Héloïse. There is no fire or tempest in her
love for Renzo, and no questioning. Like her love for God

and the Madonna, she has been born for it, and it awakes
no more surprise than the air she breathes or the radiance
of sunlight. Such is her passive rôle through the whole
story, save for the one moment when terrified she cringes
at the feet of the Unnamed; and there it is only terror,
the terror of the unknown and sinful, and she commends
her innocence to the Mother.

Banal, commonplace, and unworthy of serious consideration is she? Not quite. The author has a purpose
in avoiding realism and in turning almost to the personifications of virtue of the old allegories, with her and with
the other characters. Rousseau as we remember with *The
New Héloïse* had done the same thing with his characters,
but he had likewise been as allegorical with the background. Renzo is no more a real character, or exactly a
type, either. He is practical courage, diligent and faithful
love, and love of justice; the masculine counterpart of
Lucia, and as innocent as she, and as devoid of open passion. There is about him the dogged perseverance of the
peasant who has learned to cope with the uncertainties by
means of single-minded toil. One can't be temperamental
with the phenomena of nature, one should not allow oneself likewise to be temperamental with the experience of
the other sex. He too takes love as the peasant takes
seed-time and harvest, with dogged perseverance and
loyalty.

Rodrigo is the incalculable evil, the unexpected tyranny
of nature, the power of destruction, malicious and over-
weening. Again there is no shading. It is suggested that
he might once have had a conscience allied to fear, but
like nature he rests secure in his irresponsibility, and
there is never a doubt that appetite, will, power are with
him their own justification. The girl for him was at first
a mere caprice, but because her attainment was made

difficult, she finally became a justification of his own existence; and he would move his heaviest artillery for her capture. Nothing short of a visitation of the plague can stop his career of destruction. Is this love a lust or sheer vindictiveness? Hardly either, for he is farther from being a real character than the two lovers he would destroy. Even Tartuffe, the most sinister of Molière's figures, or Iago, has his moments when he drops his mask and stands out as a clear personality. Rodrigo never.

Don Abbondio, the curate, is of all the characters the most interesting, shifty cowardice and absence of any moral compunctions. All the resources of this man of God, who should be shepherd of his flock, are turned to saving his skin. He is neither good nor bad, one can't call him unscrupulous, for he has never dreamed of scruples, any more than the mouse with a cat complex. He fears Rodrigo, he fears invading armies, he fears plagues, and he has cleverly devised runs and holes for escape. Abbondio is a superb comic figure of whom Molière might have been proud. But he is no real character. Nor are his spiritual opposites the Cardinal Bishop or the good friar, Cristoforo. They are Christian love and Christian service that know no difficulties too severe, and no bounds too remote for their virtue. They love and they serve all comers without question of merit or hope of reward. Rodrigo dying of plague is as near an object of charity as Lucia, perhaps nearer for his offense had been greater; and perfect love has long since cast out all offense. It is difficult not to love them, as it is impossible to call them real. They are human only because they are human aspiration.

In this last we have it, the secret of the charm of Manzoni's characters, unreal as are they all. For they are human ideals, not personifications of ideals, but expressed ideals in conflict with a world of bitter reality. How much more vivid this, and more significant, than Rousseau's fancy, where all is ideal, in *The New Héloïse*. For such is Manzoni's idea of history; it is a conflict between the human ideal and the historical real, and through this conflict comes progress, or, if one prefers the word, evolution.

How different this from the characters of the historical novel as it was given by Manzoni's best contemporaries. Scott, and I quote from a recent critic, "traveled into history to find gallantry and courage, loyalty and service, cleverness and oddity, the aroma of aristocracy and the savor of national character in new shapes and picturesque costumes. Essential humanity was his delight." He is looking for the essentials of noble, downright manhood, and the grounds for loyalty to human nature, that he may fortify the spirit and increase the delight of living. Because he did so he belongs to the tradition of the classical Greek, more than to the searching nineteenth century. Others, like Hugo, poke into the debris of romantic history for the grisly or the superhuman figures of romantic terror; and are always on the threshold of the supernatural even when they would be most real. Thus the romanticist would add "strangeness to beauty" and find compensation for the commonplace. Manzoni is looking for a formula for human destiny and for a vindication of the human ideal.

With Manzoni there is always an ideal around the corner, and hidden away in the most unsuspected places, yes even in the hearts of the most lowly. But it is always in conflict with the real, unhappy or suppressed or the victim of tyranny, right opposed to force, purity to corruption. The moral world, or the ideal, lives only in people's consciences. The real world would obscure this, or deny it, or destroy it. But only in the conflict is it realized and its significance seen for human welfare; and the fact even that it gets itself expressed is its victory. For daily Lucias are violated and Renzos overwhelmed and Abbondios and Rodrigos escape without penalty; but even defeat for the ideal is, if it be expressed, a moral victory of which humanity becomes conscious. The fact that in this story all ends well is of relative insignificance; be good and you will be happy in conscience, even if one's goodness gain no sugar plum, is an abiding law in this universe of ideals. This, as I take it, is the philosophy of the religious thinker and artist of the post-Napoleonic and troubled Italy of the nineteenth century.

This conflict of the real and the ideal is the story of history. Each age has its own ideal which in its characters it strives to express, as the conflict with the real by repercussion urges it to activity. Or to put it in another way, the ideal of each age is aroused to indignant activity by the unworthiness of the real. Manzoni then deliberately chose the most unworthy of the epochs of Italian history to illustrate the truth of his "law." But he had an eye, too, on his own age, after the fiasco of the revolution, when the Metternich policies of Imperial Austria again held Italy in subjection, and foreign armies again were invading the plains of Lombardy. In the sturdy conscience of the Italian peasant he saw the only hope of the unredeemed country. That conscience was vindicating his dream of an Italy liberated and morally conscious of its dignity. It is one of the gratifications of history that Manzoni lived to see the day of Italy's final triumph.

Trust in the conscience of the humble. We have seen the same doctrine in Rousseau. Wordsworth found love in the huts where poor men lie. This side of Manzoni's creed is going to be very popular in the succeeding decades of European and American letters. It might seem extravagant to look for it as the cause of the great popularity of *Uncle Tom's Cabin*, a book which even today is a testament in many countries of Europe, though sophisticated Americans have chided its lacrymose sentimentality. Better perhaps is a story like Balzac's *Country Doctor*, which one medical school, and a large one, a few years ago required its graduates to read as a text book on the doctor's conscience. For the picture there of devoted service and sacrifice, even to death, is full of the same trust in the human conscience.

But the English Manzoni is no less a figure than Charles Dickens. In him the awakened English conscience of liberalism and democracy is speaking, with overworked sentimentality at times—Manzoni was never sentimental —but with the same consciousness of a conflict between conscience and historical fact. One hardly needs to mention *Barnaby Rudge* and *Bleak House* as examples, to see how much the Englishman and the Italian have in common. Or to return to where we began, Scott, the eighteenth century Tory squire, has the same fundamental trust in genuine human nature that transcends all man-made classes and stations. His lowly characters have the same admirable soundness of conscience and action: "The likes o' us maun to our work again if our hearts were beating as hard as my hammer."

Manzoni is not promoting a war between the classes, nor pleading the cause of the proletariat. Conscience and the essential nobility of man knows no bounds of a social hierarchy. Borromeo is a noble by birth and a saint, Cristoforo is a bourgeois, Lucia is a peasant, and they meet on a common level. The Unnamed in his humility abases himself to the peasant. Again one is reminded of Walter Scott and of the remark of Edie Ochiltree in *The*

Antiquary, when noble and peasant are caught by the in-coming tide: "Our riches will soon be equal—they are sae already; for I have nae land, and you would give your fair bounds and barony for a square yard of rock that would be dry for twael hours."

True. But Manzoni's ideal is penetrated deeply with a consciousness of a vital religion. Lucia, who has every reason to hate the person of the villain Rodrigo, will not hate nor even endure the thought of his punishment.

" 'No, no, mother; no!' interrupted Lucia; 'don't predict suffering for him; don't predict it to any one! If you knew what it was to suffer! If you had tried it! No, No! rather let us pray God and the Madonna for him: that God would touch his heart, as he has done to this other poor Signor, who *was* worse than he is, and is now a saint.' "

Here is a Christian virtue that also knows no bounds. These meek ones have the great inheritance, the con-sciousness of victory.

VII. A VOCIFEROUS FAITH

WALT WHITMAN

"This is no book;
Who touches this touches a man."

Leaves of Grass

AMERICA was a warning or an inspiration or an interesting political experiment in the first half of the nineteenth century for all Europe. As journalists and philosophers today go to Russia to confirm their faith or to lift their hands in horrified surprise, *absit omen,* so they came in those days to America to return with their Notes or to write *Martin Chuzzlewits,* or to raise panegyrics for the "New Day." Goethe was thinking of a people freed from the dogmas of tradition and cleansed from superstition when he wrote the last scenes of the Faust.

"Such busy crowds I fain would see,
Upon free soil stand with a people free."

Chateaubriand is not less interested and enthusiastic when in his *Memoirs* he described President Washington and the American People as he met them on his visit during the days of the French Revolution.

"Placed on the ocean road, at the head of progress in opinions as new as his country, the American seems to have received from Columbus a mission to discover fresh worlds."

De Tocqueville was elected to the French Academy for a serious study of America and its institutions in the thirties. It is a book all Americans should be proud to read today, and give to it some quarter hours of serious thought.

"The Americans never use the word 'peasant,' because they have no idea of the peculiar class which that term denotes; the ignorance of more remote ages, the simplicity of rural life, and the rusticity of the villager, have not been preserved among them; and they are alike unacquainted with the virtues, the vices, the coarse habits, and the simple graces of an early stage of civilization. . . . As soon as the pioneer arrives upon the spot which is to serve him for a retreat, he fells a few trees and builds a log-house. . . . Who would not suppose that this poor hut is the asylum of rudeness and ignorance? Yet no sort of comparison can be drawn between the pioneer and the dwelling which shelters him. Everything about him is primitive and unformed, but he is himself the result of the labour and the experience of eighteen centuries. He wears the dress, and he speaks the language of cities; he is acquainted with the past, curious of the future, and ready for argument upon the present; he is, in short, a highly civilized being, who consents, for a time, to inhabit the back-woods, and who penetrates into the wilds of a New World with the Bible, an axe, and a file of newspapers."

Before Whitman literature in America had with becoming modesty, as a younger sister, followed the tradition of Europe, a city literature in the main, and, if on American themes, refined and conscious of the large models that Europe supplied. Whitman, with ample lungs and vociferous, is the America that De Tocqueville saw and felt in his cool and detached paragraphs. He is the poet of the America before the Civil War, and the America in the amplitude of its faith that made the war into a Crusade for humanity. His is the protest of the pioneer and the dreamer, the protest that conquered the wilderness and spanned the continent, the protest of the new individualism that broke into excess in the new industrialism, and that even today talks of "industrial democracy." His is the spirit of revolt carried out into practice and conquering a continent.

This is a far different thing from the revolt from society and the return to nature of a Rousseau, or the love of the primitive of a Chateaubriand, or a dreaming of worlds to come of Shelley. Whitman, as we shall see in the sequel, ignores the primitive and desires complexity and variety. He has the optimism of Shelley, but will put it into instant use. For Whitman was the buoyant, restless, assertive, crude always, but deeply sensitive, and titanically energetic spirit of these early States.

One should feel some diffidence in attempting an analysis of Whitman's ideas. For he has left the plain warning: "Do not attempt to explain me; I cannot explain myself." Yet seldom has a poet left in his poetry so complete an account of his varied ideas. But the pattern is baffling, for to Whitman, as to few others, poetry is a response to the sheer ecstasy of living; it is his joy or pain translated into ideas. To him it was allowed to "warm both hands before the fire of life," in a way that would quite have shocked the statue-like propriety of the New England poets. He himself has told us of his growing volume of poems, the *Leaves of Grass*,

> "This is no book;
> Who touches this touches a man."

Nearly every poem in it owes its thought or its imagery to actual experience. There is no continuous argument here, as in Wordsworth's biographical *Prelude* or *Excursion*. There are no flashes of insight that came, as they came to Emerson as he rambled alone in the Concord woods or along the Merrimac. His responses are like those of the organ when life, like the organist, presses the key.

A curious farrago of interruptions this life of his appears as one studies it chronologically, a curious pattern of tangled threads. Though his father was a poor carpenter of Long Island, yet he had intellectual decision and independence enough to break with orthodoxy and range himself with the Deists. This stubborn individualism was about all the young boy inherited from his parents. Walt, as he preferred to call himself, was country bred, though he lived near the city and made numerous visits to Brooklyn and New York. The education he received was caught on the fly in a printer's shop, and later as editor of papers from Brooklyn to New Orleans. He taught school, wrote for magazines and papers, wrote poetry in the conventional manner. With quick sentimentalism we see him making friends on the water front of the city, with truck drivers, and laborers. He held no position long. He was indolent or dissatisfied with the routine, or unable to compromise with his principles. He traveled south and west to New Orleans, then returned to New York by way of the Mississippi and Great Lakes. It was not until the Civil War, when he met reality face to face on the battlefield, that there slipped into his life the controlling purpose that made him the poet of American democracy. It was then also that he contracted the ailment that made him a sufferer until his death. But there is never a murmur nor complaint. He bravely faced the world, received an ever increasing circle of friends, and wrote his greatest poems. There are in truth two Whitmans, the young and the old, the irresponsible youth and the mature man ripe in experience.

Whitman is the poet of individualism. He had seen early that this faith is no mere chance theory haply chosen by American democracy to translate into practice, but is the secret of its growth and the promise of its future greatness. Into his faith had entered his earliest instincts. He early gained for it a philosophy by reading Mill *On Liberty*. There he found the idea that a democracy to be vital must have a large variety of characters and allow full play of personality. Any narrowing or restricting creed, which makes much of conformity and convention, or of class consciousness and class legislation, things not entirely unfamiliar today to a brood of social reformers, he would abhor as stifling the amplest freedom demanded by democracy. Nor must it restrict the free play of personality, even of eccentricity, which alone can give it richness and savor. Thus he revolted against the prevailing Puritan or Quaker asceticism, and took pride in draining the cup of experience even to the dregs. To his friend John Burroughs he confessed that he had "sounded all experiences of life, with all passions, pleasures, and abandonments." [1]

Instinctively he was drawn to the gospel of "Transcendentalism." Whether he caught the contagion from Emerson, or whether it was in the air, is a matter critics have yet left unsettled. The question does not matter. He had met Emerson, admired him, and in places seems almost to quote him. Emerson was one of the earliest to catch the original note in Whitman's poetry and to proclaim its potency. Emerson introduced him to the charmed circle, to Bronson Alcott, to Thoreau. But the new doctrine was like new wine to young enthusiasts; and for Whitman there was in these early days no Puritan conscience or orthodox creed to restrain his intemperance.

---

[1] It makes little difference whether Whitman's confessions are true or not. The exuberance of life is there, whether he carried it out into exuberant action or not. It is his state of mind that is interesting, and this appears best in his poems. Hence I am only remotely interested in the findings or speculations of his recent biographers.

Already he was a soul in revolt, the unrestrained vitality of this inspiration gave him a philosophy for his impulses. It was the dawning of a new day, and the freeing of the imagination for unexplored flights.

> "From this hour, freedom!
> From this hour I ordain myself loos'd of limits and imaginary lines."

Transcendentalism gave him a philosophical creed. To it truth is not a thing of books, or of the slow process of logical proof, or even of human utterance. It is grasped only by the intuition, by flights of the fancy or imagination, by the deeper instinctive knowledge of man and nature. Thus he launched himself into the welter of experience and into the joyous abandon of nature to catch the eternal secret. But it is not man and nature as it has been catalogued and indexed by science; from this the glory of truth has departed, it is the husk from which the spirit has flown. It is the unknown, the unique, the bizarre that he would seek, for life to him now is a great adventure into the Unknown, a search of unexplored regions with the imagination and instinct as his guide.

> "What is known I strip away:
> I launch all men and women forward with me into
>   THE UNKNOWN."

> "Here is the test of wisdom;
> Wisdom is not finally tested in schools;
> Wisdom cannot be pass'd from one having it, to another
>   not having it;
> Wisdom is of the Soul, is not susceptible of proof, is its
>   own proof,
> Applies to all stages and objects and qualities, and is
>   content,
> Is the certainty of the reality and immortality of things,
>   and the excellence of things;
> Something there is in the float of the sight of things that
>   provokes it out of the Soul."

There is a subtle intoxication in all this quite unknown to the devotee of pure science. Indeed, Whitman goes farther to turn his back on all that civilization has hitherto termed good, lest it act as a clog to the freest human endeavor. Even good manners must go, and conformity in dress and action. Thus he has himself portrayed in his 1855 edition of the *Leaves of Grass* in open flannel shirt and ranger's hat. There is a youthful abandon here, a lifting the heel against every convention, almost a pure spirit of mischief like that of a boy on a stolen holiday, before hunger and fear of the dark drive him home.

> "I am he who tauntingly compels men, women, nations,
>   Crying, Leap from your seats, and contend for your
>   lives!"

> "If you would be freer than all that has been before, come
>   listen to me."

> "Fear grace—Fear elegance, civilization, delicatesse,
>   Fear the mellow sweet, the sucking of honey-juice;
>   Beware the advancing mortal ripening of nature,
>   Beware what precedes the decay of the ruggedness of
>   states and men."

Yet he has his note of seriousness as well. He reveals the responsibility those must assume who, like him, would cut themselves loose from the path of convention and law. For it is a lonely path, this open road of self-reliance. He can but point the way—

> "My right hand pointing to landscapes of continents,
>   and a plain public road.
> Not I—Not anyone else, can travel that road for you,
>   you must travel it for yourself."

This is nothing but Emerson's doctrine of "Self Reliance," but with what utter abandon and joyous absence of restraint the youthful Whitman plunges along the lone highway. It is the morning song of youth, before the evil days come; later he saw that heaven could not be reached at a bound and utter freedom achieved by declaring in a loud voice that one is free from all restraint. Later we shall see, though he never abandoned his philosophy—one would not want him to do that—that he feels the need of discipline even for individualism, a discipline that cannot be had for a mere shrug of one's shoulders. But now the sky is bright, the breeze cool, and the road to "landscapes of continents" lies open and inviting, and he is without care.

"Afoot and light-hearted, I take to the open road,
   Healthy, free, the world before me,
   The long brown path before me, leading wherever I choose.

"Henceforth I ask not good-fortune—
   I myself am good fortune;
   Henceforth I whimper no more, postpone no more, need
      nothing,
   Strong and content, I travel the open road."

"From this hour, freedom!
   From this hour I ordain myself loos'd of limits and
      imaginary lines,
   Going where I list, my own master, total and absolute,
   Listening to others, and considering well what they say,
   Pausing, searching, receiving, contemplating,
   Gently, but with undeniable will, divesting myself of
      the holds that would hold me.

"I inhale great draughts of space;
   The east and the west are mine, and the north and the
      south are mine!"

The world, great draughts of space, the north and the south, are his for the asking. This is invigorating, and a heady tonic, like the wind from a snowy mountain peak on an early morning. It is the frenzy of jubilation, the beating of the tomtoms to exorcise the evil spirit and restore humanity to its pristine joyousness and endeavor. One can love Whitman for the abundance of his early morning faith, before the sun becomes hot and the road dusty and long, and the distant continents shimmer in the heat, and mirages dance before one's eyes. But democracy and individualism if they are to justify themselves must do more than make a noise of shoutings. The battle is yet to be joined.

But this was the individualism of adolescent America, breathing the freshness, the vitality of the new emancipation. It had yet been unchecked by experience, and unmellowed by time. Whitman "is the Declaration of Independence incarnate." The crudeness and unloveliness of those days we can see now, as it struck superficial foreigners, in the *Notes* by Charles Dickens and in his *Martin Chuzzlewit*. It was the time of Jacksonian democracy. The ideals in the new west—and Whitman belongs to the west in spirit at least—were those of the pioneer, the rugged homeliness of speech and manners, the contempt for refinement as an effete reminiscence of an outworn culture. But the spirit was justifying itself in the large. A continent was being opened up; forests were being felled to make a path for the railroad and spaces for cultivation; rivers were being bridged; already the mountains had been crossed, and the new democracy was sprawling over the valleys of the western coast. It was the inarticulate creed of every covered wagon that crept its way across the great plains. Whitman has justified the faith of the American pioneer. He is the faith.

Hence there will be crudeness and restlessness and irresponsibility in his life. Youth of this sort will quickly feel the uselessness and bondage of routine and long for large creative effort. Think of imprisoning within the narrow walls of a country school the spirit that has ordained itself "free from all limits and imaginary lines." How shall one, whom faith teaches that "wisdom cannot be passed from one having it, to another not having it," be content to pass his time teaching the "rule of three" and the multiplication tables to youngsters, or writing editorials for the *Brooklyn Eagle*. Had he spoken his real thoughts in either place there would have been much bewilderment among the children and parents and a horrified newspaper owner. There were doubtless both on more occasions than one; and one smiles at the picture of young Whitman, the editor and carrier of a country weekly, losing his position for failure to be prompt in his deliveries. He had other and larger matters to occupy his time; and to these he turns his restless, irresponsible, and creative imagination.

But judged by the standards of excellence and taste—though Whitman would have been the first to reject these as standards—his early poems are wanting in several important particulars. There is a lack of discrimination that is disconcerting, even discouraging. Here again one thinks of Dickens' strictures on the lack of excellence in much of American democracy. Determined to use the language of everyday life and eschew the paraphernalia of current poetic diction, we yet find him dropping into foreign expressions or imitations of foreign words, "camerado," "salut au monde," "libertad," "en masse." What would the democracy which Whitman professed to address make of such drawings of French and Spanish waters from the undefiled spring of the American muse? Nor is he always quite happy in his choice even of English. But these faults critics have played with since the beginning. They mar the perfect symmetry, but they do not destroy the picture. More serious is the lack of discrimination which must be traced to an essential lack of humor—militant youth ever takes itself seriously, and forgets in its enthusiasm that all objects of its adoration are not equally valuable. His *Salut au Monde* though it has some of his finest poetry, is also a lesson in geography. He has forgotten nothing in his eagerness to set down all races and peoples. There is a large grotesqueness in the ample catalogue he furnishes us at times, and not seldom, of the objects of his contemplation. This is not poetry, it is a capricious plundering of the dictionary, it is the large garrulousness of untrained youth.

In his revolt against the niceties he shocked even Emerson. What the Concord sage's defiance of social conventions had unconsciously implied Whitman shouts from the housetops. Prudery also and false shame and the fear of exposure of the human body were conventions that this young iconoclast must shatter. So unashamed he sings the beauty of nudity and the mystery of parenthood. If both body and soul are divine then both are equally available for poetry. The thought gives him his theme:

> "I am the poet of the Body;
> And I am the poet of the Soul."

And he proceeded, much to the consternation of even his chiefest admirers, to exploit what Puritanism had always shrouded with careful decency.

Learning from the Transcendentalist that evil is but a subjective hallucination, possessing no objective or external reality, he proclaims with complacent fervor, "Evil propels me and reform of evils propels me—I stand indifferent." Here is again the sublime confidence of unsophisticated youth in this denial of evil, making a curious parody of Pippa's song in Browning's poem: "Walt Whitman's on this earth; all is well in heaven." But at least this confidence is wholesome, born of good digestion and an unfailing appetite. He is far different from Wordsworth whose spirit became queasy at the sight of the evil in the world, and who to escape suffering put himself upon a restricted diet. Whitman glories in evil, for it is one more opportunity to show the infinite potency of self-reliant individualism.

There is egotism in this, egotism at times blatantly vocal. "I am the acme of things accomplished, and I am encloser of things to be." But this is not to imply that the poet felt or proclaimed himself better than the rest of humanity, in regal splendor thinking thoughts for them to digest; far from it, he is proclaiming to America, and to the world, the significance of this new power, when each man and each woman shall realise the significance of individual personality. Each then may make his own pattern of life, not bounded by any constraints, unbewildered by convention or tradition. At least he will show how easily it is done; and he writes a poem of some thousand lines about himself. It is not an apology, it is a creed and a defiance and a mystery.

> "Walt Whitman am I a Kosmos, of mighty Manhattan
>   the son,
> Turbulent, fleshy and sensual, eating, drinking, and
>   breeding,
> No sentimentalist—no stander above men and women,
>   or apart from them;
> No more modest than immodest."

> "I too am not a bit tamed—I too am untranslatable;
> I sound my barbaric yawp over the roofs of the world."

But Whitman, though he has this large grossness, this love of the pure animal life, is by no means to be confused with a more modern school of realists who have called themselves disciples of naturalism. Our poet's view of the world is that of a perfectly healthy, normal being with large appetites and keen emotions, but it is never morbid. Man's life is divided between the activities of the body and those of the soul or mind, and these must each have due proportion. The school of naturalism is often not a little inclined to show a diseased imagination, to dwell with the morbid, the sickly, the socially, mentally, or physically unbalanced. Whitman, though he recognises the charm of sex and its vital claims, would never for example, have been of the school of Freud who finds the demands of sex at the bottom of most unconscious and instinctive action. The problems of sex with Whitman are like the problems of food, recurrent and normal, and hence human, but not to be exaggerated or to control all conduct.

Indeed he gets one very significant thought from the contemplation of animals. They are always wholesome and well, and act fully up to their instincts and from moment to moment. Tradition, law, custom, history, religion, conscience, mean nothing to them; they are individuals living each one on the dictates of its own immediate needs.

> "I think I could turn and live with animals, they are so
>   placid and self-contained:
> I stand and look at them long and long.
> They do not sweat and whine about their condition;
> They do not lie awake in the dark and weep for their
>   sins;
> They do not make me sick discussing their duty to God;
> Not one is dissatisfied—not one is demented with the
>   mania of owning things;

> Not one kneels to another, nor to his kind that lived
>   thousands of years ago;
> Not one is respectable or industrious over the whole
>   earth."

But there is more than the mere love of the physical in Whitman's youthful creed displayed at such length in his poem to himself. It proclaims his secret of life, the common humanity of man, and the spirit that breathes through all man and nature.

> "And I know that the spirit of God is the brother of my
>   own;
> And that all the men ever born are also my brothers,
>   and the women my sisters and lovers;
> And that a kelson of the creation is love;
> And limitless are leaves, stiff or drooping in the fields;
> And brown ants in the little wells beneath them;
> And mossy scabs of the worm fence, and heap'd stones,
>   elder, mullen, and poke-weed."

He recounts the varied experiences of life to show the heroic stuff of mankind, heroic in action or suffering—the hounded slave wincing at the bite of the dogs, the Yankee clipper captain on his distant voyage, the butcher boy, the singer, the artilleryman wounded in battle, Whitman is all of them; they are he. He draws vivid pictures of the massacre of four hundred and fifty prisoners, of the capture of a British sloop of war, with its heroism and carnage, and he again is the action and the actors.

> "I embody all prisoners outlawed or suffering.
> Not a mutineer walks handcuffed to jail, but I am hand-
>   cuffed to him and walk by his side;
> Not a cholera patient lies at the last gasp, but I also lie
>   at my last gasp."

Democracy to be a national or world creed must not stop with individualism. In this poem to himself he proclaims the mystic union of all humanity with the pervading spirit of love. It was this lesson, with others, that was brought home to Whitman by the fires of the Civil War. There will henceforth be less of egotism, less of grotesque posturing, and less of the flaunting of his eccentricities. For after all one is tempted to think that much of Whitman's egotism and parading of himself, his youthful gawkiness and unrestrained imagination, was a mantle of self-protection hiding what was really a sensitive spirit. The calmness of conscious power was to come later.

When the Civil War broke out Whitman was at first indifferent. It was not until his brother was wounded and he went to the field hospital to nurse him that his imagination caught fire and he saw the significance of the conflict. Here were things that were evils, and could not be denied, war, hate, bloodshed. Then throughout the long years of the war he gave himself utterly, in hospitals, on the battlefield, to the ministry to the wounded and dying. He came away from this experience "the good grey poet."

American Democracy also has never been quite the same thing since the Civil War. The agitation of the abolitionists, the reforms sought by the Transcendentalists, these were only in part the cause of the war. One may speak also of the economic causes of the struggle, the inevitable conflict between slave labor and free industry. But the North that went into the struggle with a lofty idealism was looking not only for the freedom of the negro slave, but for the sweeping away of the accumulated rubbish of generations, and for the coming of a brighter and better day for all humanity. Language was used then, as we have used it since, to describe it as a war of ideals, a war for the triumph of democracy. The freeing

of the slave was but the symbol of the freedom that was
to be offered to all humanity. It was in this spirit that the
West spent and was spent in the four years. For the pioneer West was the heart of the cause of the North. The
idealism of the Pioneer was never more clearly seen than
on the battlefields of Antietam, Gettysburg, and Lookout
Mountain. It saw in the feudalism of the South the denial
of individualism which to the pioneer was the heritage
and secret of democracy.

But the horror and waste of the war and the hates en-
gendered and the slow process of reconstruction sobered
the North. For though idealism unchecked by the school
of experience might pour out its life unselfishly on the
battlefield, though it might be the stuff of which martyrs
are made; yet after the martyrdom, after the victory
was won, there remained the yet nobler task of reuniting
the fragments of a country lately so torn with anger and
horror. The North and the South could not go on forever with bitterness in their hearts. If democracy was to
be real it must show now even a finer idealism, and learn
by experience the gentle art of "binding up a nation's
wounds."

This was precisely what Whitman was doing on the
battlefield and in camp hospitals even before the war was
over. The word hate was never less in his vocabulary
than when as a wound dresser he moved with the armies,
giving his aid equally to friend and foe, and seeing in both
the wrecks of a common humanity, the children of a
common mother.

But first he saw clearly that the war must be fought to
a successful termination. There was no possibility of
compromise when the forces were once engaged in the
final appeal to arms. He was no pacifist. He had suddenly awakened and discovered evil threatening his ideal

of democracy; and until this evil had been conquered there was no time to sing the beatitudes of peace and quietness. Instead he cried with exultation:

"Thunder on! stride on, Democracy! strike with vengeful stroke." He knew the cost of war, the horror of the carnage and the arguments on the uselessness of it all, the economic loss, the thing we are again hearing today. He had seen in his imagination the horror of war long before 1861. But the drums were beating, the enemy already had taken the field, and he exulted in the spirit that calls for the noblest self-sacrifice:

> "Beat! beat! drums!— Blow! bugles! blow!
> Make no parley—stop for no expostulation;
> Mind not the timid—mind not the weeper or prayer;
> Mind not the old man beseeching the young man;
> Let not the child's voice be heard nor the mother's
>   entreaties;
> Make even the trestles to shake the dead, where they lie
>   awaiting the hearses,
> So strong you thump, O terrible drums—so loud you
>   bugles blow."

Above waved the flag, the symbol of the ideal of democracy—

> "O you up there! O pennant! where you undulate like
>   a snake, hissing so curious,
> Out of reach—an idea only—yet furiously fought for,
>   risking bloody death—loved by me!
> So loved! O you banner leading the day, with stars
>   brought from the night!
> Valueless, object of eyes, over all and demanding all—
>   (absolute owner of all)—O banner and pennant!
> I too leave the rest—great as it is, it is nothing—
>   houses, machines, are nothing—I see them not;
> I see but you, O warlike pennant! O banner so broad,
>   with stripes, I sing you only,
> Flapping up there in the wind."

Whitman is never better as a poet than in his poems of the battlefield and hospital. Where before there had been posturings and mouthings, though much sincerity too, here is sincerest of emotion and restraint of expression. The pain he sees, he himself feels.

> "I onward go, I stop,
>   With hinged knees and steady hand, to dress wounds;
>   I am firm with each—the pangs are sharp, yet unavoidable;
>   One turns to me his appealing eyes—poor boy! I never knew you,
>   Yet I think I could not refuse this moment to die for you, if that would save you.
>
> "Then to the third—a face nor child, nor old, very calm, as of beautiful yellow white ivory;
>   Young man, I think I know you—I think this face of yours is the face of Christ himself;
>   Dead and divine, brother of all and here again he lies."

In the days of Reconstruction that followed, his ideal of democracy became more and more tempered by reflection. His stormy youth had passed; he acquired the needed restraint, that is restraint for Whitman, and he proceeded to a fuller and nobler exposition of his theme. He saw early that the Union, preserved by force, could only be united by the spirit of love:

> "Over the carnage rose prophetic a voice,
>   Be not disheartened—Affection shall solve the problems of Freedom yet;
>   Those who love each other shall become invincible—they shall yet make Columbia victorious.
>   It shall be customary in the houses and streets to see manly affection;
>   The most dauntless and rude shall touch face to face lightly;

> The dependence of Liberty shall be lovers,
> The continuance of Equality shall be comrades."

The war left Whitman more than ever convinced of the essential truth in the theory of democracy; and to the end he retained his essential faith in individualism:

> "Oneself I sing—a simple, separate Person:
> Yet utter the word Democratic, the word *en masse.*"

It became the poet's task to reconcile these two ideals by means of the active spirit of love. To him, with his Quaker tradition all of which he had revolted against save this spirit of love, the task was not a difficult one. He had a far wider and more generous scope of affection than Emerson or any other of the colder New England group. They had drawn their traditions too deeply from the acid well of Calvinism.

Whitman, too, came to realize slowly what America has not yet quite consented to, that Democracy is a late, a very late stage in a people's progress. He even confessed in his *Democratic Vistas* that all people are not ready for it, and that a period of tutelage may be necessary. Carlyle in his *Chartism* and his *Shooting Niagara* had prophesied darkly of the dangers of the American experiment. Democracy was with him a wiping of the slate, a clearing out of old rubbish against a new form of government and society. It was itself a zero, an empty stage on which new properties are to be assembled. In a way all Whitman's later poems are a prophetic utterance in answer to Carlyle. With a rude, robust people, crude in sentiment and intelligence, there may be much misunderstanding of liberty, the kind of thing perhaps painted by Plato in his warning against an excess of democracy, where "Subjects are like rulers, and where rulers are like subjects."

"In such a state of society the master fears and flatters his scholars, and the scholars despise their masters and tutors; young and old are all alike; and the young man is on a level with the old and is ready to compete with him in word or deed; and old men condescend to the young and are full of pleasantry and gaiety; and they are loth to be thought morose and authoritative, and therefore they adopt the manners of the young. . . . And the horses and asses have a way of marching along with all the rights and dignities of freemen: . . . and all things are ready to burst with liberty."

Equality may also be sought by suppressing all individuals of superior ability to the level of the majority; and there may always be a plentiful lack of fraternity for all who differ either in ability or theory or practice from the gross majority. And who shall judge between Plato and Carlyle, and Whitman and Shelley?

But whether people liked it or not, the drift of the world was then toward democracy. America had long been committed. Whitman was keen enough to realize this fact, and he gloried in it, and foresaw the triumph of a world democracy, self-restrained, peaceful, and at work. For him the present stage is transitory. He saw the crudeness and ignorance of its youth, with its bad manners and intolerance; it was his belief that with riper years and experience these will disappear and give place to settled wisdom. In his own life he tried to be an allegory of America.

In the first place Whitman loved America with an intense passion as is seldom revealed in literature. He had a pride in its size and its complexity, even in its crudeness, imperfection, vices and caprices.

"These States are the amplest poem,
   Here is not merely a nation, but a teeming nation of
      nations,
   Here the doings of men correspond with the broadcast
      doings of the day and night,

> Here is what moves in magnificent masses, careless of
>   particulars,
> Here are the roughs, beards, friendliness, combative-
>   ness, the Soul loves,
> Here the flowing trains—here the crowds, equality,
>   diversity, the Soul loves."

It is not a meaningless boast and love due to the accident of his birth, but a true pride because America had a destiny in the world, a destiny commensurate with its size.

"Sole among nationalities these states have assumed the task to put in forms of lasting power and practicality, on areas of amplitude rivalling the operations of the physical cosmos, the moral political speculations of ages, long, long deferred, the democratic republican principle, and the theory of development and perfection of voluntary standards and self-reliance."

He has no hazy notion of the State as a thing apart from the individuals that compose it. Though he may personify America in his poems, he has none of that power of abstraction possessed by some modern theorists—he is unable ever to think abstractly—who think of the state as a thing distinct from the citizens, and to which the citizen must duly subordinate his instincts and his interests. Whitman does not even think of humanity in the abstract.

> "O I see now, flashing, that this America is only you
>   and me,
> Its power, weapons, testimony, are you and me,
> Its crimes, lies, defections, slavery, are you and me,
> Its Congress is you and me—the officers, capitols, armies,
>   ships are you and me,
> Its endless gestations of new States are you and me,
> The war—that war so bloody and grim—the war I will
>   henceforth forget—was you and me,
> Natural and artificial are you and me,

Freedom, language, poems, employments, are you and
me,
Past, present, future, are you and me."

In order that Democracy may survive the experiment
that America is making, the first duty of all is to preserve
the ideal of individualism, to redefine it, and to spiritual-
ize it. It is possibly true that the greatest periods of human progress have been the times when this ideal was
strong and full of meaning; and that the ages of stag-
nation, of living on the past or with the past, have been
times when man allowed himself to forget this first duty
to himself. For this reason Whitman distrusts organized
majorities.

"It behooves you to convey yourself implicitly to no party, nor
submit blindly to their dictators, but steadily hold yourself judge and
master over all of them."

In this it would seem that Whitman is proposing what
in essence is but a general biological law—the species is
for the sake of the individual.

"I swear nothing is good to me that ignores individuals,
The American compact is altogether with individuals,
The only government is that which makes minute of
individuals,
The whole theory of the universe is directed unerringly
to one single individual—namely to You."

But the individual must be worthy of the trust that
nature has reposed in him. The individuals must not be
weak or sickly, puny in body and shrunken in soul, mouth-
ing their unfulfilled wishes and their infinite desires.
There is such a class today who cast the burden of their ill-
assorted aspirations and abilities upon the shoulders of
this wholesome giant. But he would never recognize the

brood as his offspring. They speak neither his language nor think his thoughts. His great individuals are the Lincolns, the Miltons, the Cromwells, men who leaned on themselves, for theirs was perfect self-reliance. It is his essential faith that only in a democracy will full opportunity be found to develop such unafraid and unashamed spirits; and he would have a multitude of them. A critic once wrote of him: "In his conception of equality he is least American—as in his ideal of democracy the ideal of excellence is wanting." It is curious how far wrong even a celebrated critic of American literature may go. When speaking of equality, Whitman is speaking of individuals like Lincoln and Grant, of the right heroic stuff, though their lives may never be celebrated in poetry or history; and when he thinks of excellence it is of the possibilities hitherto unexplored of self-reliant men.

There is no question about what Whitman would say in answer to the pleadings of the humanitarians, who look with compassion upon the forgotten man and would sacrifice the alert and the vigorous, that the weak and the halt might live in comfort. To do this would be to stop all social and spiritual progress; his remedy for social ills would be more intelligent individualism. The race is to the strong; and yet there is no reason why all should not be strong. So far from being affected by the ideas of communism, Whitman looks quite in the opposite direction. The very basis of democracy is the ownership of property, for largely by its means can come that essential self-respect and pride. "The poor are a disgrace to a democracy. She asks for men and women with occupations, well off, owners of houses and acres, and with cash in the bank—and with some cravings for literature too." He hated equally the predatory individualist as a menace to democracy, for he was often the cause of poverty. Instead of a society with economic extremes exposed to the danger of repression or rebellion, he would have a society stabilized by individuals each working according to his powers, and proud in self-dependence.

It is curious too that Whitman rarely or never uses the word "service," which today is urged so feelingly by theories of reform. The best service one can perform for an individual, he would say, is to arouse his pride in himself alone, to give him "this image of completeness in separation, of individual personal dignity, of a single person, either male or female, characterized in the main, not from extrinsic acquirements or position, but in pride of himself or herself alone." For society as a whole will be no larger nor better than the individuals that compose it. They give it its character, for good or evil, for weakness or strength; and "perfect individualism is indeed that which tinges and gives character to the idea of the aggregate."

To be sure there is the example of Thoreau who in his individualism retreated to Walden and lived on eight dollars a year, a rebel against society and a recluse. At the other extreme is the criminal who in his "pride in himself" exacts his heavy toll from his neighbors. There is also Hawthorne's warning in his *Doctor Rappaccini's Daughter*, that individual eccentricity, though benevolent, may go so far as to blight with poison those who come near it. Self-reliance may thus weave its own halter and society perish of the very excess of its virtue. All this seems possible; and there are other evils, in these days of new deals on all continents, that democracy is heavily charged with.

All these thoughts seemingly had come to the poet, but caused him no doubt of his theme. "Democracy too is law," he would say to some, "and of the amplest, strict-

est kind." The law will not be one of an external authority, imposed from without; but an expression of man's
own best nature. "Man properly trained in sanest, highest
freedom, may and must become a law, and series of laws
unto himself, surrounding and providing for, not only his
personal control, but all his relations to other individuals
and to the state."

During the period of transition there may be much
contempt for the rights of others, and much disorder;
but where is the progressive state, he would exclaim, that
is not in the excess of its energy a trifle disorderly? It is
like a growing infant, showing its vitality in part by its
destructiveness and noise. But on transcendental grounds
Whitman trusted the individual, his deepest desires must
per se be good; and as deep and as fundamental as his
desire for self-expression will also be that other demand
for sympathy and love.

Whitman calls it solidarity, this second trait that must
be possessed by a true democracy. No state can be held
together by any other tie. Constitutions and laws, and all
the paraphernalia of state-craft, unless they express this
deep motive of national affection, are of no avail.

> "Were you looking to be held together by the lawyers?
> Or by an agreement of a paper? or by arms?
> —Nay—not the world, nor any living thing, will so cohere."

There is a word here for those who would set up revolutionary governments founded upon the motive of class
hatreds, or who would think in terms of class legislation.
But Whitman never shows his desire for concreteness
better than when he speaks of this unselfish bond of affection that holds together the nation. He is least of all a
mystic here. He does not vaporize over universal benevolence, brotherly love, and the other stock phrases that

are much in the vocabularies of social reformers. He prefers rather the word comrade or as he often playfully uses it "camerado." His heart goes out to the dead rebel soldier, to the poor savage woman, to the tanned plains-boy who newly joins the regiment. Always with him it is the affection of person for person, and thus must it be "in Democracy en masse."

With this motive would disappear that menace to democracy, greed and a desire to excel at the cost of one's neighbor. With it also would go, as the poet fancies, the other ills that drive the criminal to his crimes, and the recluse to his woods and Walden. Even a Doctor Rappaccini would see the essential danger of his form of individualism to society and would turn and cultivate less dismal vegetables. The same spirit that prompted John Woolman to sigh over the hard fate of post-boys is working here in the serious democratic promptings of Walt Whitman. One can read it also in well known passages in the New Testament. The fact that it is not yet universal is no blemish on its beauty or on its power to inspire prophet and poet.

But Whitman saw also its universal significance to Democracy. He saw clearly that, whether statesmen and philosophers, the Bismarcks and Nietzsches liked it or no, the trend of the world consciousness was toward democratic principles. Europe already was learning to speak a democratic language, Asia and even Africa would follow in time. He saw the triumph of its ideal in the "universalizing" of all humanity in "loving comradeship." "Democracy," he exclaimed, "alone can bind all nations, all men, into a brotherhood, a family." There are many captious critics today who decry the notion of universal benevolence and world brotherhood. The war has left us with its aftermath of jealousies and hates, and national boundaries are more forbidding than even when Whitman saw the devastation of a half dozen wars in Europe and America, but it is none the less edifying today to read soberly lines like these:

> "This moment yearning and thoughtful sitting alone,
>   It seems to me there are other men in other lands yearn-
>   ing and thoughtful,
>   It seems to me I can look over and behold them in Ger-
>   many, Italy, France, Spain,
>   Or far, far away, in China, or in Russia or Japan, talking
>   other dialects,
>   And it seems to me if I could know these men I should
>   become attached to them as I do to men in my
>   own lands,
>   O I know we should be brethren and lovers,
>   I know I should be happy with them."

This is far less unrestrained in expression than the earlier "Salut au Monde," but it is inspired by the same wish, "By God! I will accept nothing which all cannot have their counterpart of on the same terms." It is not un-fitting to call Whitman the poet of a sublime and serious world Democracy. Such is the ideal that he places before America.

To Whitman, America has three supreme tasks, to create a political organization which shall be commensurate with her size; to organize science and industry for her physical and mental welfare; and finally to discover a new art, literature, morals, and religion. The first two tasks have been partly performed and are progressing rapidly. The last remains. Whitman proposes to speak with confidence on the need of a new literature and poetry, to suit the needs of the new culture of Democracy. "The poet of the modern is wanted, or the great literatus of the modern." He, when he comes, will do more for America than all wars or all political or social legislation. He must no longer look to the past or to Europe for inspiration; rather he, above all others, will speak with the voice of authority for he will know the doctrine of utter self-reliance. To him the seer turns:

"Are you he who would assume a place to teach, or be
a poet here in the States?
The place is august—the terms obdurate.

"Who would assume to teach here, may well prepare himself, body and mind,
He may well survey, ponder, arm, fortify, harden, make
lithe, himself,
He shall surely be question'd beforehand by me with
many and stern questions.

"Who are you, indeed, who would talk or sing to
America?
Have you studied out the land, its idioms and men?
Have you learn'd the physiology, phrenology, politics,
geography, pride, freedom, friendship, of the
land? its substratums and objects?
Have you consider'd the organic compact of the first day
of the first year of Independence, sign'd by the
Commissioners, ratified by The States, and read
by Washington at the head of the army?
Have you possess'd yourself of the Federal Constitution?

"Do you see who have left all feudal processes and poems
behind them, and assumed the poems and processes of Democracy?
Are you faithful to things? do you teach as the land
and sea, the bodies of men, womanhood, amative-
ness, angers, teach?
Have you sped through fleeting customs, popularities?
Can you hold your hand against all seductions, follies,
whirls, fierce contentions? are you very strong?
are you really of the whole people?

Are you not of some coterie? some school or mere
    religion?
Are you done with reviews and criticism of life? animat-
    ing now to life itself?
Have you vivified yourself from the maternity of These
    States?
Have you too the old, ever-fresh forbearance and im-
    partiality?
Do you hold the like love for those hardening to
    maturity; for the last-born? little and big? and
    for the errant?"

Within limits Whitman strove to be the poet of the
New America. More than any other we have had, he has
expressed the ideals of early and enthusiastic America
and spoken more clearly from its heart of hearts. More
than any other American poet he is perennially modern
and ready for the challenge of a crisis. We can read him
today with even more confidence in his essential grasp of
at least one elemental truth concerning democracy, that
it is not by political organization nor by deftly planned
new deals that a crisis may be averted or difficulties con-
fronted and mastered, but by alert and self-reliant citizens
who like the poet know the world and its needs.

VIII. THE TRAGIC SENSE OF LIFE

FRIEDRICH HEBBEL

"Die Blumen, so hoch sie wachsen,
Sind blass hier wie der Tod,
Nur eine in der Mitte
Steht da in dunklem Roth.

"Die hat es nicht von der Sonne,
Nie traf sie deren Glut,
Sie hat es von der Erde,
Und die trank Menschenblut!" [1]

Waldbilder

The tragic sense of life. There have been times in the classical age in Greece, and again in the days of Shakespeare and Cervantes, when poets turned to tragedy, not as a refuge from the unsupportable burden of life, but as an ironic compensation for the rich adventure of living. It was a sign of the natural color of health, when death seems the intolerable and last of life's ironies. There are

---

[1] It would be a pity to leave this untranslated; but the effort here offered may be a greater pity.

"The flowers, though high they are growing,
    Are pallid here as death,
Save one that stands in their center
    Is red with poisonous breath.

"She got it not from the sunbeams,
    Nor knew their glowing flood;
She's of the earth and earthly
    And drank of human blood."

142

other and quite paradoxical times when tragedy is not the irony of life, but its only acceptable meaning, when its flowers have the pallid hue of death, or are crimson with human blood.

Such times came to Germany after the bright promise of the long wars for German liberation and liberalism fought against Napoleon and the epochal victory of Waterloo. Immermann calls it "the age of the afterborn." The Holy Alliance, Prussia, Austria, Russia, systematically set themselves to undo all that the Revolution had begun. The end of freedom after the War for Freedom, it was the day of censorship and banishment; ardent spirits, like Heine, fled to Paris, Hegel, the orthodox philosopher of a stiffly orthodox Prussia, wrote his *Philosophy of Right* in his professional chair in Berlin, dedicated to the doctrine

"What is Rational is Real
What is Real is Rational."

Nothing was more real than reactionary government; nothing less real than any striving of a liberal spirit. The state was all powerful, before it the individual will was exactly nothing. *"Die erste Bürgerpflicht ist Ruhe."* "The citizen's duty is peace and contentment." The only voices and gestures in opposition were from students, the athletic societies; irresponsible youth that built bonfires and sang songs in their beer-halls, and indulged in rucksacks and cross-country hikes. Not much danger from them; but their professors were watched anxiously, and decorated as "privy councillors" if they kept their *Bürgerpflicht.*

Schiller, the great poet of freedom, had died in 1805. The members of the Romantic School were all dead or doing penance for their unorthodox youth in the chilliest of ascetic practice. Fichte, the philosopher of freedom, turned socialist and died in the year before the Battle. Only Goethe of the old light, but he the brightest, was left; but even he, living as he was in the only liberal state in Germany, with the liberal Grand Duke, Karl August, was more concerned with the welfare of the individual and of society than with politics, and least of all with Germany. "Germany as a whole is nothing; the individual German is everything." To the alarmist patriot, he gave no sympathy and cold advice.

> "Be at ease. . . . In a country where the prince is always accessible, where the classes and the masses think kindly of each other, where no one is hindered from his proper activity, where sound views and knowledge are spread abroad,—there no parties can come into existence. What goes forward in the world will claim our attention, but the seditious sentiments of entire nations will have no influence. We in our quietude will be thankful that we see above our heads a calm heaven, while miserable tempests are devastating boundless tracts of country."

Let each citizen keep his own doorsteps clean, and there will be no social or political problems. Goethe himself was a *Geheimrath*. In 1832 he died, and his last work was the celestial vision of the Second Part of *Faust*.

The German genius seemed exhausted, fatal and complacent mediocrity; Germany, as was said, cultivating the "kingdom of the air," philosophy and scholarship. Scholarship—the witty Saint Marc Girardin twitted the German hope of "liberating the world with Sanscrit." Philosophy after Kant, the vigorous Fichte, the poetic and erratic Schelling, and the absolutist Hegel, gave Germany as its most gifted contemporary thinker, Schopenhauer. His call is a return to death, and the cultivation of tragedy as the artistic approach to the gospel of self-annihilation. The tragic sense of life as a philosophy of life, tragedy as a code, a profession, tears not for sentiment's sake but as the reminder that death is better than life.

Into this world in the then Danish province of Holstein was born the boy, Friedrich Hebbel, almost from his birth at odds with the world, convinced of the tragic significance of life, convinced of the malignity of his surroundings, the *feindselige Welt* of humanity. A spirit in agonized revolt against things as they are, and convinced that a true philosophy of life can be discovered in the essential necessity of tragedy, he devoted all his life to its search and definition. As the philosopher-poet he early decided to become, he used his art as the means of arriving at the discovery. For a man of his means he traveled extensively, for a man of his limited schooling he read intelligently and voraciously. In his fifty years of life he managed to squeeze in a rich variety of experience at all levels. His fertile mind and imagination turned all into a rich harvest. Unlike Rousseau and Chateaubriand, for whom he had no sympathy, he was no vagabond or fugitive. As a boy he had lived in an imaginary background of conflict, the stories of the wars of the Hebrews, the legendary heroes of Germany, Siegfried and the Nibelungs. His later life is a fight with objective fact and, if not a conquest, an honorable truce.

He had learned, in the German tradition, the dignified necessity of art, and the philosophical significance of the artist for life. But he gave the tradition a new direction, and one of large significance for the nineteenth century. Kant had given art, as it were, a metaphysical slant, with the corollary that without art human nature could not arrive at complete self-expression. First, to him, there comes in its order the world of science. This originates with the data of sense, and to it the pure reason is assigned, which builds up the organized system of phenomena, working with its categories of relationship such as time and space and causation. Here is the tight world of natural phenomena organized by the laws of the mind into the world of Science. The next is the world of human conduct or practical living, in which the high necessities of ethical duty appear, and whose precepts are similarly organized by the mind into the tight little world of Ethics. Finally comes the world of Art, as necessary and as natural as the other two, and again organized by the creative mind, with now a higher freedom than is possible in either science or morals. For "the artist creates as nature creates" with inner laws of his own, and bound only by his own sense of values.

Thus the tradition in German philosophy for a metaphysics of Art, as for a metaphysics of Science and one also of Ethics; and a corresponding feeling of its importance for an understanding of human nature which freely through the creative aid of art reveals its own powers. Art for a long time will be spelled in Germany and then in Europe with a capital A; and the artist will be exalted as the highest of creative philosophers. Hebbel will assume in his melancholy, serious way the problem of undertaking the aesthetic-metaphysical explanation of life through the high agency of philosophical art.[2]

What I mean to say is this. Chateaubriand, in his revolt against life, fled to the primitive and to the mystic past, in a search for peace and harmony; Shelley, to the distant future where a fuller discipline of man will restore to him his lost heritage; Manzoni and Whitman flee each to the ideal of a perfectable democracy; Hebbel flees to metaphysics that by its aid he may understand the *feindselige Welt*,

---

[2] I hope I have not been too cavalier in this brief assault on the Kantian and post-Kantian metaphysics of art. The doctrine, as I conceive it, is not nearly so profound as its metaphysicians have labored to make it. Of the moderns Croce is most indebted to it.

this malicious world that drives him into inner and instinctive revolt. He will through the agency of art study it face to face in its worst maliciousness, that he may understand the cosmic significance of his ever present consciousness of the tragic in life.[3]

If life is a tragedy, it cannot, to him, be an unmeaning or merely ironic gesture; tragedy must in some way be connected with the whole tissue of life itself, which it is the business of metaphysics to explore and chart. He will gaze at it steadily and, as a philosopher, coolly. He will analyze character and situation, and find their hidden springs and relations. He will plunge deep, even to the motives that to most are unconscious. He will not be looking only for the bizarre and the dramatic, nor even for the grotesque and repulsive, merely for their own sake; but it will be his aim to lay these out in a plain tale of convincing sequence, that he may below its flow see the web and woof of that thing scientists were beginning to call human evolution and understand the meaning of the story of the human conscience.

Hebbel had learned from recent German philosophy, and probably Hegel, to think of life as a universal process, as an evolution in the growth of ideas and institutions, and of history as the story of that process. But it is also a process, according to Hegel, due to the result of a clash of opposite forces, and the emergence from the catastrophe of the new and more fit. The doctrine of survival, thus with him, has a moral and historical as well as a purely scientific significance; and behind it is the metaphysical idea of the ceaseless urge of the whole cosmic process of life. Tragedy thus, instead of an ironical accident, or a mere sport of malicious caprice, is essential to the very

[3] I hope it will be clear to students of Hebbel that I am drawing his philosophy from his later plays where it is explicit. But his idea is implicit even in his early work.

nature of life itself in its continuous adjustment to the new. It is of the essence of human progress itself; and the tragic figures become the benefactors of humanity, allowing life to rise on the stepping stones of their dead selves to higher things. Sense of the tragic? There will then be in Hebbel sense of little else of human nature but the tragic that is of cosmic value. Here is a definition of tragedy that neither the Greek nor Shakespeare ever dreamed of.

But Hebbel, though he will in this sense explore the metaphysics of art, never suggests the abstract philosopher; nor is his art ever that of the allegorizing moralist. His characters and his situations are farthest removed from abstract types. For he recognizes clearly the difference between philosopher and poet.

> "To make poetry and to speculate are quite distinct processes, the one excludes the other, as I see more and more clearly."

Nor is he quite sure which comes first.

> "For it makes a very great deal of difference, whether our metaphysics is born from life, or, on the other hand, if life must be born from metaphysics."

But at least one thing is certain. The poet must stand unbewildered before the pageant of life. If his tragedies are to discover the cosmic harmony to which tragedy is a prelude, he must in his own life have arrived at complete harmonious self-possession. In his own life, conduct and theory must correspond. Both the thought of the metaphysical process and the concrete and emotional experience of the poet must be blended into one harmonious picture.

> "I am not sure that I am right, but to me it seems a sin against the holy spirit of truth, if the poet, who seeks in his art a harmony

in the way things go in the world of men and affairs, is in his own life far from such a harmony. It seems to me in that case that the work of art loses all value."

It is in this state of mind of cool intellectual detachment and warm emotional interest and at the same time perfect sincerity, that he approaches the study of life itself.

"The dramatic poet must approach every variety of human character in the same spirit as a student of nature every species of animal and plant, no matter whether they be beautiful or ugly, poisonous or wholesome, so long as he has to exhibit them in their completeness."

This is to this German to see life steadily and to see it whole. It is realism, but realism with a philosophical or even scientific purpose. But it is only genius that is able thus to see that "art is philosophy realized." To most, life is only a meaningless or ironical complex or flux of individuals and their personal relations. They come and go like the debris floating on a river and blown by contrary winds; only the poet can catch their meaning for life as a process, and read the forces that give them movement.

"This is also a sign of genius, that it stands ever in relation with the infinite and engenders in each of his works an anagram of the process of creation."

Each of the poet's works is a creation, like that of nature, the infinite itself, and, like nature, obeying nature's law of progress by tragedy. Again like the scientist, the poet by generalization on the individuals whom he in his poems has created, is able to read the universal tragic law of nature. You have it either way; he gains the sense of the tragic from experience, he discovers the same tragic sense of life in art. The question we asked a moment ago— which came first, the metaphysics of tragedy by speculation, or the experience of tragedy in life?—for the genius is quite irrelevant. Tragedy is inescapable.

It is thus that Hebbel, who first recoiled from this *feindselige Welt,* could through his metaphysics and his art discover the *Versöhnung* or harmony or reconciliation his poetic nature craved. For by looking at the process *sub specie aeternitatis* he discovered that what seemed the cruelty of malicious irony was in reality nature's way of vindicating herself, and of laying a bridge to the better.

For this reason there are no unqualified villains in Hebbel's tragedies, no Iagos or Iachimos. The nearest approach is Golo in the early play *Genoveva,* and there the plot as he received it demanded unspeakable villainy, but he gives Golo intelligible and ungovernable passion, aroused by the saintliness of Genoveva, who should be to the man unattainable, for she is the affectionate wife of his feudal lord. The reason for no villains in his plays is not far to discover; undiluted villainy is a sport in nature, a monstrosity, and not natural, interesting as a hybrid, but unfertile. Nature works with its own materials. And tragedy which is the exploration of the natural process must not confuse the issue by raising moral problems like the conflict between the good and the evil, and show how the wicked prosper, or, what would be infinitely worse, hand out liberal soporifics of "poetic justice."

No, the characters are all "cases," even Golo, persons who at the beginning were quite normal and good, even admirable. Indeed, that the tragedy may be the more striking, they are models of their variety of excellence, driven by motives that under ordinary situations would be above reproach. It is the situations that play them false, and the characters with whom they are thrown in conflict. The nearest approach in Shakespeare to this method are his problem plays *All's Well* and *Measure for Measure.* Angelo and Helena, each at first good after its kind, are excellent models for the sort of individual in a problem conflict that would attract the inquiry of Hebbel; and the plays, as with him, show how each character grows in power as the inevitability of the conflict becomes finally clear.

But with Shakespeare the interest is in human nature alone, the way of the once just judge with a maid in his power, or the way of the single-minded and resourceful Helena with the wayward youth Bertram. With Hebbel the tragedy always marks an epoch in the history of humanity. Hence his situations are epochs in human history, situations that mark the death of an old order and the emergence into consciousness of a new. Or, as Hebbel himself describes it in the Preface to *Maria Magdelene*, the highest drama is produced at times of crises in human history, at periods of spiritual revolution, when one tradition gives way to another; and the vindication of the new is the tragic desolation of both of the contending characters. They are erased, because their characters and their motives had become outworn. Their defeat is nature's victory. Sometimes it is given to the characters to attain to this spiritual insight and peace; but always it is granted to the poet and the spectator. This to the German poet is the katharsis, the purgation of tragedy. It clears and gives freedom to men's souls and reconciles them to their destiny.

Of all his plays the most intimately human, and the most moving, is his bourgeois tragedy of *Maria Magdelene*. It is the nearest to our time, and suggests all sorts and conditions of later dramas of lowly life, from Hauptmann's *Lonely Lives* to Masefield's *Tragedy of Nan*. It is the kind of thing to which the cinema loves to give a Sunday School conclusion. But Hebbel is not picturing in this the unfortunate lot of the poor or the oppressed;

least of all is he, as Ibsen later, writing a sociological treatise. It is his interpretation of a spiritual revolution then taking place in Germany, the revolt of the younger generation against the tradition of the German family. And in those days the German family was the one organic unit in the state that was feeling the stirrings of new ideas and was free to respond. The group of small town characters in this play were then engaged in questioning the social codes. It is of the conflict between the old and the new that these characters are the symbols. It is domestic tragedy in a day, when alone, either the old or the new domestic code, if accepted by all, would have made such tragedy impossible. But such is the universal interest of the characters, that the play has its points in common even with the *Antigone* of Sophocles.

The story is of the stark disaster that overwhelms a family. Old Anton, an upright master workman, affectionate but austere, prides himself, and justly, on his place in the little world. He has come from poverty, but his uncompromising steadfastness to his code has given him success. He dominates his family, a wife just recovering from illness, his daughter, somewhat like him, Klara, and his wayward son Karl, loved indulgently by his mother. Klara has long been secretly in love with Friedrich who seems to have forgotten her while away at his studies; and reluctantly she has engaged herself to Leonhardt, a timeserver, but good natured, who fearing Friedrich's return demands her complete surrender.

Then things happen that completely upset this orderly though uncomfortable situation. Friedrich returns and learns the truth. Karl is falsely accused of theft; the mother dies; and Anton has only one assurance to which he can cling, the rectitude of his daughter; and before this can fail him and prove his utter desolation, Klara takes

the only step she can to save his integrity. She drowns
herself. She might have borne it had she been alone.

"If it meant only me, I'd bear it; take it patiently, as a well-
deserved punishment for I don't know what. . . . But I'm not the
only one. And when the Judge asks me on the last day, 'Why did
you kill yourself?' it will be an easier question to answer than 'Why
did you drive your father to it?' "

"Well deserved punishment for I don't know what." It
is no wonder that before a world thus suddenly gone in-
sane the old man, broken and bewildered, cries out in
agony "*Ich verstehe die Welt nicht mehr.*"

Hebbel's own comment in his diary on this tragedy is
illuminating. "Life's habitual one-sidedness from which
in the past and in the present every evil in the world is
born." One sidedness, partiality of view, inability to grasp
the situation as a whole, the inability of the old code to
accommodate itself to life ever renewing itself—this or
these are the fatal "*unbedingteste Notwendigkeit,*" the
remorseless necessity, that drives to this catastrophe. It
is human nature responding as only human nature can
respond when it finds itself so fettered against the emer-
gency.

Human fetters that must be broken, but are only perceived after the tragedy has intervened. And these are
all the more inexorable because they are states of mind,
the *Einigseitigkeit,* or better, the moral tissue of the character itself. With the impact of the unexpected situation
these bind the reaction of the character, and the inexorable
law of nature makes escape impossible.

The *Maria Magdalene* is unique among Hebbel's plays
because of its intimate and every day realism. In his
more usual grand style is the *Herodes and Mariamne.*
Here are figures that belong to the romantic past of the

days of Antony and Cleopatra, and a love story almost as exalted. The story is one of the best in Josephus' long history of the Jews, and the New Testament has made the name of Herod a by-word. Again it is the story of the conflict of the sexes and motives misunderstood and pride that can drive to destruction.

Herod is a dominating personality, a king worthy of the throne, just, resourceful, even admirable in his innate greatness. He has for his wife Mariamne, the last of the line of the Maccabees, a race distinguished in Hebrew history, fighters all and deliverers of their country; and she has the unbending pride and regal bearing of her race. Not a queen to be taken lightly, but a woman great as Herod and as unyielding. But they are in love, sincerely, passionately as is their nature, and this love strengthens their special attributes. Between them, however, lies the shadow of her brother Aristobulus, drowned presumably by royal order—he was an obstacle to Herod's complete security—for Herod is a *parvenu* to the once royal house. Were all to go smoothly her love could ignore the suspicion of her brother's murder; but should unexpected complications arise, how would this proud, reserved creature meet them?

And the situation comes in its most unexpected manner. Herod, on the accusation of the Aristobulus party, is dragged off to Egypt to give an account of himself before the court of Antony and Cleopatra. He knows Antony's character and his weakness as well as strength. He knows the unique loveliness of Mariamne, rivaling even that of the great Egyptian queen. He knows the danger of his mission. Will his life be forfeit? What then of the woman he so passionately loves? Can he trust her? Will she be one more oriental queen for this Roman connoisseur of beauty? The thought is maddening, and he asks her for an assurance of her undying devotion—the last question a man can ask of a woman—will she willingly sacrifice herself on the news of his death?

Now here is an assurance that a wife lesser than her husband and equally devoted might have gladly given. Or a greater had it not been exacted of her. But this daughter of the Maccabees, how can she reduce herself in her own eyes?

> "And if I gave that oath, what surety yours
> I'd keep it? Always I am only I myself,
> My nature's as you know it. . . .
> Go, go! Act otherwise I cannot! At least today!"

To Alexandra, her mother, she is perfectly explicit.

> "Only, be well assured of this—the barb
> That reaches Herod reaches Mariamne.
> The oath that I withheld and he demanded
> In leaving me, I swear it now."

But to Herod, the king that made the demand, her lips are sealed by the very consciousness of her own dignity. And as naturally he cannot read her nature. Each character is now distrustful of the other; and the king responds in the way of the absolute potentate, if he dies she must be sacrificed with him. He leaves orders with his viceroy, and she with clever woman's perception gains the secret. The motives for a complete tragedy of distrust are in the open and the action hastens to the painful catastrophe.

Here are two superb characters, who might have left the world better for their union. But Mariamne is a futile sacrifice, and Herod at the end, now an unrecognizable tyrant, sends off his soldiers to the slaughter of the innocent babes in Bethlehem. The pity of it. Their tragic guilt? Surely not a moral delinquency, any more than the guilt of Klara or of Anton. It was only that each surpassed his rôle; there was in each that excess *Unmässigkeit* of will and personality, that made perfect harmony between them impossible. The old order, like old wine skins, could not accommodate itself to the new ferment; and with their tragic sacrifice is ushered in the new. For the play closes with the visit of the Wise Men who had seen the Star, and were on their way to pay homage to the new King. The conflict of these two regal wills, symptomatic of a conflict between two potent motives for life, can be resolved only by a new will that shall transcend them both.

There is something so redeemingly simple in the play *Agnes Bernauer* that it has been from the beginning for all readers Hebbel's most popular tragedy. The motive is as old as human institutions, the conflict between the individual's debt to himself and his debt to society. The scene is laid in mediaeval Bavaria, but change the characters and the situation, and it might be true of the remotest village anywhere, any time. It is the old conflict between love and duty, only here each is perfect and the two wholly incompatible.

Agnes is the daughter of a commoner, in the days of feudal loyalties; Albrecht is the son of a prince of the Empire, the ruler of Bavaria. Agnes is beautiful and all that a spirited prince might aspire to. Albrecht is the prince *par excellence*, and his devotion is wholehearted and passionate. Theirs is a love that brooks no interference, and rouses only admiration even among the most calculating. And contrary to all precedent, and in defiance of all authority, the two are married, the commoner and the heir to a throne. For a time even in their revolt against convention and with the astonished yet loyal aid of their friends both are defiantly happy.

Albrecht: "Oh, Agnes, if ever I shall attain God's presence I must begin
with you; for me there is no other path to him. Is it not
so also with you?"

Agnes: "Were death to come to me now, I could no longer say, you
come too soon."

The words are prophetic. For Ernst, the Grand Duke,
sees too clearly the impossible which the ecstatic lovers
will not recognize. Albrecht is heir to a throne, pledged
to a trust which no one else can fulfil. And behind is the
power of the Emperor who can brook no rebellion. The
sacrifice is not a judgment, least of all is it punishment
for disloyalty. It is plain duty shorn of every personal
motive, devotion to the welfare of the state. And the
Grand Duke who demands it is the first to recognize its
purity: "The purest sacrifice that Fate in all its centuries
has been pleased to make." "There are things that a man
must do only in sleep. This is one of them." Even the
devoted Agnes goes with loyal acceptance of the truth
to her death. "No, no, you must not carry the sacrifice
so far that the victim stain itself. Pure was my first
breath, and pure shall also be my last! Do with me what
you ought and must. I shall endure. Soon shall I know
where the justice lay."

Sacrifice, *Opfer,* for the welfare of the state, that here
demanded the sacrifice. Were Agnes less Agnes, were
Albrecht less the prince, there would have been no tragedy, only sentimental romance. But both are too fine for
the rôle in which love cast them. Here is not a judgment condemning guilty lovers as when Paolo and Fran-
cesca were condemned, or Lancelot and Guinevere. These
tragedies are comprehensible on the level of the viola-
tion of an ethical law or on the motive of justifiable revenge. Here it is purity and exquisite romance being
sacrificed by the impersonal will, the remorseless neces-

sity of a mediaeval code, against which their beauty is an agonized protest.

Of all his plays this philosophical and symbolical background for tragedy is most obtrusive in the *Ring of Gyges*. It is at the same time perhaps the most poetic. Gyges is a wandering Greek soldier of fortune at the court of Kandaules, King of Lydia. The two become fast friends. Now the king has a wife Rhodope, the most exquisite of women, with whom he is most deeply in love. He possesses a jewel, but how enjoy its possession when there are none to whom he can boast or communicate its rarity, for she lives in voluntary and devoted seclusion. Possession in secret is scarce possession at all, a gem worn in private is no treasure unless there are others who can know its priceless rarity.

> "And I'll ne'er be
> A happy man till your lips say I am.
> Come, ask you—if the crown were to your liking
> Should you be bound to wear it but in darkness?
> Well, that's the plight I'm in with her. She is
> The Queen of women, but I hold possession
> Of her as Ocean holds its pearls—none dreams
> How rich I am, and when I'm dead and done with
> There's not a friend can set it on my tombstone."

But Gyges has in his wanderings picked up a magic ring which makes its wearer invisible. It is no treasure for a common soldier and he gives it to the King. Now Kandaules solves his predicament. He urges his friend with the aid of the ring to slip into the royal apartments, that he may catch one glimpse of Rhodope and forever after know to its utmost the beauty of woman. Reluctantly Gyges is forced to accept the challenge. He goes with misgiving and the event is overwhelming. Deliberately he slips the ring that he may be visible for a moment and force his friend to slay him. But Kandaules glides between them to hide the fleeting view, and is jubilant that the experiment has justified his boast.

But unwarranted liberties have been taken with two much more than commonplace people. Gyges has fallen in love—against his will to be sure—and he will not smirch his loyalty to his friend. Rhodope suspects that her rights and her devotion to seclusion have been violated. Kandaules' love, like Herod's, has gone too far. Herod wanted the assurance of absolute possession, the Lydian King wants the assurance of absolute uniqueness. And both invaded the rights of women as great as themselves. And the ring becomes the symbol of a power, no man should have, to transgress beyond the limits of human right.

Kandaules, the proud husband and king, Gyges, the sensitive and affectionate friend, Rhodope, the unpolluted spirit of beauty, the balance in their exquisite relationship was too precarious to be maintained. The rights of a friend, the rights of a husband, the rights of a wife, when the harmony between them has been destroyed and each has become an agency of pain to itself and to all, can only be restored by the sacrifice of all. And with eyes open to its significance each of the three chooses the path of self-erasure and tragedy. Here is no resentment, only pained consciousness of moral duty. Each becomes the priest of a higher ethics. As such Kandaules falls willingly before the instructed hand of Gyges; as such Rhodope accepts self-inflicted death; as such Gyges, as King of Lydia now, begins a new day.

Now that Germany is with renewed enthusiasm offering incense to its old legendary history, it is above all interesting, when Germany was only a geographical convenience, to see what service Hebbel put the old epic of the Nibelungs. Siegfried, Gunther, Hagen, and above all Brunhild and Kriemhild, these majestic figures that Wagner has raised to godlike proportions, and made their actions thrill to imaginative music, it is interesting to see how another great poet responded to their power. For the *Nibelungenlied* is a powerful poem, full of undiluted heroic personality, stark, remorseless, and gigantically human. He must be a brave man indeed who will put his hand into matters that look like the debris of divinity.

Hebbel has lost none of the stark grandeur of these old heroines and heroes. He has not attempted, as did the Greek dramatists, Sophocles and Euripides, to bring them down to human level. But rather like Aeschylus, with the legend of Prometheus, another fragment of divinity, he puts into their mouths poetry of superhuman majesty, and gives them a station and a gesture that has nothing in common with the routine of science and sociology. In a way they are no more real as human beings than Wagner's music makes them, but are also quite as compelling; and far more significant in their motives for tragedy.

There are three plays—the first a brief Prelude: *The Invulnerable Siegfried, Siegfried's Death,* and *Kriemhild's Revenge*. It is the old pagan order that he is painting, a time of blood and revenge, of passion given full scope, of hate unqualified, and loyalty to the death. How can poetry be given the rein to express in full those passions, to speak and act with none of the restraints that a later age discovered, and unsoftened by any of the graces of the New Faith? These are Nietzsche's super-men and super-women, "blond beasts" speaking unchecked their hearts, and acting their treacherous or loyal rôles in a day when life was as simple as it was intense. One must forget all inhibitions of restraint when one reads in this clear, cold and rarified atmosphere of a legendary heroic and yet human past.

For notwithstanding their heroic stature Hagen and Kriemhild, Siegfried and Brunhild are for Hebbel utterly human, only they are human nature undiluted by any of the subterfuges of more recent convention. Their story is so direct and simple that it alone would be impossible in an age of more complex natures. Siegfried the victor over the dragon, now invulnerable save at one spot, the possessor of the Rhine Gold and of the magic cap and the irresistable sword; valorous simplicity itself, he falls in love with the Burgundian princess, Kriemhild, and to win her must assist her brother Gunther, the king, to win and possess the Amazon of the North, the redoubtable Brunhild.

Then the quarrel between the two rival heroines, and the anger of the duped Brunhild when she learns how she has been achieved, complicated too by her attraction to her real victor. Now the sinister, but yet utterly loyal Hagen, who must atone for the wrong done his queen, by the treacherous slaying of Siegfried. All this moves with a swiftness that almost takes one's breath, and the body of the dead hero is brought and laid at the door of the wife who could not keep a secret. It is cruel; it is devastating. And the quiet, self-effacing wife rises to heroic, implacable revenge. She too is a Nibelung. Now the contest is between her and the grim and loyal protector of the Burgundian tradition, Hagen. These are the two characters, embodiments of the two stark pagan loyalties, on which the poem comes to a final focus—Kriemhild, fiendish and insatiable through loyalty to her dead, and Hagen, grim and unyielding through loyalty to his lord.

In the final clash between them everything goes down in ruin. Husband, child, family, love, romance, nothing but is tinder to this last ecstatic lust of battle—the sheer zest of destruction and blood—blood and iron, until there is nothing left. The conflict has destroyed its own agents; and the serene Dietrich von Bern, the prophet of the new era takes command, "in the name of Him who died on the Cross."

This tale, moving with single passion to its swift catastrophe, is to Hebbel the virtue of the old Paganism, admirable in its simple heroic grandeur but, when thwarted or opposed, the author of its own passionate destruction because it had nothing in it to qualify its nature. The heroes are the saurian monsters of a geological past. So Hebbel reads the lesson of the epic and gives it a philosophical significance in the cosmic process of human evolution. Is the modern revival today of the code of the antique Teutonic loyalties and the antique worship of power missing the meaning of the tragedy as seen by the philosopher poet? There will be one more philosopher of the same nation who is to have something also to say concerning the "will to power" and its significance for tragedy, as also of the daemoniac or Dionysian ecstasy of tragedy and annihilation. I mean Nietzsche.

Thus Hebbel feeling the tragedy that lies at the heart of all existence, with his earnest resentment against the enmity of the world, turned to an idealistic philosophy which might give its malicious irony a meaning and restore for the poet harmony. It is the age-old problem of the individual and the world; no longer the concrete world of the Greek or of Shakespeare, but the ideal world behind and beyond all concrete phenomena, the remorseless cosmic process of evolution, the spirit that informs all things and gives them meaning. An abstraction? Yes, but one that the intuitive poet or the philosopher has always felt profoundly. Virgil called it Providence, and gave it the name Jupiter, the guardian of Rome, in the *Aeneid*. Dante in his rapt vision sees its human lineaments in the *Paradise*. Goethe finds it as the indwelling and informing spirit of cosmic evolution. Hebbel also finds in it the *Versöhnung*, the harmony, the reconciliation, without which all life is meaningless gossip and scandal.

The philosopher explores with his logic, like Hegel, the metaphysical formulas of this dynamic spirit, and orders the universe of acts into a system of abstract thought. But he cannot minister to men's imaginations nor carry the formulas into the region of human conduct. Here is the function of the intuitive poet, who, lost in the concrete complexities and mischiefs of life, finds his way perilously through them to their reconciliation in the mystery of the law for all nature. His eyes in a vision are raised above the quarreling individuals to the stream of existence which gives their quarrels meaning and form. This is the mystery that his poetry reveals. "*Jedes echte Kunstwerk ist ein geheimnissvolles, vieldeutiges, in gewissem Sinn unergrundliches Symbol.*" [4]

It is the way of all life to pit the individual against the cosmic order. For the universal spirit of progress can only be quickened into activity by the stirrings of opposition by the individual. And the finer the individual the more inevitable the conflict. Here, and here alone, is the true significance of human grandeur and human sacrifice and human progress. The heroes must go down that the world may be better for their having lived and suffered; for their sacrifice is never in vain. Tragedy is thus a baptism into a new life. Here is the doctrine of vicarious punishment raised into a philosophical and artistic creed. And

[4] Each true work of art is a symbol, full of mystery, ambiguous and, in truth, unfathomable."

at the same time it is offered as the spiritual corollary of the biological mechanism of evolutionary survival.

Klaras in despair may leap into wells to drown their shame, Mariamnes march resolutely to the executioner, Rhodopes stab themselves in outraged modesty, and Kriemhild's bloody bath of vengeance raise against her the outraged arm of a loyal henchman, Agneses may be put out of the way by political expediency; all these and the multitude of the unnamed who daily suffer because they are too fine for the gross rôles for which life cast them. But we who stand above with the poet and read must not be dismayed at life's cruelty, at the tragedy that is at the heart of things. The flowers that bloom in this garden may be pallid as death, or radiant with the stain of human blood. We must not be dismayed. For the poet tells us to raise our eyes to the heavenly vision of the mystery of life. And in it we read the demand that these beautiful things must suffer and die, that from their sacrifice the world may be ennobled and we edified.

The tragedy may not be understood by Klara or Kriemhild, to each it may be a fiendish irony, for each was utterly guiltless in any ordinary human sense. Or it may be the serene martyrdom of an outraged Rhodope, or an affectionate Agnes. Their claims are of no consequence beside the higher claims of that mystical Absolute, the *Weltprocess*. It sweeps away the offender, the individual who opposes, indifferent to his unique exquisiteness; and then as impersonally makes of him the motive for a new and better order. It was on the shoulders of the Absolute that Hebbel laid his burden of a malicious world he found too heavy to bear alone.

Is this a creed too breathless for the clear objectivity of a Shakespeare or a Sophocles? Does it make for the annihilation of the democratic faith in the sanctity of the individual? Has it any consistency with a modern trend toward the ruthless suppression of the individual for the welfare of that abstraction, the State? Does this last offer any hint why Hebbel has never been popular in Anglo-Saxon countries? These are interesting questions.

IX. THE PERPLEXED IN SPIRIT

TOLSTOI

"These words and the conceptions they stood for satisfied his mental requirements, but they gave him nothing for life, and he suddenly began to feel himself in the position of a man who has given up his fur coat in exchange for a gauze garment, and at the first approach of the frost realizes that he is little better than naked, and must inevitably die a painful death."

Anna Karenina

To escape a painful death, more painful because it was of his moral nature, Tolstoi made the great renunciation to the consternation of the nineteenth century, and to the bewilderment of the twentieth. And in spite of his denial of nearly everything that cultured society thinks it lives by, and by drawing up a code of conduct the mediaeval ascetic might have envied, he remained to the end Tolstoi the Unhappy and the Lonely. Martyrdom brought with it no peace of mind. And though he had, and has, many disciples, his mode of life had no imitators. Yet when the history of the century's thought can be written with adequate perspective, Tolstoi may well be discovered to be its most critical and qualified thinker, and most sensitive. Was this in large part due to the fact that Tolstoi was of Russia, a late comer upon the drama of European thought, and because a late comer the more sensitive both to its allurements and its danger?

166

There is a verse in the New Testament that feelingly describes the significance to the Deity of even the fall of a sparrow; what then must be the loss of an immortal human soul? The poets who had theorized about human frailty or tragic human worth, like Hebbel, had comforted themselves with a metaphysical creed, persuading themselves that only by such tragic experience of the individual can humanity in the large reach its destined heights. Prometheus must be bound that later he may be enlightened and triumph. Klara must leap into the well and be self-drowned, that her sisters to come might meet their situations with a more enlightened code. This is a curious erasure of the problem of human conduct, or at best seeing it in a higher dimension. It was precisely the refusal to look at human conduct from the perspective of infinity that characterizes that group of brilliant Russian writers of the mid-nineteenth century and later. To them humanity is the aggregate of individuals and not an abstraction; and it was the welfare or the tragedy of these millions here and now that is of significance. The ultimate future, with its spacious depths: there is now no telescope that will descry for us its pattern.

One of the most interesting institutions in the history of modern Russia was that more or less self-contained group that came to be called the *intelligentsia*. In it all sections of society co-operated. Unlike the French *Salon* or the English Club, which lent color to society and was always a decorative fringe to the government, the Russian intellectuals were always a force in opposition, and as a group always under the suspicion or active persecution of the government. They were drawn from all classes, from the workers in the factories to university graduates and members of the nobility. But their ideas and ideals never touched the life of their generation except negatively, as a criticism of things as they were and as rallying cries for planned revolutions. Much that is unique in Russian history from the reign of Catherine the Great, after the explosion of the French Revolution, may be traced almost directly to the unfortunate inability of the government and the vital intellectual life of the nation to speak the same language. It explains clearly how as the nineteenth century progressed the distance between them became greater and greater, until the possibility of compromise was forever lost.

For Russia was a late comer into the tradition of the West. The reign of Peter the Great seems infinitely farther removed than that of the English George I, and the times of Addison and Steele and Pope, who were his contemporaries. The court of Catherine the Great near the end of the century might imitate the culture of Versailles, but the peasants of Russia were nearer to the times of Abraham than to village and town life of England or France. By the middle of the nineteenth century there were the brilliant groups about the court at Saint Petersburg or at Moscow, a few islands of culture at the chateaux of the aristocracy, and all else a vast sea of a rude, unlettered, superstitious, and yet strangely good natured and complacent peasantry. They had only very recently been freed from serfdom, but their freedom had brought yet neither light nor restlessness of ideas. And above the whole yet inert body were the divine institutions of the Holy Orthodox Church and the White Father, the Czar. It was either a social panorama for self-congratulation for its willing subservience, or a caricature of absolute degradation, depending upon the point of view. And that chosen by the *intelligentsia* could not bring happiness or even patience.

The two institutions, the orthodox Church and the orthodox Empire were divine, each was revered, each seemed omnipotent. They laid down with perfect precision the whole pattern of human life, and insisted upon a perfect conformity. New ideas that might, like grit thrown into bearings, mar the harmony, were not only deplorable but damnable. Hence the censorship was a wholly benevolent institution, in its own eyes, like another institution called the Holy Inquisition, patterned to save men from going the heretic's way to damnation. And the *intelligentsia*—it is a difficult word to use flippantly today—chose the dangerous road of thinking for themselves. It is not to be wondered at, then, that government of state and church looked at them askance, and invented special corps of police to spy on their meetings and report their conduct. Siberia was a new country needing opening up, and these restless ones could find plenty of means of satisfying their restlessness in that remote region. For more serious offenders there was the swifter and probably less painful silence of death.

Thus with an active and aggressive censorship, when all possibility of an exchange of ideas through journalism was forbidden, and public meetings banned, what was more natural than that these restless souls with ideas that burned should turn to the apparently more harmless pastime of literature? Here in fiction, at least, there would be fewer restraints. Here in a purely fictitious picture of life with invented characters and situations, authors could discuss ideas that, though the censor might not like them, his bungling finger would find more difficulty in pointing out as heresy. In any case the author would disclaim any desire to be a reformer; he was only showing what any one with eyes could see, the life about him. His truth to life could hardly be laid to his charge as a crime. Thus began the tradition in Russian fiction of painstaking realism.

It was a realism with ideas, but concrete ideas, not set out in the prophetic manner of denunciation, nor in the journalist manner of exposition, but in the artist's manner of creations of flesh and blood—the panorama of Russian life, uttering the thoughts of which the real Russia was as yet only dimly conscious. Turgenev's *Sportsman's Sketches* came out only ten years before the emancipation of the serfs. And who can say where the *Lear of the Steppes* stops in its delineation of the life of the Russian peasant? Such ideas are vital and move into regions far beyond the little intimate details of one family or one village tradition. So it was with Gogol's *Dead Souls*. The novelist was in no sense afflicted with any personal grievance or possessed by the itch for any one social reform. He was intelligently and morally uncomfortable, and his novel is the imaginative picture of the discontent.

Nowhere was the ground for discontent with things as they were more vital and moving than with the lot of those who were least conscious, the one time serfs. Only recently emancipated, knowing nothing beyond the narrowest of village horizons, poor in the extreme, impotent, harrassed by superstition, good-natured even gay, abysmally ignorant, and yet with a native shrewdness—as splendid material for worthy citizens as any in Europe, but contributing nothing save the toil of their hands. Among them came to be found the largest theme in Russian fiction. Then the peasant transplanted to the factories, not yet urban-conscious, but loosed of the communal ties that bound the peasant, frequently a vagrant, always living in unsightly and unsanitary tenements: from studies of these sunken folk emerged the cult of the people, the pictures of the lowly that were such a heavy majority of the population of Russia.

Russian Revolutions. Certainly the nineteenth century in Russian thought prepared the way for the twentieth century in Russian action.

In more than one way Tolstoi is an epitome of the triumph and the bewilderment and defeat of the nineteenth century. A Russian count, the brilliant lion of a brilliant society, quickly recognized for the genius he was by all Western Europe; in contact with nearly all the intellectual movements and interests of the century; then peasant and cobbler, living the life of the lowly that in their narrow lives he might find the peace of soul not to be discovered in progress, or in the philosophies of any human creed. It is not to be wondered at that critics and biographers have sought to interpret his vagaries by the methods of psychologists and alienists, that they have sought to discover the two, three, or more interfering personalities that go to make up this complex man.

Tolstoi is the symbol of the restless and searching century. He knew the new science and the new industry that rapidly was transforming the West, even Russia, and above all challenging the old creeds by which Europe had lived. He saw the new industrial aristocracy which now, not in Russia alone, but in all Europe, was displacing the old feudal aristocracy that had maintained its contact with the land, and in theory at least was the guardian of the peasant. He saw them devoted to the pursuit of wealth for its own sake or for its impersonal power. He saw through their brilliancy to their emptiness of any resolute moral significance. Above all he saw the profound social changes that involved every one, and which had substituted a purely mechanical for the older personal bond between classes. Because the change in Russia was the more sudden, its effects were the more bewildering. But

the difference was only one in degree between Russia and
the rest of Europe—islands of comfort and security for
the fortunate few, and a sea of the employed and unem-
ployed, their old securities gone, slender as these might
have been, restless and foot-loose in the cities, complacently
ignorant and in cruel poverty, most, in the country. All
thinking people of the nineteenth century were none too
happy at the prospect.

In Russia there was the burden beside of a heavy beau-
rocracy, and of the army, but no state to bind the whole of
Russia into one common purpose, nothing but the autocratic government, and an equally autocratic church.
And above all there was a middle class that as yet, unlike
the one in the West, had not found itself, or a rôle in the
political or social scene. It was in this atmosphere that the
young Tolstoi grew up. He was sensitive to it all, his
ideas came in concrete images of what he saw and heard
and felt. From the beginning he was obsessed with the
desire to discover a plan in what seemed a miscellany, and
above all, a moral purpose, and a place he might call
home. In a way, again, Tolstoi is the Ulysses of the wandering century, and his journey is beset with greater dangers than Scylla and Charybdis and the Clashing Rocks.
And the tragedy of this familiar figure is that the home
he did finally make for himself brought not peace but
the sword.

It would be interesting and instructive, were there
space, to follow the character of this genius as it unfolds its
complexity, from sensitive and affectionate youth to restless young manhood, to the experiments and powers of his
maturity with its enthusiasms and its doubts, to its obsession with the question of questions, the meaning of life
and the fear of death, to its age when it put its heel
upon all that was most beautiful in youth and manhood,

striving to ease bewilderment and pain by still greater pain and bewilderment. Yet through it all runs like a scarlet cord the overmastering love of life and all things living, a desire to drink its draught to the dregs, and yet the fear that its joy is deadly and its intoxication death. Fearful of his natural gifts, especially his intelligence, and yet keen in his analysis of what he sees and knows; an epicurean is his love of the sensuous, and yet appalled by the wages of sin; seeing God in all things, and yet never sure that his deity may not play false; finally setting up humanity and its love as the goal of all endeavor, and dying alone and self-exiled; it is no wonder that Tolstoi is a mystery to those who would find an even pattern in his life or a psychological consistency in his actions. He was many millions of personalities, who without him would be inarticulate.

Combining all these paradoxes and giving them life is his all embracing poetic imagination, even when in his later years he strove to crucify it. Hence the strange melancholic pain that occurs at increasing intervals in all his work, a nostalgia, as though he longed to look backward at the myth of man's lost innocence, when these contradictions could not prevail against his naïve happiness, and which he was too clear sighted to regard as other than a myth. Loving the whole of life, he was unable to hate that part of it he felt he must deny; morally convinced he must hate falsehood, giving his life to discover its nature. Such is Tolstoi, the sympathetic and realist artist, and at the same time the ascetic of an almost oriental mysticism.

Though a work of fiction and done in his earliest manner, his *Childhood and Youth* is a superb piece of self-revelation. Here is a boy precociously vain, and yet failing at nearly every trial, and with a growing conviction of his own social inferiority. Terribly sensitive and affectionate, erotic and yet terrified at the prospect of love.

"I crept closer to the pillows, imagined to myself her lovely face, covered my head over with the bedclothes, tucked the counterpane in on all sides, and, thus snugly covered, lay quiet and enjoying the warmth until I became wholly absorbed in pleasant fancies and reminiscences."

He is passionate, but never daring self-assertion. How he longs for innocence, as for the Golden Age.

"Do in after life the freshness and lightheartedness, the craving for love and for strength of faith, ever return which we experience in our childhood's years? What better time is there in our lives than when the two best of virtues—innocent gaiety and a boundless yearning for affection—are our sole objects of pursuit?

"Where now are our ardent prayers? Where now are our best gifts—the pure tears of emotion which a guardian angel dries with a smile as he sheds upon us lovely dreams of ineffable childish joy? Can it be that life has left such heavy traces upon one's heart that those tears and ecstasies are for ever vanished? Can it be that there remains to us only the recollection of them?"

This is almost Rousseau. But more, for he is conscious of problems of moral conviction that go much farther than Rousseau:

"Has it ever befallen you, my readers, to become suddenly aware that your conception of things has altered—as though every object in life had unexpectedly turned a side towards you of which you had hitherto remained unaware? Such a species of moral change occurred, as regards myself, during this journey, and therefore from it I date the beginning of my boyhood. For the first time in my life I then envisaged the idea that we—i.e. our family—were not the only persons in the world; that not every conceivable interest was centred in ourselves; and that there existed numbers of people who had nothing in common with us, cared nothing for us, and even knew nothing of our existence. No doubt I had known all this before—only I had not known it then as I knew it now; I had never properly felt or understood it."

There is a seriousness here that has little in common with carefree youth, this early consciousness of the trinity of body, mind, and spirit, and this instinctive search for what is to prove an unattainable harmony.

"I have said that my friendship with Dimitrieff opened up for me a new view of my life and of its aim and relations. The essence of that view lay in the conviction that the destiny of many is to strive for moral improvement, and that such improvement is at once easy, possible, and lasting. Hitherto, however, I had found pleasure only in the new ideas which I discovered to arise from that conviction, and in the forming of brilliant plans for a moral, active future, while all the time my life had been continuing along its old petty, muddled, pleasure-seeking course, and the same virtuous thoughts which I and my adored friend Dimitrieff ("my own marvellous Mitia," as I used to call him to myself in a whisper) had been wont to exchange with one another still pleased my intellect, but left my sensibility untouched. Nevertheless there came a moment when those thoughts swept into my head with a sudden freshness and force of moral revelation which left me aghast at the amount of time which I had been wasting, and made me feel as though I must at once—that very second—apply those thoughts to life, with the firm intention of never again changing them."

In this little sketch, done while he was a soldier at Sebastopol, when, save among friends, he was yet utterly unknown, are discoverable all the ingredients of the experiments that were to be Tolstoi.

Then ten years later he astonished the world with one of the greatest explosions of sheer genius. It was the *War and Peace.* He had planned a panorama whose like there never had been, possibly could never be. It was to begin with the Russia of the Napoleonic Wars in 1805, and to carry through, a moving narrative of the Russian scene, for two generations to the end of the Crimean war in 1856. But if his book, compared with his plan, is fragmentary, it nevertheless paints the Russia of those

vital years of national consciousness and national endeavor, 1805 to 1812, the Russian campaigns against
Napoleon, which by an Emperor's promise were to give
Russia a liberal constitution. Russia for the first time
in conflict and in alliance with Western Europe, in a war
that was not a dynastic problem, but a struggle of ideas.
Then he followed it with the story of the Aftermath, the
abortive Revolution of 1825, when the liberal stirrings
of the Russian nobility were sternly suppressed and punished. But the theme of the novel is neither social nor
political, it is Russia itself in all its ideas and its manifold
aspects, that marches past in this prodigious review.

Its effect was prodigious. It is a panorama of all Russia, and also of all mankind. Here are hundreds of characters from servant girls to Napoleon. It is a historical canvas that leaves nothing unnoticed. It is also a philosophy
of history and an exposition of human progress, and a
treatise on the meaning and place of human greatness.
How do characters like Napoleon or Alexander arise?
What is the final aim of history? How do such events as
the burning of Moscow and the French retreat, or the
battles of Tilsit or Borodino come about in the fulness
of time? There seems to lie over such catastrophes some
heavy fatality that makes human history an ineluctable
tragedy.

But Tolstoi's sensuous love of life is never more apparent than in this great novel. He feels it with every
sense, and he responds with this full gallery of portraits,
Russian and foreign. It is more than a wide acquaintance
with human nature, it is a sensitiveness to the moods, feelings, overtones of the minds of his characters. And the
reader reacts as does the author with a wider and sympathetic love of life. It is Tolstoi's first great thrust at life,
a great theme—perhaps the greatest ever conceived by

the nineteenth century. But its very magnitude leaves the author and the reader a bit breathless. Its ideas are too vast; to study patiently and understand better he will select a somewhat smaller canvas.

The result came a few years later with *Anna Karenina.* Here the author is at his mature best, but also ready to make his next attack in a new direction. Here it is the panorama of the Russia of his own time that is slowly unfolded for us. He sees and knows it all from the prince and court to the lowliest peasant, and its issues. And always now the pertinent question—to what end? A world is made more visible than the one we live in, and its motives laid down plain for all to read. Yet the author stands aloof. Over and over again the patient question repeats itself, to what end; and to the last the question is left unanswered, save in the spasmodic actions of the characters themselves. None are villains, though many are unworthy; none are unsympathetic, they are too like ourselves. And none are wholly successful, for success depends upon the answer to the eternal question. Some are tragic, but the author will not condemn. "Judgment is mine, saith the Lord, I will repay." Some have called it, and I think not unjustly, the greatest novel ever written. At the least it has an unexcelled universality.

The story, unlike the *War and Peace,* has a plot, about which are gathered more or less intimately the concerns of a great many people. The plot is the love of Anna, the wife of a high government official, the Prince Karenin, and Vronsky, an attractive and dashing young officer, and the web of tragedy they finally weave. But Tolstoi is far from condemning love outside marriage. It is against the background of this tragedy that move the other restless incidents in the story, like the love of Kitty and Levin, until at the end this strange searcher after peace, Levin, becomes for his very doggedness the prince of the novel.

For Levin was no other than Tolstoi himself, and his search was Tolstoi's inner biography. Tolstoi had acted in his novels before. He is the child, boy, youth, of the *Childhood and Youth*; he was Pierre Bezukhof of the *War and Peace*; but now at the time of the writing of the *Anna Karenina* he had been stirred deeply to search anew for a meaning of life and death; and Levin was his attempted answer. The courtship of Kitty is Tolstoi's own love story, and their efforts to effect a mutual accommodation. The death of Levin's brother is the story of the death of Tolstoi's brother Nicholas. But the parallel is much more far reaching. Levin's restless mind, searching forever among land problems, peasants' shortcomings, political careers, science, scholarship, everywhere, for something that will not only occupy his mind but fill his soul: this is Tolstoi.

For one remembers that it was at this time that he set himself up with huge enthusiasm as school teacher to the peasants on his estates. And then came his effort with a text-book for their salvation. (He will do this later for all peasants with his moral folktales.) For a time he is held by this new exercise. "Angelic faces—I am seized with fear and anxiety, as though I were beholding drowning people: Lord, how to save them, and whom to save first." This again is both Levin and Tolstoi.

There is no moral to the story, as there is no moral to life, except as one brings the moral oneself. Over it floats the anxiety of the man who sees and strives to understand, or as Levin, to mould it into an intelligible pattern. Only then he must begin with himself, and he is his own severest problem. "If I wanted to sum up," wrote Tolstoi, "that which I tried to express in my novel, I would have to write another novel, and it would be precisely the novel I have written." Perhaps the comment by the brother novelist Dostoevsky comes nearest to a moral.

"—The evil existed before men. Caught in the whirlwind of life, men commit crimes, and perish ineluctably.— No triumph of 'democratic elements,' no annihilation of poverty, no organization of labor can save mankind from this abnormality, and, consequently, from sin and crime. Tolstoi has expressed it in a tremendous investigation of human souls, with a frightening depth and power, with a hitherto unprecedented realism of artistic expression. It is evident to perfect clearness that evil is rooted in man deeper than our socialistic healers believe, that no organization of society can do away with the evil, that man's soul always will remain the same, that perversity and sin grow out of it itself and that finally, the laws of human spirit are as yet so entirely unknown and mysterious, that there can be neither real healers, nor *final* judges, and that there is but He who says: 'Vengeance is mine: I will repay.' As for the human judge, he must know that he is not a final judge, that he himself is a sinner, that the scales and sword in his hands will be a monstrosity unless, holding the scales and the sword, he bows his head before the law of the as yet unfathomable mystery, and resorts to the only solution open to him—to clemency and love."

But who is the Lord of vengeance? Is it the God Jehovah of the Hebrew Ten Commandments? Or is it any supernatural Being? Is it only an ethical idea? Or, to put the question in another way, are we not here close to the theme of the Greek tragedy of Euripides? Life, life has its own tragedies and when driven by the power of passion it wrecks itself. There is a sistership that Anna can claim with the impassioned heroines like Medea or Electra. And Tolstoi at this stage of his writing was not unlike that other profound student of human nature and its overtones, the poet Euripides; both in love with life and both in perplexity over its meaning.

So the book has no one point of view, but the points of view of each of its characters. It has no philosophy of

life, but examines all the motives that have entered into
the pattern of the nineteenth century. Here we see liberalism, and its shortcomings, also conservatism, its excel-
lences and its paralysis; humanitarianism, social uplift,
the gospel of service, all have their day in court; here
also are besotted and contented ignorance and prejudice,
in high life and in low; religious faith and mysticism
sit in the witness box, and also religious nihilism; science
and industry speak their pieces and show also their impotence and dangers; scholarship and politics are ruthlessly shown for all they are; asceticism is here and against
it sensuous epicurianism, and the unthinking joy in life;
and over all hangs like a cloud Tolstoi's obsession with
death and his doubts. He has peered into the motives
and the life of all conventions, creeds, thoughts, ideals;
into the whole scope of western life; into its lies as well
as into what passes as truth. All this is the pageantry of
this remarkable novel.

Life gathers headway and flows in this novel. Characters emerge and are slowly transformed as they move
from situation to situation. Here is Levin at the beginning.

" 'Well, what shall I do? How shall I do it?' he asked himself,
trying to give expression to what he had thought and felt during the
short night. All his sensations and thoughts seemed to have run in
three different directions. One was the renunciation of his former life
and his utterly useless education. This idea afforded him great pleasure,
as it was easy and simple. His other thoughts had reference to the
new life that he wanted to lead now. It seemed to him that in the
conditions of this new life, in purity and simplicity, he would find that
resignation, contentment, and dignity the lack of which he felt so painfully now. The third line of thought brought him to the question
of how to effect the transition from the old life to the new. Here,
nothing definite presented itself to his mind. 'I must have a wife and
work. And there must be an incentive to work. . . .'

" 'How beautiful!' he thought, gazing up at a fleecy cloud, the colour of mother-of-pearl, that had stopped just overhead in the middle of the sky. 'How lovely everything is on this glorious night! And when did that shell have time to form? It is only a moment ago since I looked at the sky and there was nothing on it but two streaks of light. And my views on life have changed just as imperceptibly.' "

He is nearly unrecognizable as we take leave of him.

" 'Formerly I used to say that in my body, in this grass, in this caterpillar, a transmutation of matter takes place according to physical, chemical, and physiological laws. And in all of us, in these aspens, in the clouds, evolution is going on. Evolution from what, to what? An eternal evolution and struggle? As if there could be any direction and struggle in the infinite! And in spite of all the efforts of my reason in that direction, until now, the meaning of life, the meaning of my own impulses and strivings were not revealed to me. Now I know that life consists in living for God, for the soul.' "

But what assurance is there that this transformation is his last? The flux of life makes character, and it is only death that puts an end to its morphology. What should be its goal? Does one wonder that the thoughtful Tolstoi was himself perplexed?

How many blind alleys discovered themselves in this ceaseless struggle to discover a pattern to peace? Here are the Tom, Dick, and Harry of the miscellany called "society." There is a picture of society.

"There were the same ladies in the boxes, with the same officers in the background, the same gaily dressed women, the same dress coats, the same dirty crowd in the gallery. In all that mass, in boxes and stalls, there were only about forty people that represented *society*, and to these Vronsky turned his attention."

It is made up of such people as Stepan Arkadyevitch Oblonsky, a good natured, irresponsible aristocrat, with his domestic irrelevancies and his meaningless life, the bureaucrat whose duties are his least care. Against him is the serious Prince Karenin, the unfortunate husband, becoming the oriental mystic under the aid of the Countess Lydia; but his life is tragically empty. Or there is the harmless, lovable trifler, Vasenka Veslovsky, with his ribbons and dainty nothingness. These and many like them are the obvious failures or misfits, or pleasing excrescences.

But even serious and admirable pursuits bring nothing in the way of a solution. Sergei Ivanovitch, the diligent scholar, though he may resolutely seek an aim for his own life, finds that his pursuit is only up a blind alley.

"And the more he observed the more he felt that Sergei Ivanovitch and all those other people who were busy working for the public good, did so, not through the dictates of their own hearts, but for some intellectual conclusion that made them consider it the proper thing to do. It seemed to him that his brother was no more concerned about questions relating to human welfare, to the immortal soul, than he was about a problem of chess or the clever construction of some new machine."

Even Vronsky, who ought to be the villain of the piece, has a code that is not unadmirable, but its futility is seen in the tragic conclusion of his life.

"This code embraced only a limited circle of duties; but as they were strictly determined, and Vronsky never had occasion to go outside this circle, he was never uncertain as to the course of action he had to take. The code prescribed that it was essential to pay a gambling debt, but not a tailor; that it was wrong to lie to men, but allowable to women; that it was wrong to deceive any one except a husband; that an insult should not be endured, but that you had a right to insult others, and so on, and so on. All these rules might be senseless and bad, but they were indubitable, and in observing them Vronsky felt that he could hold his head high. Later, however, on account of his relations to Anna, he began to feel that this code did not embrace all conditions of life, and that in the future doubts and perplexities might present themselves to which it did not apply."

He is not a bad man, and his love for Anna is never condemned. But what of the dilemma of poor, and once
radiant Anna?

"Will I get a divorce and become Vronsky's wife. Will Kitty cease
looking at me as she looked at me to-day? No. And will Serioja stop
asking or thinking of my two husbands? What new sentiment will grow
up between me and Vronsky? Can I possibly hope if not for happiness,
at least for peace? No and no!" she replied to herself without the least
hesitation. "Impossible! We diverge along different ways; I am the
cause of his unhappiness and he of mine, and it is impossible to change
either of us. Every attempt has been made . . . There is a screw
loose somewhere. There goes a beggar woman with her child. She
thinks she ought to be pitied."

And through it all goes the inquiring character of Tolstoi himself, Levin, checking, testing, and rejecting one
after another all the varied motives, as they seem to promise much, then wither under his piercing analysis. He
sees the value of an aristocracy, and yet is willing to renounce his own, for it has been futile for him. He loves
the country and country work, and the contented peasants
in their labor, and yet there is never the answer, to what
end? If work is only an anodyne it is of doubtful value
or even dangerous. But what of leisure? He is sincerely
in love with his wife, but he finds that in spite of love
each lives a separate life, and there is between them a wall
that never can be crossed. He studies science, but can it
bring happiness; and his inquiry pushes deeper than the
romantic generalizations of Rousseau.

In the same manner Tolstoi takes up remorselessly the
various ideals for proposed reform that might make life
more happy. Is happiness, as proposed by Rousseau, now
to be found only among the industrious and uncontami-
nated huts of the peasant? Is their content a genuine tribute to their higher and purer nature? Or is their

conservatism and ignorance a handicap that should be removed by education? There was much being said in those days, as much has been said since, on these subjects. But Levin sees to the heart of the matter. Their conservatism is innate dulness, or almost a religious fear of change. And any effort at education for them, as things are, is useless. So he takes up the land problem, the question of dividing up the great estates among the peasants, the reform most advocated by the liberals. Indeed liberalism itself in the character of Sviajsky is shown to be as empty as it has so often proved; and this was in the days before liberalism acquired its patina of moss. So he takes up also the easy knowledge and culture carried so jauntily by the modern omniscient journalist.

> "At one time if a man, let us say a Frenchman, had wished to educate himself he would have begun by studying the classics, the theologians, the tragedians, the historians, the philosophers—all the vast scope open before him. But now he immediately turns to journalism, gets some smattering of science, and thinks he's finished."

And with this jauntiness comes also the cockiness of free thought, which is in effect a refusal to think, and indifference, which is so often confused with tolerance. There is little in the way of new ideas or proposals for reform that this straight-eyed, objective Levin cannot see through and give its right name.

But all the while he is burning with apprehension about the question of human fate. Something is wanting to give the right motive for life. Where shall he find it? There is the essential knowledge of the unlearned peasantry. But he cannot put himself back into the state of the unlearned peasant. Love also is necessary for all work. But love is not a motive that is always at one's beck and call. Once, after a hard day's work and a night alone with nature, he caught the vision. But these poetic moods of transcendental peace are fleeting. Tolstoi is not a Wordsworth. He must act. Where shall he turn? And the peace that he gained at the end? Is it after all the peace of victory, or only an illusory truce? Will not the adjustments that next day's experience requires again leave the heart empty? Levin is Tolstoi now at the cross-roads, and a finger seems remorselessly pointing to the final sacrifice that will be required of him.

"I shall continue to pray without being able to explain to myself why, but my life, my whole life, independently of what may happen to me, every minute of it, shall no longer be senseless as before, but every moment, every action shall be invested with meaning."

Dostoevsky with the same irrelevant complexity of life, and with a personal motive in it quite as poignant as Tolstoi's, is later going to come to a quite different solution of life's puzzle. But life at this time, sensuously as he bathed himself in it and absorbed it at every pore—and perhaps for this very reason—made Tolstoi dizzy. Instead of art discovering to him a clue and a philosophy, as to Goethe, it seemed to contribute to the general confusion by offering a palliative or a means to forget. And he looked at the work of his hand and pronounced a bitter judgment. "Then I looked at all the works that my hand had wrought and on the labor that I had labored to do; and behold, all was vanity and vexation of spirit and there was no profit in them under the sun." Or again, "I live—what for? and what then? a miserable, duped fool." It is the intoxication of life repenting the night's extravagance.

These were the years of climax of the doubts and bewilderments from his youth onward. Read his *Confession* which is the commentary on Levin in the *Anna Ka-*

renina. And inexorably, as many before him, like Levin, Tolstoi is driven to religion. It, and it only, will offer the formula for the simplification he demands. But it is going to be at a tragic cost. There are emotional and social needs that must be satisfied. These must be reduced to the simplest possible terms. Only the simplest formula for religion—one that a peasant gives him—can bring the desired peace.

"People are different; one man lives for himself alone, like Mityuha, who only thinks of filling his belly, but Fokanitch is an honest man; he lives for his soul. He thinks of God.

"What do you mean by that? How does he live for his soul? Levin almost shouted.

"It's quite simple, according to the truth, according to God's word. There are all kinds of people. Take yourself, for example, you would not hurt any one . . .

"Yes, yes, good-bye! Levin said, hastily, and turned away. He took his cane and walked rapidly towards the house, in a state of great agitation. The peasant's simple words about Fokanitch living for his soul, according to God's word, set a whole chain of thoughts whirling in his brain, blinding him with their light."

The very vehemence of his sensuous love of life drove Tolstoi, as many a mediaeval ascetic, to renounce its allurements as promptings of Evil. The sensuousness of his nature drove him to a repentance that would inflict the severest of sensuous pain; again as the mediaeval ascetic indulged the ecstasy of flagellation. One would like to point to the illustrious example of Saint Francis, the pleasure loving youth who embraced Lady Poverty and bare-footed sought the stony path of salvation through love of God and man. Only for Tolstoi this is the nineteenth century, and God is not so simple a concept as in the thirteenth, and human institutions are not so receptive to this simple creed. One would like to point to Gandhi who in a revolt against the western creed in our day has again chosen the way of simplicity and love; but India has not yet adopted western ways and has since the beginning known the "blessings" of poverty. Tolstoi's voluntary martyrdom became a tragedy to him because he could never deny wholly the thing he renounced.

But from now he takes as his text-book the *Sermon on the Mount*, or its summary in the two great commandments: "Thou shalt love the Lord, thy God with all thy heart, mind, strength and spirit; and thy neighbor as thyself." Only the second command has the greater significance and emphasis. These texts he makes the occasion for the *Tales* he wrote for peasants and others who could read. These he elaborates in pamphlet and book, like his *Confession*, the *Criticism of the Four Gospels*, and *What My Faith Consists in*. The doctrine is simplicity itself, and terribly attractive to souls like his in a tempest of doubt. He calls himself a discoverer and dates this time as "my regeneration," "my awakening." Now "peasant life, obscurity, poverty, rudeness, simplicity of food, furniture, clothing, and manners appear to me as good and lofty."

And again I am reminded of the simplicity of the garb of Mr. Gandhi, as I saw him, and the austerity of his home. His bed a mat on the floor of a bare room; his desk before which he works, seated on the floor; a row of books where Tolstoi's writings were prominent; a simple cotton floor cloth; and that was all, except for the spinning wheel. This last for the cobbler's bench that Tolstoi selected, and the shed where he now preferred to live and work, and the peasant's plow on which at times he set his hands. He even went farther and tried to speak with the peasant's accent.

His attitude toward literature was revolutionized. There must be a new art and a new artist with new motives for writing. So he rejected the idea of royalties as compensation for his books. He rejected Shakespeare, as well as Beethoven and Wagner. World-wide fame is now a superstition, an "epidemic mental disease." He turned savagely against his own writings. "Absolutely insignificant works" they are now. And he tried the cultivation of a peasant circle of readers—with the *Peoples' Tales* to teach Christian love. To be sure his old readers took to him avidly, to his consternation. He tried the *Power of Darkness* on a peasant audience. The comment of a peasant neighbor was, "What shall I tell you, Leo Nicholayevich? At first Nikita managed his affairs cleverly, but in the end he proved to be a fool." That was all. But in Saint Petersburg the reception was thunderous. Two hundred and fifty thousand copies went in three days. And again a prophet was not without honor save—.

His creed is Christian anarchy, with a contempt for Church and State, that he is teaching, and literary anarchy, with himself against himself. And of course he was never without the protest of those who saw in him a traitor to his own century. To discuss "True and False Light" in a pamphlet, as he did when he paraphrased the Scriptures, is in itself comparatively easy; others have felt in the same way. A simple creed of Love, God, and Work is beautifully attractive even in a drawing room or laboratory.

"Blessed are the poor, the property-less; but blessed only when they are not only poor externally, but poor by their spirit, their desire; as salt is good, not when it looks like salt, but only when it has saltness in itself."

"For know, that God requires neither sacrifices nor prayers, but only peace, agreement and love among men. And you can neither pray nor think of God if you have but one man with whom you are out of love."

"Therefore, Do not judge, do not use law courts, do not punish; and you will not be judged or punished. Forgive everything, and you will be forgiven. But if you judge men they will judge you."

"But I say to you: Love not only the people of your own land but of other nations also. Let foreigners hate you, let them attack you, offend you;—speak well of them and do them kindnesses."

Such things, almost, are read daily in orthodox churches. But to act as a literal commentary on such injunctions, this involves the acceptance of values quite out of contact with an enlightened and progressive century. And for genius to renounce its gifts and turn bunglingly to farming and cobbling! It is no wonder that Turgenev wrote in pained remonstrance.

For Tolstoi's definition of art and the artist implies a revolution which goes much farther than man's return to the calling of the peasant. It means the clipping of the wings of the imagination and a substitution of a new purpose, and a simple, definite, and moral one, for the large license of the artist. The *What Is Art* raises fundamental questions. And there are countries in Europe today that, twisting Tolstoi's purpose, are prescribing simple, definite, and moral or political programs for the artist.

Art and science, to Tolstoi, must be used for the regeneration of the world. But of the two art is the more needed. It must have a purpose, definite and potent, and must be judged solely as it contributes to that purpose.

"Christian art, *i.e.*, the art of our time, should be catholic in the original meaning of the word, *i.e.*, universal, and therefore it should unite all men. And only two kinds of feeling do unite all men: first, feelings flowing from the perception of our sonship to God and of the brotherhood of man; and next, the simple feelings of common life, accessible to every one without exception—such as the feeling of merriment, of pity, of cheerfulness, of tranquillity, etc. Only these two kinds of feelings can now supply material for art good in its subject matter."

We can call this effect in his own words the "ripening of men's conscience." It is in this spirit that he wrote those exquisite little moral tales: *The Kingdom of God is Within You,* or *How Much Land does a Man Require.* And it is with something of the same purpose that came the amazing remark from him at a time of famine that it is not man's duty to "feed the hungry" so much as to "love the hungry."

His ideas on the place of science are equally downright. Science to which the nineteenth century was devoted, was for him on the wrong path. It had been "occupied with the study of subjects unrelated to the conduct of human life"; and hence had come its absolute divorce from life. It therefore, like art, must be regenerated and given a human purpose.

"Astronomical, physical, chemical, and biological science, as also technical and medical science, will be studied only in so far as they can help to free mankind from religious, juridical, or social deceptions, or can serve to promote the well-being of all men, and not of any single class.

"Only then will science cease to be what it is now,—on the one hand a system of sophistries needed for the maintenance of the existing worn-out order of society, and, on the other hand, a shapeless mass of miscellaneous knowledge, for the most part good for little or nothing,—and become a shapely and organic whole, having a definite and reasonable purpose comprehensible to all men; namely, the purpose of bringing to the consciousness of men the truths that flow from the religious perception of our times."

When these, the two highest activities of man, have been redirected to a nobler purpose and co-ordinated to man's moral regeneration, then and then only will they be truly beneficent.

"The task of art is enormous. Through the influence of real art, aided by science guided by religion, that peaceful co-operation of man which is now obtained by external means—by our law-courts, police, charitable institutions, factory inspection, etc.—should be obtained by man's free and joyous activity. Art should cause violence to be set aside."

Thus the first Tolstoi, the sensitive, objective artist, became Tolstoi, the troubled thinker, and last Tolstoi the prophet of a new moral Absolute. And the transformation was due to the complex motives of life, its varied manifestations, that he could not fuse into any aim that seemed consistent with man's moral nature. With an insight that reminds one of the old Hebrew prophet, his world appeared as a world of conflict between the moral and immoral, between evil and good. To him good was the old moral law with the two commandments of love. He chose, and the last thirty years of his life were a recurring tragedy.

Tragedy—for the Tolstoi, who from the beginning had eagerly and seriously sought the sheer joy of living, to the very end could not remain crushed and passive. One sees his early love of life rise in such novels as the *Kreutzer Sonata*, where it struggles with the problem of sex—a motive whose power the prophet could never forget. And though the patent moral purpose loses much for us in its second half, his last novel, *Resurrection*, written in the closing year of the century for the emigrating Dukhobars, is his apology to life. In it again is the panorama of Russia. The nearly twenty years of self-denial had not clouded his eyes; and his old power had scarcely abated. But he paid for his recusancy by much trouble of conscience and his apology has clearly a double meaning. "Yes I have a great reputation. It proves that I have not achieved anything worth while in all my life." Had he done so, he implies, his reputation would have been small, for the world and he were not treading the same path.

It is easy for the modern critic to see in this great genius something psychologically aberrant, a personality divided. One of them calls him a "satyr with a horror of the flesh," his ethical code "a house built upon an ice pack." It would be equally easy to find names for the prophet Isaiah, who also lived in a century of divided counsels, loved life and its poetry eagerly, saw the vision, and had coals of fire placed on his lips that his utterance might be clean. Tolstoi is the nineteenth century in a Russia that has cut the cables from its old moorings and is adrift upon an uncharted sea. Not able to see the other shore—and has the vision yet been granted to this our next century?—he would desert the ship and swim back even if he must go alone, and the ship he abandons be full of the enchantment of life.

He at least will not compromise as some strove to do with science and religion, or with science and art. The claims of each are seen by him in all their full details. Where he cannot reconcile he will reject, and strive to live his rejection down to the last instruction.

So he stands apart from the social and political controversies of his time, and yet lent them new meaning. So Russian orthodoxy, though it felt him to be the latest *fantaisiste,* was never comfortable in his presence. For his criticisms of the state and the church were neither political nor social, but moral and spiritual, and hence the more devastating, because their immediate effects were imperceptible. It is quite within reason to say that Tolstoi was probably the single greatest power toward the Revolution, though he would have been the first to be horrified at its motive and direction. For the Soviet regime is again an attempt to simplify life and give it a direction.

The nineteenth century, though it understood, could

not accept Tolstoi. And the reason for the rejection of this prophet, like the reason for the rejection of his Hebrew ancestor, was plain. His way was far too simple, and his words therefore seemed only fit for babes and sucklings. But he was not, as a recent critic has said, a prophet with an ethical code without a metaphysics. He had an innate and immediate consciousness of spirit, his God; and though this deity had little in common with the traditional God of the theologians, it was a very real, though mystical, source for an apprehension of a transcendent spiritual motive for life. His code of ethics had transcendental origins. It is the purely human and intellectual origins of the world of science and of human institutions that made him reject their claims, when they conflict with the mystical "Thou Shalt" in his sensitive conscience. There is a world of Rousseau here.

To him it is because of their purely intellectual origin, that human political, social and ecclesiastical institutions, unlike the inspirations of the moral conscience, contribute so little to human happiness and good will. Rather they tend to promote the very forces that drive men into open hostility. Thus arise class distinctions, and idle classes, and a fear of work. Thus arise all the complications of vanity that disfigure man's moral excellence. And above all, thus arise the gradual suppression and loss of the vital emotions, which alone can give life its value. So thought, so spoke the prophet Tolstoi. But the young Tolstoi had, even in childhood, much of the same instinctive fear of a life divested of an emotional guide. Tolstoi's revolt against the life of the century and its thought is a perfectly natural revolt, though, as naturally, for the century it was impossible. So Tolstoi remains, as he was when alive, now a generation after his death, the great solitary: the tragedy of the century.

Others like Rousseau had talked charmingly of the return to the simple life, some like Wordsworth had gone to the villages and the mountains, but carrying the culture and language of the century in their baggage. Tolstoi alone gave up the fur coat of civilization and knew the bitter cost of the sacrifice.

X. A RETURN TO LIFE

DOSTOEVSKY

"Certainly, love life, regardless of logic as you say; it must be regardless of logic, and it is only then one will understand the meaning of it."

The Brothers Karamazov

LOVE life: but one must know also what life is to which one must give all in loving. And what will life offer in return? These are the problems that perplexed Tolstoi, and drove him into monastic seclusion. To escape from its bewildering complexity he chose simplicity and solitude. The path for Dostoevsky lay from the solitude and simplicity of the political prisoner in Siberia to the larger and richer life of the world of human behavior, where he strove to discipline his love with understanding. If Tolstoi is the Russian who strove to become a mediaeval saint, Dostoevsky is the Russian who succeeded in becoming a modern Western European.

Yet it can be said that Dostoevsky is the most Russian of all the Russians. An eagerly curious intelligence, only recently freed to explore the riches of modern life and thought, and as hungry a bundle of nerves that must translate this into passionate sensations. To think in sensation, to transform a syllogism into sense and action, to discover a logic of passion; this is the manner of the Rus-

197

sian temper when it pursues its amorous conquest of life;
to compass its physical thrill with understanding, and to
know the logic of each heart throb; to be at the same
time metaphysician, psychologist, biologist, and lover—
a bewildering program. Can any such lover stand before
his beloved object, asking such revealing questions and
not be dismayed by the answer? I remember a medical
student friend of my student days who broke off his en-
gagement after intimately studying the anatomy of the
abdomen. Tolstoi's revolt had something of the same
motive. Will Dostoevsky fare any better?

Thus it is that no experience for the Russian is significant only for its own sake. Even so commonplace a
thing as getting drunk has facets that reflect eternity.

> "And what have Russian boys been doing up till now, some of them,
> I mean? In this stinking tavern, for instance, here, they meet and sit
> down in a corner. They've never met in their lives before and, when
> they go out of the tavern, they won't meet again for forty years. And
> what do they talk about in that momentary halt in the tavern? Of the
> eternal questions, of the existence of God and immortality. And those
> who do not believe in God talk of socialism or anarchism, of the
> transformation of all humanity on a new pattern, so that it all comes
> to the same, they're the same questions turned inside out."

Thus was Levin constantly tortured in the *Anna Karenina*.
Thus will nearly all of the characters in Dostoevsky's
novels be unable to give themselves wholly at any one
time to any single experience. And this is one reason why
the uninitiated reader feels there must be something exaggerated, something essentially abnormal in Russian
fiction from Gogol to Gorky.

There is another side to it that adds to the difficulty
for those who have been trained in the discreet fiction
of, let us say, Thackeray or Meredith. The western mind
has been accustomed to the manners of restraint and "good

form." Compromise, half-statement, suggestion rather than complete expression, inhibition, those Aristotelian virtues of nothing too much, have become standard and matters of inheritance from the old classical tradition. The Russian coming on this tradition very late in his career has never regarded it except as a polite mask or irritating lie. Hence his more expressive exuberance, his gaiety that knows no bounds, or his depression that is extravagant with tears. We dread "to make a scene," the Russian takes to "scenes" as truth to life. So to the tender-minded, Fyodor Pavlovitch Karamazov is a monster of incredible and voluble debauchery. He puts even Zola's worst to shamed silence. But he merely has set no bounds to his self-expression; on the contrary shame would detract from his artistic self-satisfaction. Where his western counterpart would be circumspect, he is boastfully open, and more according to nature. One must be willing to see, indeed enjoy seeing, human nature nakedly displayed, and, admirable or hateful, without bondage or restraint in its action and speech, before one can pretend to understand this perhaps most contemporary of Russian novelists.

Dostoevsky loved life, and experience had made him as passionate and temperamental a lover as any in his novels. It had its first crisis in his youth, at a time when the western boy is acquiring "good form" in a university, with his sentence to be shot for belonging to a daring debating society. A reprieve came in the nick of time to save his life. The story is best told in his own words.

"Twenty times the fatal words were repeated: "Sentence, to be shot! And so indelibly were the words graven into my memory that for years afterwards I would wake in the middle of the night fancying I heard them being read. But at the same time I distinctly remember another circumstance: the officer, after having finished the reading, folded the paper and put it into his pocket, after which he descended from the scaffold. At this moment the sun broke through the clouds, and I thought, 'It is impossible, they can't mean to kill us!' and I whispered these words to my nearest companion, but instead of answering, he only pointed to a line of coffins that stood near the scaffold, covered with a large cloth.

"All my hope vanished in an instant, and I expected to be shot in a few minutes.

"It gave me a great fright, but I determined not to show any fear, and I kept talking to my companion about different things. He told me afterwards that I had not even been very pale.

"All of a sudden a priest ascends the scaffold, and asks if any of the condemned wish to confess their sins. Only one accepted the invitation, but when the priest held out the crucifix we all touched it with our lips.

"Petroschevsky and two others, who were considered the most culpable, were already tied to the poles and had their heads covered with a kind of bag, and the soldiers stood ready to fire at the command 'Fire!'

"I thought I might perhaps have five minutes more to live, and awful these moments were. I kept staring at a church with a gilt dome, which reflected the sunbeams, and I suddenly felt as if these beams came from the region where I was to be myself in a few moments!

"Then there was a general stir. I was too short-sighted to discern anything, but I felt that something extraordinary was happening. At last I descried an officer, who came galloping across the square, waving a white handkerchief. He was sent by the emperor to announce our pardon. Afterwards we learned that the sentence of death had only been a threat, intended as 'a lesson not to be forgotten.' "

The sentence was commuted to eight years of life as a convict in Siberia and many years more of exile.

A lesser man, or a more commonplace, would have been broken by this tragedy in youth. But this man loved life the more passionately the more severely it repulsed him. When in Siberia he was associated with the most atrocious of criminals, he discovered that they were men, and questioned the meaning of the word criminal. He never forgot the experience; but this does not mean that he never was able to live it down; on the contrary it is from it that he dates the beginnings of his efforts to seek a reconciliation with life, or, as a rejected lover might, to discover some philosophy of hope. He is convinced of tragedy and horror. Life never made its peace with him. But in spite of tragedy and horror, in spite of the conviction that peace is a fiction, is there possible somewhere a philosophy of hope?

Hence there is the essential lack of serenity in his own life. This has perhaps been overdrawn by recent biographers, who see chiefly the agitations on the surface, and forget that below there may be a larger calm. The *Letters from the Underworld* show how he is passionately drawn to the humanity of men jettisoned by society. His *Journal of an Author* shows the moral resolution and fortitude and higher faith that will give substance to his great novels. But at best his career was tempestuous, harried by debt and exile, always unsettled; he was a born gambler, and generous to folly. It is not to be wondered at that those who, with Milton, would hold that he who would write a great poem must make of his own life a great poem, shake their heads over this career of drab shreds and purple patches.

And things of shreds and patches, and not serene security, are also his novels. *Crime and Punishment, The Idiot* and above all *The Brothers Karamazov* are at first sight a series of situations disintegrating under successive charges of emotional dynamite. They lack the flow and assured progress by logic of the old fiction. They detonate and the flying debris at first overwhelms us with passion and thought, exclamation and exposition, in a blinding and deafening shower. Reading these novels at first is like trying to describe one's thoughts and sensations in the midst of a typhoon.

But this is only because after his *Letters from the Underworld* he has explored for us vaster regions for mental adventure. There is no time and space in his novels, at least as we have been accustomed to think of time and space. There is no local color. There are none of these definite lines for orientation in a typhoon. Whereas the ordinary two volume novel covers a period of years, here it is crowded into days, one or two or three—we never know just how many—and we don't care. Chronology as clock time or almanac time is utterly absent. What counts time is the mind; when it is occupied time is ignored, when it is vacant time ceases. And so it is with space—a city, or a countryside, or a room, or any object, is important only as it registers its presence and uniqueness on the sensitive mind. A crack in a door or a torn strip of wall paper may be of the utmost significance, or the slant of the sunlight, but a street, a city, a bridge or a monastery, if they record no impressions, their existence may be acknowledged and ignored. Dostoevsky allows the sensitive minds of his characters to make their own records of their impressions. The result might be called, if one must name it, a psychological impressionism.

In a way the backgrounds are a series of revolving stages for his characters, but managed so as to be perfectly appropriate for the immediate situations. And these must be brought together just at the time when they are ripe for the discovery and its effects. It is the dramatist's art, but here transferred to the huge canvas of a long novel, and its much looser plot. In the hands of one less absorbed in the main issue of the intense inner experience of the characters, the result would be the mechanical play of coincidence. For example, how appropriately just at the moment when Raskolnikoff, perpetrator of the crime in *Crime and Punishment*, is shuddering over his deed, he is summoned to report at the Police Station where his landlady has lodged a complaint. This is "stagey"; but for the purpose of this novel is profoundly appropriate. It is Raskolnikoff we are interested in, his inner responses to his own desperate action, and we pursue him remorselessly from stage to stage, situation to situation, as the sky clears or the tempest closes, remorselessly to the last scene where he is finally restored to life and peace.

The effect is cumulative, for we are watching an adventure that is occurring in two dimensions. It is not only the outer act that holds our eyes and its effects on the character in agony or relief, but what is far more dramatic for this writer, the inner tragedy of conflicting impulses and emotions. More recently we have learned to call this the story of the flow of consciousness. Dostoevsky shows how intense and how significant is the making of a single decision, even a trifling one perhaps; and carrying it farther, how a dream may be more vivid and far-reaching than external act. Was it the loneliness of the convict's life in Siberia and the exile's later, or his internal conflicts when he sought reconciliation with life, that opened these hitherto little explored regions for adventures in fiction? The effect of these adventures on the reader, as on their victim, is cumulative. It is no wonder that to many the reading of even *Crime and Punishment* or the *Idiot,* to put aside *The Brothers Karamazov,* is an exercise in emotional crescendo from which they shrink. And they caution the reader against the extravagance of Russian realism.

Tolstoi in his search was looking for a philosophy of hope, that would give life meaning. Dostoevsky is not so much concerned with the philosophy as with the psychology of hope that might reconcile man to life. For philosophy implies a creed, hence an abstraction, while life is a vital and sensitive process, and man is a delicate organism, whose actions and thoughts are as vital and sensitive. Tolstoi had found a creed that satisfied his reason and conscience, but left his life desolate. He could live it only by a constant civil war with life itself, and his victory was only the compromise of the ascetic. Dostoevsky will begin not with reason and conscience, but with life itself, the human personality, and strive to discover the reconciliation with life in a search for harmony within. How modern, how contemporary this is, with our new psychological clinics and the new science of psychiatry. And yet again, how old; for was not Euripides doing the same thing nearly twenty-five hundred years ago in his *Electra* or *Alcestis?* [1]

The frequent antagonism between reason or conscience, on the one hand, and psychology, that is, the demands of the human personality, on the other, this becomes his theme. The needs of the one are fairly clear, and find themselves expressed in the formulas of science and of ethics. But the other is elusive, and its needs as elusive as its protean shapes. These shapes it is that one must discover; and Dostoevsky's novels are a pursuit into its hidden labyrinths of the mystery of human conduct. There may be a philosophy behind it all, biological or metaphysical, but this is not the question now. Much more important is the question of an attitude toward life. "Man's whole business is to prove that he is a man and not a cog-wheel." So much for the affairs of the new sciences of biology and sociology with their deterministic theories of life. "That two and two make four is not a part of life but the beginnings of death." So much for

---

[1] I have tried to raise this same question in the chapter on Greek Tragedy in *The Golden Thread.*

the laws of consistency and logic. "Surely I haven't suffered, simply that I, my crimes and my sufferings, may
manure the soil of the future harmony for somebody
else." So much for those who like Hebbel took refuge in
a metaphysical creed. All these things of reason and
conscience, with their formulas and creeds, touch so remotely the immediate question of this act of conduct or
that fact of suffering, or the other of stark tragedy, that
the sufferer has no will, nor means, to look upward for
the divine vision. He desires vindication, as did the pursued murderer, Raskolnikoff, and immediate harmony.
Can he be ministered to, and how? It is for the new
psychology to answer: so runs Dostoevsky. He loves life,
and he longs to live.

"Where was it that I read of a condemned man who, at the hour
of death, says or thinks that if the alternative were offered him of
existing somewhere, on a height or rocks or some narrow elevation,
where only his two feet could stand, and round about him were placed
an ocean, perpetual gloom, perpetual solitude, perpetual storm, to remain there standing on a yard of surface for a lifetime, a thousand
years, eternity!—rather would he live thus than die at once? Only
live, live, live!—no matter how, only live! How true is this? Oh,
Lord, how true! Oh, miserable race of men! . . ."

In consequence Dostoevsky refuses to judge and condemn with a very different motive from Tolstoi's. For
though Tolstoi understands his characters far too well
to condemn their vagaries—Oblonsky and Anna are too
human for any judge's sentence, save God's—yet the
obliquity of their destiny is forever a vindication of reason and conscience which are God. There must be some
Absolute which must prevail, or the universe becomes a
mad and illogical terror; and Tolstoi, like Levin, never
abandons the hope that it will finally be discovered. But
Dostoevsky in his pursuit of concrete reality, which is

human experience, will follow it through scepticism and pessimism, wherever it may lead, even if as in Dante's *Inferno* across the portal be written the fatal warning of hope abandoned. So *Crime and Punishment* and *The Brothers Karamazov* are not judgments implied or even self-confessed. Raskolnikoff never thought of the murder as a crime, but as "a silly *error,* which might have happened to any man." What are criminals? The question puzzles the characters as well as the author. He had once been branded himself, and lived with those under society's ban. Who is he that he should pass judgment for any individual act, tied up as it is with circumstance and personality? For this is a region where the laws of reason or of conscience in the abstract have no meaning.

Good and bad, customary and uncustomary, these pairs of words are almost interchangeable, for every concrete situation in life is unique, as must be the response to it of personality. Is the mountain fir that is buried by the avalanche immoral or bad because it stood in the way of the scientific law of moving bodies? So the comment seems to run as we watch the pilgrim's progress of his characters, which at times is a macabre dance of death, at others a flirting with the celestial vision. Are both equally meaningless? Is the same index value to be written above both? Is the man-monster Fyodor Pavlovitch in the scale to weigh as much as the saintly Alyosha? Both stood firm in the love of life, but what a difference in its manifestation. Is there a right, or better, or higher, attitude one may attain to in this love? And the answers will reveal, if an answer is possible, the value to the century, as to all time, of this Russian novelist.

The answers are found, not in his letters or his own life, but in those novels which bear the traces of his deepest experience—*Crime and Punishment* and *The Brothers Karamazov*. But they are neither plain nor easy; for neither novel is an allegory, though the stage in the latter seems at the beginning to be somewhat arbitrarily set with perfectly balanced characters. Even in *Crime and Punishment* the characters at times seem to be those of a roman *à thèse*.

"Man's whole business is to prove that he is a man and not a cog-wheel." More perhaps than in any of his other novels this is the theme of the *Crime and Punishment*, this and its corollary, that man has a *right* to life and a *duty* to translate an instinctive love of life into love vindicated by experience; and that *any* experience may be justified by its results, if one is able to pay the price. It is this last clause, with its anticipation of Nietzsche's doctrine of the *Uebermensch*, the superman, that has made some readers shake their heads.

The hero, Raskolnikoff, once a student, the son of a poor widow, under the stress of poverty and compelled to give up his studies, has become a dreamer. He imagines the one deed that will free him of all encumbrances, and let him take his place in the world. We see his attic room, its torn paper, the couch with its hollows worn deep by his listless dreaming. There is an old woman, an evil money lender, a blot on all society, with whom one by one he has left his treasures; her death surely will be a glorious service and an act of self-assertion.

Just as he is in imagination pondering the deed two events happen that seem to put the action beyond his volition, as though the deed were part of an inscrutable destiny, and Fate is pointing the way. A letter from his mother tells of the approaching marriage of his sister, Dounia, to Looshin, an impossible suitor, whom she cannot love. She is marrying, no doubt of it, to help her brother; and he will not accept her sacrifice. At the same moment he overhears the sister of the money-lender tell of an hour when he will have a perfect opportunity to carry out his plan. Everything conspires to help him; even the trifling detail of getting the hatchet is made to order. And he acts the rôle that is without his effort handed to him.

In the meanwhile he is thrown into contact with a Marmaladoff, once a petty official, now one of those drunken waifs that is "not driven out of society with a stick, but with a broom." A weak, but poetic creature is this man who in his better days had married a woman from the upper classes, but now the family with little children is living in extreme poverty, supported entirely by Sonia, his daughter, who has, to save the family, become a prostitute. Sonia's love touches Raskolnikoff, rouses his respect, and on a day of drunken trouble for the father, out of his pitifully small change, he leaves a handful as a token of his pity. Sonia and Raskolnikoff are to be the chief characters, she tender, true, and deeply religious; he broken by the deed that he thought would free him, torn by conflicting motives, a prey to his active imagination, and even contemplating suicide.

From now the story dives underground to trace the inner drama of the hero pursued by his own fears, tormented by the well meant efforts of his friend and his bewildered sister and mother, pricked to side issues by Looshin whom he insults, and by a former admirer of his sister and her would-be seducer, who wavers between bestiality and nobility, and himself writhing under the constant scrutiny of police inspectors who have no evidence against him except his own involuntary reactions.

He plans suicide from a bridge, but as he gazes into the water a girl anticipates him, and he turns from his failure with disgust. He attempts active benevolence when he relieves, with his mother's poor money, the needs of the Marmaladoff family after the father has been killed. In braggadoccio he attempts to outface the keen-faced lawyer who has interested himself in the psychology of the case; and for a moment he seems the superman he had dreamed himself.

But there is always the weak spot in his armor. He is too sensitive. He refuses to profit by the murder, and has rid himself of the unclean spoils. He dreams of strength:

"It is sufficient!" he muttered solemnly and decidedly. "Away, spectres! away, fear! away, visions! This is life. Am I living now? Did my life not leave me together with the old woman's? Heaven be hers and—enough! peace to her! The reign of reason and light commences now, of will, of force. . . . Strength, strength is necessary; without strength one can attain nothing, and strength begets strength."

But immediately after he falters, and sinks into the hollows of his couch. He boasts the value of the extraordinary man who makes his own code of values.

"An extraordinary man has a right—not officially, be it understood—but from and by his very individuality, to permit his conscience to overstep certain bounds, only so far as the realization of one of his ideas may require it."

But he confesses that there is the more tragic person, the weak man, who fancies himself to be above man made law.

"Notwithstanding their inborn tendency to obey, many of them, as a result of some freak of nature, fancy themselves men that ought to be in the van, and consider themselves in the light of 'regenerators' —think themselves selected to bring about a 'new state of things,' and this illusion is perfectly genuine in their case."

And it is these who are their own most efficient instruments of torture.

> "Yes, I am, *de facto*, so much vermin; first, from the fact that I am now considering whether I really am so; secondly, because during a whole month I have been pestering Divine Providence. Taking it to witness that I was contemplating this attempt, not with a view to material gains, but with ulterior purposes—hah! hah! . . ."

Nor in all this is there any trace of the thing one would expect, active remorse. The worst he can confess is that the crime was a "silly error," that for a better man would have meant success, but for him was a tragic illumination of a truth that, "suffering is part and parcel of extreme intelligence and a feeling heart." This is neither reason, nor conscience, but agonizing consciousness of loss of self, loss of freedom and self-direction. "Liberty and power, but above all power," this is what he had sought, and in its stead, helplessness, emptiness, and hopeless disintegration.

This is not punishment, as the word is used in criminal courts, or in text-books on ethics. It is not tears and remorse for guilt as it would be in a religious manual. It is not even self-inflicted penance, prompted by a motive for guilt. This is what was meant when I said Dostoevsky substitutes psychology, the study of the reactions of the single mind, for the older generalizations of ethics or reasoned conduct.

Raskolnikoff is a bundle of conflicting impulses, and none able to be satisfied, though he craves for action. The lawyer investigator advises peace through confession. He spurns it as a sign of the inferior mind. But Sonia, the symbol of suffering humanity,—before her he bows. She is greater than he. And he tells her the story. He asks her to read from the only book that she knows.

"The dying piece of candle dimly lit up this low-ceilinged room, in which an assassin and a harlot had just read the Book of Books."

And her advice is good. He will find himself only through some action. He had fancied himself a Napoleon who could go from action to action, not touched by any scruples or emotional bar. His one act had paralyzed him; now he must, if he would be free, undo so far as possible that one act, and that can only be through public confession with its consequences. She will remain at his side to share his guilt, so far as might be possible.

He is sentenced to Siberia. The torture is less, but yet life has for him no open road. The past has been swept away, but there is yet no future, only a blank wall, convicts among whom he finds no welcome, and Sonia in the distance whom yet he cannot see. But illness, and a dream which in allegory revealed his own meaningless-ness when alone, and the crying out of his heart for love, conspire at last for his final surrender. Complete self-surrender, love, Sonia; only with this can the "new tale" of his rejuvenation begin.

Self-assertion is not freedom. Freedom comes only in self-submission, surrender, to what? Sonia? But Sonia is self-surrendering love, active and enduring all things. When he returns from her to the prison, with this new insight, the convicts to him seem changed. He is in a new world, transformed by this new attitude. He can love life.

The novel *Crime and Punishment* in its conclusion suggests that this new attitude is comparable to a religious conversion. These last words will cry for definition. But how far does Dostoevsky go, like Tolstoi, in declaring that this new attitude toward life must be prompted by a motive that can be called only religious. To answer this question in all its bearings it will be necessary to analyse his last and greatest novel, *The Brothers Karamazov*.

The Brothers Karamazov was written in the years when the effects of the new definition given to the process of evolution by Darwin were being most strongly felt in all Europe. This so-called law of survival or selection had reinforced the mechanistic theory of life proposed by the French philosopher Auguste Comte, was interpreted by Zola in his novels, showing that character and personality were the results of heredity and environment alone, and was laid down as a thesis by Zola, in *le Roman Expérimental*, that from now on the art of the novelist in no way differed from the technique of the biological scientist.

To Dostoevsky the question of how to love life differs by the whole human horizon from the *élan vital*, the vital urge in plants and animals, that is the motive for the struggle for existence and survival. It is not alone survival that is demanded by his characters, but freedom, if not for action, at least freedom of the will to assert the value of personality against the pressure of heredity and environment, even at the cost of tragedy. This seems to be the motive behind all of the characters of *The Brothers Karamazov*.

There is heredity and environment in plenty in this picture of a large portion of Russia, but Zola again is handling toys of children in comparison with the stark figures that Dostoevsky puts into this panorama of passion and motive. Tolstoi had surveyed Russian life in the large, in its social classes and in its varied creeds and pass-words. Here we have the inner panorama as complete, though one hardly ventures beyond the streets of a little town, and sees not much farther than the members of one family. That town and that family are Russia, and in their more general characters all Europe.

It is a family of five: a father Fyodor Pavlovitch, one son, Dmitri, by a wife he had driven away to die in desperation, two sons, Ivan and Alyosha, by a second wife he had killed by cruelty, and a fourth son, Smerdyakov, unacknowledged, fathered on an idiot mother in his debauchery. Save for the last, who has been brought up as a menial in the household, all of the sons have been rescued from the father's sensuality and cold indifference by relatives, and educated. They have now returned with one motive or another, and for the first time in the family history meet under the same roof. Alyosha the youngest is nineteen. The other two sons are in the twenties. Smerdyakov is cook and present at more than one interview. The novel is the criss-cross of motives, and the resentments, angers, jealousies, and explosions that such meetings engender. It is never, except in rare scenes, a pretty picture.

Dmitri has been tricked by his grasping father out of much of his mother's inheritance. He has been a soldier, but now comes home to demand a reckoning, a thing his father will under no circumstances give. He has fallen in love with Grushenka, a young woman with an uncertain past, but who exudes life and gaiety. Dmitri has the same passionate love of life. But the girl is desired by the old man now, who offers a lure of money; and Dmitri has wasted half of a sum entrusted to him by another woman to devote one hour's orgy to this burning love.

But the other woman, Katerina Ivanovna, her character too is worth study. Daughter of an officer of high rank threatened with disgrace for misappropriated funds, she had saved her father by bending herself to the will of Dmitri. But he, and this is important, instead of accepting her sacrifice, had been generous. And so exalted did he feel at his unexpected nobility, that he drew his saber to stab himself, but kissed the hilt and trod on air. She now partly feels herself pledged to him, partly has fallen in love with him for his noble gesture, and will overlook his new infatuation, if only he will accept her hand and her new found fortune.

Dmitri has the passionate child's love of life and utter abandon, and the child's natural disorderliness. Debauchery with him is not, as with his father, an end, but a means to something richer, a higher love, now Grushenka. He hates what is ugly, and as a commentator says, would have been a poet had he been vocal. Put in a less sordid background he would be beautiful.

Against him is the cold and intellectual Ivan. He is reason. All the Karamazovs are sensual, but his sensuality has been suppressed, and at first his aloofness and cultured hatred of the family "scenes" make him a stranger in his own home. But his father fears him above all, as a force the older man cannot understand. Convinced that any standard of morality must rest upon a supernatural basis of immortality, and denying the supernatural with his scientific logic, he arrives at the maxim that "everything is permissible." And this last is going to prove his tragedy. To complicate his relations with his family he has fallen in love with Katerina Ivanovna; and this may prove his final salvation, for when reason finally proves unavailable against life, he learns that "two and two make four is not a part of life but the beginning of death."

Alyosha, the younger brother is the mediator in this family of crossed motives. He is the saintly one, the embodiment of conscience and naïve belief. He has at-

tached himself to the monastery which he hopes to enter
and avoid the guilt and ugliness of the world. Zossima
the saint, the love of God on earth, has attracted him
even to the belief in miracles. But his world, though he
loves it, and his life, are not of this earth. So far he
has been able to ignore suffering, and to him the cry of
Ivan, "I must have justice, or I will destroy myself.
Justice now," is a shriek of bewilderment. He has never
stopped in his adoration of the Christ of history, to think
of the suffering of the helpless. Will he ever be able to
reconcile conscience with the tragic fate of humanity?
He too must discover the vision.

Smerdyakov is hate, yet pliant and soft-spoken. He
had been born in the basest of degradation. His life was
to him a constant reproach. He is cowardly and shrinking. But he has caught the argument that "everything
is permissible"; and this shrinking coward will carry
out his act before the eyes of Ivan who has taught him,
to the better man's undoing.

Dominating them all is the father Fyodor Pavlovitch,
the man who gave them all life, and who pursues it in
perfect *insouciance* of others. "He stands on his voluptuousness as if it were stone." Confidence never forsakes
him. He "swallows life like brandy," and life to him
is the pursuit of wealth and woman. He despises his
children, for they have scruples, inhibitions, the sense
of decency, "with the milk of children in their veins instead of blood." Now his object is Grushenka. That his
son Dmitri loves her only adds to his confident appetite.
He has cheated his son out of his inheritance, now with
the aid of his money he will cheat him out of his love;
and he smirks, chatters, and giggles, as he goes about
setting the snare. Women are avaricious. Soon or late
she will come and he will be ready.

There is not much more in the plot. There are two deaths that give the motive of suffering and its effects that constitute the story—the death of a saint and the murder of a monster—Zossima ripe in years and rich in good works in the world and in the monastery, Fyodor slain by one of his sons. Was it in revenge by Dmitri? He was ready to do it, but his will faltered at the last. Was it by Smerdyakov, whose hand committed the deed? Was it by Ivan whose philosophy calmly contemplated or even encouraged the deed? "One insect will devour the other." It isn't easy to discover the real culprit.

Smerdyakov grows into a superhuman monster himself after the deed. He has vindicated himself, and thrown the moral responsibility—or the logical—on to Ivan, and quietly, methodically, hangs himself. Ivan discovers he has a conscience that is bankrupt and collapses. He disintegrates under his own teaching, as it is served up to him by the lackey. And his ruin seems complete, when he has the vision of the Devil, his other self, "the indispensable minus," ice-cold scepticism. Can it create moral values, or are "all things lawful"? Ivan breaks, and like Luther hurls at the spectre a glass. Dmitri is made and restored to life. For though he is arrested, tried and found guilty, he has the assurance of life. Yes, he has won the love and devotion of Grushenka. He is "sorry to lose God"; if God must be lost. But there is evidence higher than logic or conscience for God.

"Then if He doesn't exist, man is the chief of the earth, of the universe. Magnificent! Only how is he going to be good without God? That's the question. I always come back to that. For whom is man going to love then? To whom will he be thankful? To whom will he sing the hymn? Rakitin laughs. Rakitin says that one can love humanity without God. Well, only a sniveling idiot can maintain that. I can't understand it."

And Alyosha? It is the death of the saint, and the absence of miracle that shatters his naïve faith. There are besides his agonizing brothers that must be ministered to, and loved back to sanity and health. His master had taught him that the way to life led *away* from the monastery; like a lost child at first he is bewildered, but faith returns with love of earth and things of the earth, and in a paroxysm of joy he remembers the words of his master.

"Love to throw yourself on the earth and kiss it. Kiss the earth and love it with an unceasing, consuming love. Love all men, love everything. Seek that rapture and ecstasy. Water the earth with the tears of your joy and love those tears. Don't be ashamed of that ecstasy, prize it, for it is a gift of God and a great one; It is not given to many but only to the elect."

Love—not repentance and tears of remorse, these are futile—is the urge to life even through tragedy. It is the struggle to gain this, and through it peace and harmony in a world of tragic suffering; it is this that to most readers makes this book of profound religious significance in an age that seemed convinced, like Ivan, of irreligion. It is the struggle for this, against the barriers that heredity and environment may raise, that keeps humanity still a thing unique in nature. Russia tries to say the same thing in Tolstoi, but the prophet in Tolstoi found he must deny much in human nature in the process. Dostoevsky is able, with a more severely tried faith, to see the evil face to face and yet see beyond it to the motives in the human heart that make peace with life possible.

How does this square with human institutions and above all the Church? And how would these be regarded by the Jesus of the Gospels who strove to set men free through love? This question Dostoevsky touches in that most amazing legend of the Grand Inquisitor, told by Ivan, the sceptic, to Alyosha, his faithful brother.

It is in the days when the *auto da fé*, the burning of heretics, was a daily festival in Catholic Spain, and the triumph of the faith was born witness to by the zeal of the Inquisition. Into this scene of fanaticism came the Christ of Galilee, lowly and loving and all instantly recognized the face of the Master, and as of old he was followed by adoring crowds. But he said not a word.

Then the Grand Inquisitor, a prince and cardinal of the Church, seized him and brought him to judgment. Not a word was allowed or expected from the victim, for his message was delivered once and for all. His danger was recognized and instantly he was judged and tomorrow he was to suffer, one more victim to the triumphant faith.

For is not his message one of love and freedom, freedom of the conscience and of the individual? Did not he when the opportunity was offered in the Temptation by Satan in the wilderness,—genius only and the highest could devise such a test for his power,—did not he reject the very motives on which power could be erected? People long for food and security, and he refused to turn the stones into bread. Instead he gave them freedom. Who of the multitudes can understand or avail themselves of freedom? The choice souls that can live free are but the scant hundreds or thousands, but the untold millions want bread.

He had the chance to avail himself of miracle to strengthen the faith of the helpless and weak. Why did he not cast himself down from the pinnacle of the Temple and secure this faith? People adore and will follow power and authority; they strive for unity and the bonds of institutions that unite people. Why did Christ reject power? Authority, mystery, miracle, these things that bring peace and union among men, give food and security, and law, all these Christ rejected; and instead he gave them freedom, a thing of no worth to man, who can make nothing of it.

So the Church has consciously rejected Christ, though it speaks in his name; it has distorted his teachings, and in his name burned those who reject its miracle, mystery and power. And now Jesus comes again on earth, and would undo all that the Church had falsely done in his name. With such there can be no compromise.

"What I say to Thee will come to pass, and our dominion will be built up. I repeat, tomorrow Thou shalt see that obedient flock who at a sign from me will hasten to heap up the hot cinders about the pile on which I shall burn Thee for coming to hinder us. For if any one has ever deserved our fires, it is Thou. Tomorrow I shall burn Thee. *Dixi*"

But this is not all; the Inquisitor tells of his own struggle with the Christ. He had striven to be of the Elect and to follow the teachings of freedom.

"I fear Thee not. Know that I too have been in the wilderness, I too have lived on roots and locusts, I too prized the freedom with which Thou hast blessed men, and I too was striving to stand among Thy elect, among the strong and powerful, thirsting 'to make up the number.' But I awakened and would not serve madness. I turned back and joined the ranks of those *who have corrected Thy work.*"

And the story closes abruptly

"When the Inquisitor ceased speaking he waited some time for his Prisoner to answer him. His silence weighed down upon him. He saw that the Prisoner had listened intently all the time, looking gently in his face and evidently not wishing to reply. The old man longed for Him to say something, however bitter and terrible. But He suddenly approached the old man in silence and softly kissed him on his bloodless aged lips. That was all His answer. The old man shuddered. His lips moved. He went to the door, opened it, and said to Him: 'Go, and come no more . . . come not at all, never, never!' And he let Him out into the dark alleys of the town. The Prisoner went away."

Why the kiss? Has Christ given his benediction to the Church that has so falsely spoken in his name? Yes and no. The motive of the Church has, though mistaken in its means, still been love of humanity. The Inquisitor himself had known the benediction of search and suffering and bafflement. He is a human instrument, the Church a human institution, though with a divine message. God who knows where each sparrow falls will not utterly reject even the faulty offerings of man.

The argument of the Grand Inquisitor, if read aright, can be made to apply to every institution that would substitute authority and miracle and mystery for the essential gift of human freedom. It is as weighty, or even weightier, in its criticism of the substitute for freedom now being forced upon the world, as it was of the mediaeval institution of the Church. The Grand Inquisitor today is the political or economic dictator that pronounces the formulas of new deals when men shall be fed and made secure—at the cost of their freedom.

The kiss glowed in the heart of the Grand Inquisitor, but he could not give up his idea. And Alyosha's question, can peace and order and security be forced upon the unwilling with the consequent suffering and tragedy, still remains unanswered.

"But the little sticky leaves, and the precious tombs, and the blue sky, and the woman you love! How will you live, how will you love them?"

For Ivan has asserted and Alyosha has agreed that oppression even of the slightest is a cosmic injustice and unbearable.

"Tell me yourself, I challenge you—answer. Imagine that you are creating a fabric of human destiny with the object of making men happy in the end, giving them peace and rest at last, but that it was essential and inevitable to torture to death only one tiny creature— that baby beating its breast with its fist, for instance—and to found that edifice on its unavenged tears, would you consent to be the architect on those conditions? Tell me, and tell the truth.

"No, I wouldn't consent, said Alyosha softly."

At least for himself and his characters Dostoevsky does not choose the way of authority and power. For authority and power are often the love of death and not life.

XI. THE WILL TO POWER

NIETZSCHE

"I should only believe in a God that would know how to dance."
"And when I saw my devil, I found him serious, thorough, profound, solemn: he was the spirit of gravity—through him all things fall."

Thus Spake Zarathustra

MORE than any other, the nineteenth century has been conscious of suffering, and troubled in conscience. It was easy, too easy, in the earlier days of active faith for man to lay his burden on the ample shoulders of Deity; or what was much more rare, as Dante, to accept full moral responsibility and yet be edified by the spectacle of humanity gone astray. Man may be by nature corrupt, so the argument ran, but there is a blessed God, or an enlightened reason, to point the way to security, and unhappiness is not man's rightful heritage. Religion or science or even sound common sense, these antidotes lie ready to hand. They are fools who go the way of tragedy, or the presumptuous, or the unworthy and infirm. These last the healthy and right-minded do well to ignore.

But it was precisely these last, for whom there were once the promises of religion, that the nineteenth century could not ignore. They are still with us and one of our weightiest charges. And there have been a horde of poets and novelists who have brooded over their misery, or nakedly exposed their sores, or sentimentalized over their sweet lovableness, and pointed an edifying finger at natural goodness in distress and the obvious opportunity for worthy charity. The "naturalistic," or its opposite the "humanitarian," point of view is fairly obvious, and there will be something more to be said about both in the sequel. But to discover the joy of life in suffering and one's true self only in the fifth act of a tragedy, tragedy for the wise and not the fool or the infirm, this is something new and of the highest significance.

For the nineteenth century had by its science learned that the laws of nature are written in blood. In spite of Rousseau's benign faith, the ways of life are cruel, and fitness to survive is won after a conflict in which the weak are overwhelmed. This the new science of biology was teaching as the rule of all life. How then shall man discover freedom, a joy of living, in a world of bitter conflict and tragic suffering? For the greater the individual and the more sensitive, the more exemplary his unfortunate fate. The answer will require a new definition of tragedy—the tragedy of the individual in a world of tragic individuals; and the joy of living distilled from the tears of grief, the joy of living that can show the countenance of laughter.

"Who among you can at the same time laugh and be exalted?"
"He who climbeth on the highest mountains, laugheth at all tragic plays and tragic realities."

The answer is Nietzsche.

Dostoevsky had shown that the joy of life can be discovered through pain, only when the individual has discovered himself and established his confidence in himself. He had arrived at this goal by intimate study of character and personality through psychology. Nietzsche comes to much the same result through poetry and "vision," in the manner of the old prophets, and proclaims a new philosophy, not a system nor an abstract creed, to lift the heart and the imagination to the new horizons, a humanity transformed.[1]

Perhaps no prophet or poet has suffered so grievously from popularization as Nietzsche. For his rhapsodies are a heady draught, especially to youth, and by weak digestions can be turned to poison. He has been made the antagonist of all theories of morals and an incitement to all vagaries of mad self-expression, while the real Nietzsche was a modest scholar of Greek philology, and a poet whose ways were beyond reproach. But his outpourings are paradoxical, vain, and madly inconsistent. He glories in his disarray of thought and imagery. "The snake that cannot cast his skin dies." He talks on every possible subject from cookery to music. He rambles, repeats, has relevancies separated by chasms of irrelevancies, contradicts himself without shame, and through it all his voice thunders musically as did the prophet's of old. Reading Nietzsche requires far more care than reading a difficult, though systematic writer. His verses are "sybilline leaves" that can make some sort of sense and nonsense in any arrangement. One must be cautious in interpreting this prophet of the nineteenth century.

Like Tolstoi and Dostoevsky, Nietzsche is terribly interested in the problem of human conduct, that is, in the meaning of life. Looking about him he saw the way beset with false signs and false values. The rising tide of sentimental humanitarianism, the kind of thing that in-

---

[1] I would like to refer the reader to Schestov, *Dostoevsky and Nietzsche.* Unfortunately there is no translation in English. It has been translated into German.

spired *Uncle Tom's Cabin* for example; the fresh novelty of democracy, with Walt Whitman its American poet, and its vociferous faith in the equality and brotherhood of men; the unheard of confusion of feminism and the equality of the sexes; then the new morals founded upon the biological law of natural selection and the survival of the fittest: how can consistency of conduct and moral certitude be discovered in such a medley of contradictory cries? And in the background the reverberating echoes of the established codes warranted by revealed religion, Christian love and humility, and patience under suffering, and rewards duly administered in the hereafter.

Most of these imply a code registered by some external authority. How to liberate the individual from external authority and make him self-directing, and at the same time protect the weak who need the support of a moral shoulder? Such is the fundamental motive behind Nietzsche's quest. In all this he is not unlike Emerson, or perhaps even Whitman. Only Nietzsche does not try to teach a human morality. Rather he seeks to establish it as an attitude. He is more poet than philosopher. His answer is a dynamic call to go forth and live, and in the love of life itself to discover its moral value. One should create values by living, not live according to registered and ticketed values.

In this is the intoxicating charm and also the danger of Nietzsche. Far too many lesser spirits of us, to whom he does not address his words, make him the prophet of our easy revolts and ill-begotten vagaries. It is only too easy to fancy oneself a superman in one's childish posturings and gesturings. The same misunderstanding there was also of Emerson. But behind Emerson was the conscience of the Hebrew Jehovah and the eternal fitness of his righteousness; behind Nietzsche is the law of life

and the eternal fitness of living exaltedly. And these are
things that are not for the weak and childish, but only for
the strong and self-reliant. Nietzsche is the "anti-ass
par excellence." He is bracing, he breathes "the air of
the heights," yet there is "danger of chill—the ice is
near, the loneliness is terrible."

To see how bracing, and yet how chill, it is necessary
to follow his thought into its metaphysical background.
To love life one must know life. But what is knowledge
of life? What is reality? These to Nietzsche are fundamental questions. But can we ever *know?* "Knowing
means to place oneself in relation to something known."
But one and only one of these two objects in relation,
essential to knowledge, is available to us—in spite of our
pride in our arts and our sciences—and that is ourselves.
The ultimate reality beyond ourselves escapes our nets
and eludes our understanding. Reality may be only a
flux, but it is subject to no man made laws or categories
of art or science.

Yet art and science are our only refuge from life and
reality and its dizzying abyss. And the human mind may
be only "an instrument of power" to create these illusory
worlds of art and science, in which man may have for a
time the illusory security of understanding. Their truths
are intellect created, for there is nothing in them that
the mind has not already put there. They are useful, for
they give the ever-to-be desired sense of security and
power, but again an illusory security. For they are the
antithesis of reality. Yet how sedulous are the scientists,
how superbly convinced of their value.

"Clever are they—they have dexterous fingers: what doth *my*
simplicity pretend to beside their multiplicity! All threading and knit-

ting and weaving do their fingers understand: thus do they make the hose of the spirit!

"Good clockworks are they: only be careful to wind them up properly! Then do they indicate the hour without mistake, and make a modest noise thereby."

But how vain when blown upon by the breath of life. They will not have it above them.

"They want to hear nothing of any one walking above their heads; and so they put wood and earth and rubbish betwixt me and their heads."

Science cannot with its clocks and dexterous fingers give any thing more than its own measurements and formulas, while life, the vital thing, goes on above them; and they resent its presence. Science can offer no clue to reality; for it "finds in things only what it has put into them"—an interesting, but for life and reality itself, an irrelevant knowledge. It creates nothing but the shadows of its own reason. It is a refuge for the human intelligence that fears the unknown.

Nor is art any more useful a guide to the fundamental reality of life. For it gives form and perfection to only the imitations of the world of the senses and the reason. They are beautiful, they are satisfying, even full of edification, but only as the pictures of a dream world and possessing no more reality. They bring intelligible perfection to the unintelligibility of life. They bring pleasure to those who without them are disconsolate. But they are dreams.

"The beautiful appearance of the dream-worlds, in creating which every man is a perfect artist, is the prerequisite of all plastic art, and in fact, as we shall see, of an important part of poetry also. In our dreams we delight in the immediate apprehension of form; all forms speak to us; none are unimportant, none are superfluous. But, when this dream-reality is most intense, we also have, glimmering through it, the sensation of its appearance."

And he quotes with approval the song of Hans Sachs in the *Mastersingers:*

> "Mein Freund, das grad' ist Dichters Werk,
> dass er sein Träumen deut' und merk'.
> Glaubt mir, des Menschen wahrster Wahn
> wird ihm im Traume aufgethan:
> all' Dichtkunst und Poëterei
> ist nichts als Wahrtraum-Deuterei." [2]

Illusions, Maya,[3] the word is from Schopenhauer who in turn borrowed it from India. The world of sense is an illusion, and dreams of poetry and art are the interpretation of illusion, its perfection, its glory; and yet the subtle net in which it catches and holds fast the unwary. For the fault lies in the feeling that it encourages, that the individual is a reality, and it perpetuates the fault by giving through art a wholly false higher evidence for his individual integrity. Thus art, like science is a refuge from life and reality, a beautiful and even edifying refuge, and not by any to be ignored, but it is not life itself. The suggestion and the thrill of reality itself lie in a wholly different region. To gaze upon this, one must rend the veil of Maya and gaze with ecstatic self-forgetfulness upon the mystery of "Primordial Unity."

"We are to recognize that all that comes into being must be ready for a sorrowful end; we are forced to look into the terrors of the individual existence—yet we are not to become rigid with fear: a metaphysical comfort tears us momentarily from the bustle of the transforming

---

[2] "My friend, this is precisely the poet's task, to mark his dreams and to attach meanings to them. Believe me, man's most veracious illusions are revealed to him in dreams; and all versifying and poetizing is nothing but reading of dreams."

[3] See the chapter on the Orient in *The Golden Thread.*

figures. We are really for a brief moment Primordial Being itself, feeling its raging desire for existence and joy in existence; the struggle, the pain, the destruction of phenomena, now appear to us as a necessary thing, in view of the surplus of countless forms of existence which force and push one another into life, in view of the exuberant fertility of the universal will. We are pierced by the maddening sting of these pains just when we have become, as it were, one with the infinite primordial joy in existence, and when we anticipate, in Dionysian ecstasy, the indestructibility and eternity of this joy. In spite of fear and pity, we are the happy living beings, not as individuals, but as the *one* living being, with whose creative joy we are united."

And this to Nietzsche is gained only through intuitive and completely self-forgetting ecstasy, deep suffering or fulness of joy. "It is this gulf of oblivion that separates the world of every day from the world of reality." The real world is a *continuum* of ceaseless energy. We can by analogy of our most instinctive impulses and cravings think of it as Will, unconscious striving, craving for action, beginning with the atoms and concluding with the entire cosmic universe: "It is energy everywhere, the play of forces and force waves, at the same time one and many, rising here and falling there, a sea of forces, storming and raging, forever changing . . . with an ebb and flow of its form." "A monster of energy, without beginning or end."

What purpose has it in its "joy of unremitting creation?" To what end is its "spontaneous instability?" Has it reason? or is it for the most part "wantonness and folly?" These questions for it are wholly irrelevant, for they apply only to man's little illusory world of science and art where the phrases "reason" and "end" have an illusory significance. It can be neither measured nor foretold; its ways have no part nor lot with the momentary and illusory ways of the individuals who would ask it questions. It is as unresponsive to man's issues as the

Voice out of the Whirlwind that answered Job's impertinence with the question before which the human imagination quails. "Where wast thou when I laid the foundations of the earth?"

It has no final aim. To it reason and folly are one. To
it the destiny of man is of no more nor no less significance
than the life of the least of creatures, or of inanimate nature itself. "Life [in this planet] is something that is of
no consequence to the general character of the earth."
Quite on the contrary: "Consciousness, spirit, now seem
to us rather a symptom of relative imperfection in an organism, it is an experimenting, a groping . . . which ab-
sorbs an unnecessary quantity of nervous energy." Is
there in all this something gloomy and unpleasant? But
these words have only a human and hence an ephemeral
meaning. As one stands before It with intuitive insight it
is "false, cruel, contradictory, seductive, and without
sense." Is it a thing worthy of wonder that the human
reason quails at its restless horror and seduction, and
clings for aid to reason's two invented refuges, science
and art?

> "He who with a piercing glance has penetrated into the very heart
> of the terrible destructive processes of so-called universal history, as also
> into the cruelty of nature, and who is in danger of longing for a
> Buddhistic negation of the will, art saves him, and through art life
> saves him—for herself."

How different this vision from the universe Dante
saw, its divine plan and divine law of spirit and reason,
and the human lineaments of God himself. How different from the universe of the poetic Plato, who saw it
orderly and the region of reason and reasonable Ideas.
How different from the sceptic Montaigne even, who
saw clearly the conflict between reason and unreason, but

who yet reserved a somewhat of pride in human fortitude and dexterity. And, coming to our own century, how different the panorama from the promised land for freed and intelligently disciplined humanity that it was given the poets Shelley and Goethe to see from the heights of their mountain tops. But the vision granted to Nietzsche does not fill him with dismay or loosen the knees of his courage. It is from this sombre picture that come the most valuable texts of his poetry, and a motive for life that makes him perhaps next to Rousseau the most influential figure in our times.

There are only two alternatives for one who has once fully caught the glimpse of the essential reality that is the substrata of life, the beginning and the end of all knowledge and living. At once one knows the essential worth as well as the practical necessity, if one would keep on living, of those cities of refuge, science and art. They at least have been put in their place, and their motives and practical values accurately assessed, these children of orderliness and reason. But that greater reality behind them, and embracing the whole, the *continuum* of life, the "Primordial Spirit of Unity," this too in an alert consciousness will make its periodic or incessant demands. And it is man's relation to this that is the theme of most of that most interesting of Nietzsche's collection of poetic utterances, the *Thus Spake Zarathustra*. Two alternatives, and two only, the one cynical and dry-eyed despair, this is almost the attitude of Schopenhauer and the oriental mystic; its resulting denial of the human personality, and the will to plunge into the "Vortex of Being" in the self-annihilating bliss of *Nirvana*. The other alternative is the harder choice, and worthy only of the superman, the *Uebermensch*, the heroic effort to raise oneself to man's full stature in spite of the inescapableness of tragedy. This is the message of Nietzsche's *Zarathustra*. "Lo, I teach the Superman."

"The Superman is the meaning of the earth. Let your will say: The Superman *shall be* the meaning of the earth!

"I conjure you, my brethren, *remain true to the earth*, and believe not those who speak unto you of superearthly hopes! Poisoners are they, whether they know it or not.

"Verily, a polluted stream is man. One must be a sea, to receive a polluted stream without becoming impure.

"Lo, I teach you the Superman: he is that *sea*; in him can your great contempt be submerged."

The manly life when man realizes utterly the hardship that manliness entails; manly self-reliance that such a disharmonious universe of reality needs; heroic action, and when necessary, as it will always be, heroic self-sacrifice. For the universe of reality as Nietzsche conceives it, is the only universe, with its welter of indifference, reason and unreason, force and blind craving, ceaseless flow and paroxysms of cruelty, it is the only universe against whose inhumanity man's greatest virtue will shine with brightest luster. Without the black tyrant Jupiter there could be no benign and humanly resourceful Prometheus; without the whirling Chaos of the Walpurgisnight there could be no triumphant and serene Faust. The superman is the unconscious creation of reality, and its illumination.

And any lesser universe of reality would not serve for his triumph. A purely mechanical and scientific universe would belittle man; making him part of the machine and as irrelevant, though conscious and endowed with reason, as the least of its creatures. Man must have free will, potentially at least, that he may raise his hand and voice in protest. A purely reasonable universe whose secrets could be laid bare to the philosopher's eye, like Plato's or Dante's, would be too easy. For man must show his greatness not by the success of his penetration of the reasonableness of life and reality, but by his daring tragedy when he attempts the impossible, and perishes the victim of his own virtue. Is this a hard saying? Not to this poetic seer. Above all it must not be a providentially guided universe for this would paralyse human effort; and Nietzsche's superman is a creature primarily of action, and his virtue is courage.

"Lo, I teach the superman." The superman is Nietzsche's protest against the life as he saw it with its varied motives in nineteenth century Europe, with its insistence upon the substitutes for reality in science and art, and its large trust in science. Again he calls him the *Will to Power*, a glorious assertion of human freedom for action. It is his protest for a life of action, against the creeping paralysis of scientific determinism, physical and biological law. It is still more a protest against the new scientific sociological determinism, the more dangerous because it states its creed, not in the open manner of scientific formulas, but in the morals of poetry and plays, as in the dramas of Ibsen or Henri Becque. Fussy people who meddle, like Ibsen, with social bric-a-brac, he calls "old maids." He sees the danger to the vital individual in the growing assertiveness of the state, and in new political creeds which speak of totalitarian states and the subordination of the individual. Rousseau had implied it; Hegel, the German orthodox philosopher of the state, had elaborated and sanctified it; and other countries beside Germany today are launching huge experiments under its blessing. It is a protest against economic and sociological idealists and reformers who, with humanitarian zeal to raise the stature of the weak, would reduce the worthy,

and thus set themselves against the law of nature. It is a
protest against human weakness of every sort, that uses its
weakness as a cloak for its protection, quoting such Scripture as "blessed are the meek, for they shall inherit,"
or "blessed are the poor in spirit." Such doctrines of defeat and praise of unfitness are to Nietzsche the sin
against nature. It is above all a protest against these "hy-
brids of sickness," and deniers of the "Will to Power,"
who have founded religions based upon submission and
weakness. These are the "idols with feet of clay," who
have sought to improve mankind by encouraging its vices.
These are the farthest from the superman that life and
the century so abundantly need.

It is a call for courage against acquiescence, for will
against easy belief, for the full life against the partial,
for truth against "morals." He would rather be a "satyr"
than the accepted and conventional "saint." It is a demand for man to lose leaders and find himself. It is a
call for reality against ideas, or words, or popular con-
cepts and formulas. For man becomes divine as he reaches
the zenith of his power and the widest scope of his activity. The concept of God, if it have any meaning at all,
is of value as it inspires man to live the full life. But
those who accept a God and offer him their prayers, "do
not worship God, but something with long ears."

What does he mean by the "Will to Power?" It is for
him, as for Bergson, the *élan vital*, the motive of all
reality, of all life. The life process is a struggle, a perpetual struggle of the whole organism. And so it is for
man, if he would see his life truly, he must see it whole.
"Each instinct is a sort of thirst for power; each has its
point of view, which it would fain impose upon all other
instincts as their norm." Life thus is a compromise between instincts which must be disciplined into willed co-

operation. It is the same balance of instincts, vital and as nature wills, that gives life and form to a tree or to any animate ~eature. Man's reason is only a portion and perhaps a secondary portion of his total life. So is his sense of virtue, his justice, his pity, or any of the single motives with which he meets life. To be "true to the earth," to have the full "Will to Power," each of these must be renounced in favor of all.

"The hour when ye say: 'What good is my happiness! It is poverty and pollution and wretched self-complacency. But my happiness should justify existence itself!'

The hour when ye say: 'What good is my reason! Doth it long for knowledge as the lion for his food? It is poverty and pollution and wretched self-complacency!'

The hour when ye say: 'What good is my virtue! As yet it hath not made me *passionate*. How weary I am of my good and my bad! It is all poverty and pollution and wretched self-complacency!'

The hour when ye say: 'What good is my justice! I do not see that I am *fervour and fuel*. The just, however, are fervour and fuel!'

The hour when ye say: 'What good is my pity! Is not pity the cross on which he is nailed who loveth man? But my pity is not a crucifixion.'

Have ye ever spoken thus? Have ye ever cried thus? Ah! would that I had heard you crying thus!"

"Illustrious is it to have many virtues, but a hard lot; and many a one hath gone into the wilderness and killed himself, because he was weary of being the battle and battlefield of virtues."

But how few have the power or the will to be "true to the earth." "The majority of people are only piece-meal and fragmentary specimens of man." "The men who are nothing more than a big eye, or a big mouth, or a big belly, or something else big." "An ear big as a man . . . perched on a small, thin stalk—the stalk, however, was a man! People said that the big ear was not only a man, but a great man, a genius. . . . But it was only a reversed cripple who had too much of one thing and too little of everything else."

The "Will to Power" is to say "Yea" to life, to be "ready for the lightening in its dark bosom, and for the redeeming flash of light, charged with lightenings which say Yea! which laugh Yea! ready for divine flashes of lightening." It is to love life as a whole and not with reference to any of its effects or accompaniments. "Let your love to life be love to your highest hope; and let your highest hope be the highest thought of life." It is almost mystical, this powerful putting forth of the whole of man's nature into the act of living, like the drawing love between the sexes. "Ah, and now hast thou again opened thine eyes, O beloved Life! And into the unfathomable have I again seemed to sink." It is a love that in its ecstasy is not utterly unlike its opposite, hate. "In my heart do I love only Life—and verily most when I hate her." For there is never in it either cynicism or contempt. It is the source of all that is man's, his source and his illumination. "Verily, like the sun do I love life, and all deep seas." For only by the active acceptance of the whole of life does the will make life worth the living; to refuse to accept, to say "Nay" to it, or to accept it only in part, is to make it worthless; and to fail utterly in attaining the joy of living. The superman is a full affirmation of life.

To say "Nay" is the instinct of degeneration and chaos; it is the "death sentence of a man who is already doomed." Thus it is with the cynic, the melancholic, or those who would seek in some voluptuous anodyne an escape from the rigor of its embraces. Nietzsche, like Carlyle, seeing many who would accept it only on condition, has the highest of contempt for these fugitives from its battle and prophesies a dismal future.

"Alas! there cometh the time when man will no longer launch the arrow of his longing beyond man—and the string of his bow will have unlearned to whizz!

Alas! there cometh the time when man will no longer give birth to any star. Alas! There cometh the time of the most despicable man, who can no longer despise himself.

Lo! I show you *the last man*.

'What is love? What is creation? What is longing? What is a star?' —so asketh the last man and blinketh.

The earth hath then become small, and on it there hoppeth the last man who maketh everything small. His species is ineradicable like that of the ground-flea; the last man liveth longest.

'We have discovered happiness'—say the last men, and blink thereby.

They have left the regions where it is hard to live; for they need warmth. One still loveth one's neighbour and rubbeth against him; for one needeth warmth.

One still worketh, for work is a pastime. But one is careful lest the pastime should hurt one.

One no longer becometh poor or rich; both are too burdensome. Who still wanteth to rule? Who still wanteth to obey? Both are too burdensome.

No shepherd, and one herd! Every one wanteth the same; every one is equal: he who hath other sentiments goeth voluntarily into the mad-house.

They are clever and know all that hath happened: so there is no end to their raillery. People still fall out, but are soon reconciled—otherwise it spoileth their stomachs.

They have their little pleasures for the day, and their little pleasures for the night: but they have a regard for health.

'We have discovered happiness,'—say the last men, and blink thereby.—"

So there are degrees of fulness of life in men, or of the will to live, and therefore degrees of value. "There is struggle and inequality even in beauty." It is the super-man who, when he comes, for Nietzsche looks about him and mournfully shakes his head at the prospect in the present, will know the richness of living to its greatest fulness. He will come in the fulness of time, and it is of his coming that Zarathustra speaks. And the whole of that stimulating book is his description and the manual of his code, the table of his new commandments.

"Therefore, O my brethren, a *new nobility* is needed, which shall be the adversary of all populace and potentate rule, and shall inscribe anew the word 'noble' on new tables.

For many noble ones are needed, and many kinds of noble ones, *for a new nobility!* Or, as I once said in parable: 'That is just divinity, that there are Gods, but no God!' "

These are the sublime ones.

But all men can never hope for this nobility; and to ignore difference of degree in men is either to be guilty of falsehood and hypocrisy, or, what is worse, to impoverish the race by reducing the noble to the plane of the mediocre. The "tarantulas," teachers of equality, those who prate of equality and fraternity, are guilty of this second offense. "Ye preachers of equality, the tyrant-frenzy of impotence crieth thus in you for equality; your most secret tyrant-longings disguise themselves thus in virtue-words." And it is these who have set up the state as a hedge to restrain the sublime ones, and reduced life to a mechanism, and the love of life to an economic or political formula.

"The state, I call it, where all are poison-drinkers, the good and the bad: the state, where all lose themselves, the good and the bad: the state, where the slow suicide of all—is called 'life.' "

Is life then to be red in tooth and claw? Is it to be only the struggle for mastery? And is the "Blond Beast," the ruthless conqueror, to be the Nietzschean hero? There are many who have thus interpreted him. Or, on the other hand, and what would be infinitely worse, is he the glorifier of individual self-expression, where each and

all give free reign to each or any instinct? Dostoevsky's
Raskolnikoff fancied himself the first, and played with
murder and failed miserably. Is his failure, due to his
weakness, a sign of his offense against the code of the
superman whose "Will to Power" admits no faltering?
Is it sufficient to say that his will was feeble and hence
blameworthy; while the will of a successful murderer
which never falters is admirable? And, farther, what, in
this struggle, are we to think of enemies? Are they
necessary for the triumph of Will? And what of the
"Blond Beast" that carries out the instincts of his will on
a grand scale, the ruthless exploiter of multitudes?
Finally, and perhaps above all, what about the implications of selfishness in this cultivation of the "Will to
Power?" Is selfishness the highest virtue? These are
fairly important questions.

Fragments of men or the sublime ones, mediocrities or
supermen, there will have to be different codes of conduct for men, suited to their abilities and suited to the
ages in which they live. For, to begin with, morals are
relative, and codes must suit new times, new life, new
men. Thus has it always been in the history of humanity.

"Whoever has seen these furrowed basins which once contained
glaciers, will hardly deem it possible that a time will come when the
same spot will be a valley of woods, meadows, and streams."

So "everything good is the evil of yore which has been
rendered serviceable."

"A morality could even have grown out of an error, but with this
knowledge the problem of its worth would not be touched."

There must be a place in the revolution of morals,
that is the history of humanity, for the "breaker of the
tables" of values, for "the lion in the spirit" who is such

a danger and a calamity to the "beast of burden which renounceth and is reverent." These breakers and lions come that there may be life in the code, and that the acceptance of the beast of burden may not be acceptance of death. For life alone is the basis of moral judgment; to make a moral judgment superior to the acceptance of life is to perform the office of death. Life cannot be made subordinate to anything. Hence what makes life richer is *per se* good. The more of its instincts that are organized and active the more truly is life lived. And this is the test. "Live so that thou mayest desire to live again."

Does this mean complete self-realization? Perhaps the best example we can find in recent literature of a rich life thus richly lived is the transparent career of the poet Goethe. It is really what the poor bewildered Karamazovs were striving for and only after tragedy received. It is what the would-be Napoleon, Raskolnikoff, staked his life to attain, and caught a glimpse of within the walls of a Siberian prison camp. It is what Nietzsche himself, all his life long, strove to discover, but his tragic frailty never allowed him to taste, except vicariously in the sayings of the superman Zarathustra. It has been, from beginning to end, the quest in chief of the nineteenth century. Freedom and serenity, with a code of conduct adapted to time and place and personality.

For the superman, the lion, the breaker of tables, the sublime, the code will be an internal one, and of his own spontaneous making. But he does not allow his impulses to run wild. He knows that the way to freedom lies only through discipline of impulses that are destructive. And Zarathustra thus admonishes the youth who wept bitterly for his failure to be a superman.

"As yet thou are not free; thou still *seekest* freedom. Too unslept hath thy seeking made thee, and too wakeful.

On the open height wouldst thou be; for the stars thirsteth thy soul. But thy bad impulses also thirst for freedom.

Thy wild dogs want liberty; they bark for joy in their cellar when thy spirit endeavoureth to open all prison doors.

Still art thou a prisoner—it seemeth to me—who deviseth liberty for himself: ah! sharp becometh the soul of such prisoners, but also deceitful and wicked."

For ruthless self-indulgence there must be self-discipline, for the fruit of indulgence is defilement.

"Ah! I have known noble ones who lost their highest hope. And then they disparaged all high hopes.

Then lived they shamelessly in temporary pleasures, and beyond the day had hardly an aim.

'Spirit is also voluptuousness,'—they said. Then broke the wings of their spirit; and now it creepeth about, and defileth where it gnaweth.

Once they thought of becoming heroes; but sensualists are they now. A trouble and a terror is the hero to them."

The superman is the gardener of his life; through cultivation comes spirituality, through sensuality true love, and through hostility generous rivalry.

The true superman must learn to obey before he can hope to command. So he says to his warriors, "Let your distinction be obedience. Let your commanding itself be obeying." For when one listens to the disciplined inner voice, to obey and to command are one. Nietzsche returns to this thought again and again, for to command as to obey, when both are right, is the sign of order and organization within, and a true hierarchy of instincts.

Such then is the art of living for the great, an arranging, disposing, and valuing of the motives of life and their consequent activities, gained in moments of inspiration, until the personality is complete, adequate, and free. Free? How seldom, says Nietzsche, is this easily pronounced word rightly understood. Free, but not what

one is free *from* but what one is free *for*. And precisely
here is the severest danger. "Many a one hath cast away
his final worth when he cast away his servitude."
"Henceforth let it be your honor, not whither ye come,
but whither ye go."

This responsibility and freedom of the truly great
Nietzsche has explored in his *Will to Power* and *Beyond
Good and Evil*. It is a life of affirmation different utterly
from a system of morally prescribed duties.

> "In the main all these moral systems are distasteful to me which
> say: Do not do this! Renounce! Overcome thyself! On the other hand
> I am in favor of those moral systems which stimulate me to do some-
> thing, to do it from morning to eve, and dream of it at night. . . .
> What we do must determine what we leave undone."

But it is best of all when these incitements for conduct
come from within. So he objected to the spirit or "dae-
mon" which Socrates professed guided his conduct. For
it was a negative spirit that only forbade but never urged.
It restrained him from folly, but left him cool and
guided only by reason in his action, and left him deprived
of that dynamic force, that deeper power that is beyond
reason. So Socrates, to whom "knowledge is virtue,"
for Nietzsche fell short of the highest impulses of genius,
or wilfully restrained them, in favor of a moral sense
based upon a "penetrating critical process," and an effort
to make his life "daringly intelligible." The greatest
genius should be beyond reason.

The greatest genius thus is also beyond what is con-
ventionally called good and evil; for to him this paradox does not exist. "All things are lawful to him" that
his deepest instincts call upon him to do, for he has no
code save his own inner demand. "The king can do no
wrong," for if he does he renounces his kingship by show-

ing unfitness. For a spirit like this, life becomes an adventure without bounds into the vastness of the unknown; and he breaks into the rhapsody of song in the *Zarathustra* as he sings its ecstasy.

Is this the cult of selfishness? Has he not said it, "be not considerate of thy neighbor?" But he adds also, "great obligations do not make grateful, but revengeful; and when a small kindness is not forgotten, it becometh a gnawing worm." His great men help, but with a different motive, not pity—"So be ye warned against pity: *from thence* there yet cometh unto men a heavy cloud" —but from the overflowing and uncalculating measure of their own greatness. And such was Zarathustra himself. Cruelty and exploitation of one's fellows, what of these?

"There are enough sublime things without its being necessary to seek sublimity when it is linked with cruelty; my ambition would not be gratified in the least if I aspired to be a sublime executioner."

So much for the Teutonic "Blond Beast."

Above all, the great understand the peril of greatness, the cult of suffering. For the highest virtue of genius is always exhibited in its tragedy, "the splendid 'I can' of great genius, bought cheaply even at the price of eternal suffering." "My suffering," exclaims Zarathustra as his last word, "and my fellow suffering—what matter about them! Do I then strive after *happiness?* I strive after *work!*" Genius, the breaker of tables, the lion, must always pay the price, if he would strive after his work. For he has always opposed to his noblest effort the combined forces of mediocrity. But there is even a greater cause for his tragedy. It is that he knows of the nature and the meaninglessness of reality, the flux of life out of which for a moment he has emerged, and against which in his love for life he has striven for sweetness and order. It is not

then to be wondered at that of all heroes Nietzsche picks
the Aeschylean Prometheus as the symbol of the "infinite
tragedy of the bold individual."

But it is a tragedy that only in its ecstasy of suffering
recognizes the primordial bond that unites man and nature. Here man's intuition becomes deepest insight; and
not through abstraction and the mortification of desire,
as with the oriental,[4] but by the sharpening of desire to
ecstasy, and self-forgetfulness, the organic unity of all
reality is finally vindicated. This to Nietzsche is the lesson of tragedy. It was, to him, the spirit that prompted
the great lyric choruses of Aeschylus and Sophocles. It
was the mystery that lay behind the stories of the great
suffering heroes of Greek myth. It is the great meta-
physic that only great genius can uncover in the mystery
of his own coming and passing. Thus the philosopher
and poet Nietzsche finds a cosmic justification for pain
and tears, and sees a metaphysical solution for the paradox of joy and suffering in the ecstatic realization of
tragedy.

But the rôle of the superman is for only the lonely few.
When Zarathustra came from his lonely heights to preach
his message, at first none would hear him. The crowd
stood and laughed, then turned and watched the antics
of a rope-dancer. When he came again and preached and
there was a crowd of disciples he left them and retired
to the wilderness, for though they listened they could not
understand. For there are two classes of men, masters and
slaves, as there are two codes of conduct, for the superman
and the herd. These last must have an external code, and
it will be their virtue to be firm in their obedience. "There
are sober and industrious people, on whom religion is

---

[4] See the chapter on "The Orient" in *The Golden Thread*.

embroidered like a hem of higher humanity: these do well to remain religious, it beautifies them." For them there must be "thou shalt nots" as well as "thou shalts," for their life must be a sheltered routine, and its motives they must receive at other hands.

Nietzsche is at the farthest remove from the apostles of a democratic faith or the optimism of a Whitman or Shelley; or the meliorism of those who fancy that by doses of scientific knowledge, administered in schools, the ignorant man may be made morally strong and self-reliant; or the therapeutic faith of the sociologists, who fancy that by medicating their social ills men can be rejuvenated and a new nature be given them; or the economic naïveté of the Marxists, that by some industrial new deal man's inborn ignorance or lack of courage can be transformed into angelic wisdom and will. Most of these programs of reform he dismissed with a magnificent gesture of contempt. Their agitators are "turning the world into a hospital, so that everybody may be everybody's nurse."

The only hope for humanity lies in humanity itself and the quality of its men, and in action. Nietzsche is a worshipper at the shrine of human greatness. "Lo! I am weary of my wisdom, like the bee that hath gathered too much honey . . . I would fain bestow and distribute, until the wise have once more become joyous in their folly." "Lo! I teach you the Superman," who will unite wisdom and what is called folly in his greatness of love for life. For life is dearer to him than his wisdom had ever been. But the virtue of this superlative creature is innate, and not acquired by any training in the sciences of the human reason, his wisdom for life can be learned in no school, he is the creature of life itself. So Zarathustra implores for a love that longs to surpass itself.

"Beyond yourselves shall ye love some day! Bitterness is the cup even of the best love; thus doth it cause longing for the Superman; thus doth it cause thirst in thee, the creating one! Thirst in the creating one, arrow and longing for the Superman."

Thus does life long for excellence, and in the prose strophies of the prophet's call, it is not Nietzsche speaking, nor Zarathustra, it is life itself. Thus saith Life: "Is my experience but of yesterday? It is long ago that I experienced the reasons for my opinions. You ask me why? I am not one of those who may be asked why."

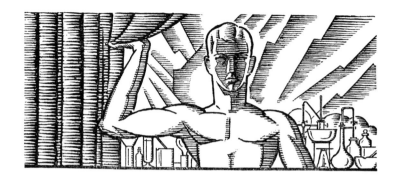

XII. THE ANSWER OF SCIENCE

"The most ardent votary of science holds his firmest convictions, not because the men he most venerates hold them; not because their verity is testified by portents and wonders; but because his experience teaches him that whenever he chooses to bring these convictions into contact with their primary source, Nature—whenever he thinks fit to test them by appealing to experiment and to observation—Nature will confirm them. The man of science has learned to believe in justification, not by faith, but by verification."

HUXLEY, *Advisableness of Improving Natural Knowledge*

"POSITIVISM"—though this word was used as the motto of a philosophical school and is associated with a man whose influence now is as dead as Pharaoh, it describes better than any long phrase the gratified complacency of the latter half of the scientific nineteenth century. Positive—it knew the theological and metaphysical mists from which it had emerged, it knew the irrefutability of its scientific attitude, it foresaw the future as the harvest for which it had already sown the seed. The sciences had all been catalogued and arranged in a hierarchy of complexity, each leading gratefully to the next. The practical application of science to life and industry had been made clear and given a working model in the bewildering new series of technological inventions. Society and the individual man were being transformed, gradually or rapidly it mattered little; for the aims of education and social adjustments were already on the circle of a not too distant horizon. And the scientific philosopher, like Comte or Spencer, and the scientific educator, like Huxley, could afford to be generous in the pride of a victory already achieved. "Mine eyes have seen," they could say with philosophic calm; "now lettest Thou thy servant depart in peace."

It was "an orgy of scientific triumph," as Whitehead describes it, and it came about the middle of the century. The aim of science was to discover the "laws of nature," the established and calculable relations between things. What these things were in the last analysis, the nature of reality, for which the metaphysics of Nietzsche for example had daringly explored, this the new scientific orthodoxy did not trouble itself about at all. It flouted metaphysics, and spoke disrespectfully of the speculations of philosophers as of the vision of poets. Spirit, matter, these two antithetical categories were only bugaboos of the imagination of man in his childhood, ghosts whom the new science, which dealt with the way relations between things should be formally set out like a table of logarithms, had successfully exorcised. The age has been called materialistic, but the phrase is meaningless, for the new science affirmed no difference between the laws for matter and the laws for spirit; both were laws of nature, and both within the region of science.

So Comte in his survey of the history of human thought sees three great epochs, two of which, like past geological epochs, have seen their day and ceased to be. The first was the age of Theology, when man, seeking for an answer to the problem of how things go in the world, gave the credit and the responsibility to deity. Man confessed his ignorance, but made him the omnipotent figure of a god who manipulated the cosmic toy to his own will. All man needed was faith and a reasonable obedience. The rest was Providence. This was the childhood of the human race.

In its adolescence man pushed his speculative curiosity farther to enquire into the essence of things, the nature of reality, and we have the next age, the age of Metaphysics. It was a splendid age for poet and philosopher, an age for vision and transcendental speculation. Naturally the philosophers contradicted themselves and each other. For there was no proof available beyond their earnestness, and for "final proof" and "first causes," the earliest philosopher was as near to an answer as the latest—and as far. The game was an exciting one, and thousands even of the best intellects had thrilled to its excitement; but for any real answer to the question, what is reality, what is its relation to these experiences that man calls life and the world about him, the game was always a blindman's-buff. Reality always was elusively just around the corner, and its mocking laughter.

But now man has grown up, and the more serious business of life permits no light-minded and futile chasing of shadows. The new age is the age of Positivism. Man will content himself with the knowable, the things within the reach of his reason and experience. These now he has learned to control by what he now calls the scientific method, which is only the right way to ask questions. Ask nature the right kind of question, and there will be always an answer. The sum of these answers is Science. So the scientist is the questioning attorney, nature is put into the witness box, the laboratory is the court room, and the record of the proceedings carefully and methodically set down is science. It looked easy. It seemed an overwhelming triumph. Science had justified itself.

As nature in all its range manifests itself from the simple to the complex, so there will be a hierarchy of science, from the simplest science to the most complex. And, in theory at least, each will depend upon the findings of its predecessor. Mathematics which is abstract, referring to no particular relations, is the first. Then comes astronomy. After follow in order chemistry, biology, psychology, and the series ends with sociology, the latest comer and the last. Thus we catalogue the laws of nature, from the purely physical, where nature is inert, to the plant and animal, until it comes to man himself, and finally to human society, a digest of law, a complete exposition of how things go in this vast complex from atoms to human institutions. Nothing was to be left out, such was the program. Every happening, whether the fall of a star or a poet's song or a revolution in the state, or a new fashion in millinery, was calculable, if astronomer, or psychologist, or sociologist only asked the right question.

It is astonishing, in these days of our little faith, to run back in memory over the span of a scant generation to see the effect upon thinking Europe of this new faith. The voices lifted in alarm, or active protest, we have heard and shall hear more. But the revolution that came in scholarship, research, and above all in attitudes toward human institutions and human history, this is a long story. Comte himself did not a little generalization. He plotted the new investigations in sociology—social statics, the study of the social nature of man, which emerges from the family and develops naturally from the relations there discoverable. How different all this is from Rousseau's theory of the social contract. On the other hand were the investigations of social dynamics, the natural law for the history of society. Herbert Spencer carried on in these lines laid down by his predecessor.

Thus the history of the human race became a series of events as scientifically related and explicable as the life history of a plant. Comte spoke of epochs here, as in human thought, of the priestly and warlike age, of the juristic, and finally of the contemporary or the industrial. The last has made life scientific. Karl Marx similarly found history a working of economic law, and comes to conclusions that even today have their significance. And Buckle wrote a history of civilization in England which made natural law the motive for national life. It was a new variety of history, a record not of events and dates, but of the gradually transforming social conditions.

For this dominating interest in the science of social institutions received its most compelling motive from the revolutionary ideas that were involved in Darwin's definition of the law of evolution in the science of biology. If the interplay of the forces of heredity and environment is the prompter who gives the actors their lines in the drama of the biological world, what simpler, more adequate, or more intelligible explanation for the drama of human institutions and human history? The divinity that shapes our ends, rough hew them how we will, is after all no mystery at all, but only the things anyone who will open his eyes sees constantly about him: the heredity of race, the geographical environment, and the peculiar quality of the particular epoch. Shakespeare and the age of Queen Elizabeth is then no miracle or accident, but as natural as the color and odor of the rose or the arch of the bones of the human foot.

But the most interesting and most fruitful application of biological law to human institutions lay in the question of conduct. It is significant, and highly so, to notice that in the table of the sciences drawn up by the new philosophy no mention is made of ethics, once the chief of the sciences; the relation of individual to individual, to society, and of social groups to social groups and to the in-

dividual. Nietzsche, following the tradition as old as the
Greek, sought for these sanctions in a metaphysics, asking
the prior question what is human nature, and what is life.
The moral realism of Tolstoi or the psychological realism
of Dostoevsky is colored and conditioned by the large
postulate of the freedom somewhere of the human will.
But if natural law is all pervasive and human conduct an
analogy of plant or animal conduct, then the description
of human conduct has no essential difference from the
biological life history of any living creature. And its success or failure is to be measured only by its survival or
death. Here are new meanings for romance or tragedy
or comedy. And thoughtful people were in no small
measure perplexed.

And human freedom? Perhaps the manner in which
this whole perplexity, when new meanings were given to
old words, mind and matter, evolution, freedom, and
ethics, is best expressed by the man who did more than
any other to popularize the new point of view in England
and America, a good scientist himself, but a better interpreter of the new method of science: I mean Huxley.
In one of his *Lay Sermons* he writes:

"Thus there can be little doubt, that the further science advances,
the more extensively and consistently will all the phenomena of nature be
represented by materialistic formulæ and symbols."

To be sure Huxley is speaking only of the so-called
natural sciences, and tactfully avoids drawing the conclusion for the social sciences likewise. But Herbert
Spencer in his text book on psychology has no inhibitions.

"And this brings us to the true conclusion implied throughout the
foregoing pages—the conclusion that it is one and the same Ultimate
Reality which is manifested to us subjectively and objectively. For
while the nature of that which is manifested under either form proves

to be inscrutable, the order of its manifestations throughout all mental phenomena proves to be the same as the order of its manifestations throughout all material phenomena.

"The Law of Evolution holds of the inner world as it does of the outer world. On tracing up from its low and vague beginnings the intelligence which becomes so marvellous in the highest beings, we find that under whatever aspect contemplated, it presents a progressive transformation of like nature with the progressive transformation we trace in the Universe as a whole, no less than in each of its parts."

And freedom of the will? He does not beat about the bush or try to dodge the issue:

"To reduce the general question to its simplest form:—Physical changes either conform to law or they do not. If they do not conform to law, this work, in common with all works on the subject, is sheer nonsense: no science of Psychology is possible. If they do conform to law, there cannot be any such thing as free will."

And he finds even some "scientific" consolation for his downright answer.

"The life must become higher and the happiness greater—must do so because the inner relations are determined by the outer relations. But were the inner relations partly determined by some other agency, the harmony at any moment existing would be disturbed, and the advance to a higher harmony impeded. There would be a retardation of that grand progress which is bearing Humanity onwards to a higher intelligence and a nobler character."

There are going to be protests. Tolstoi, Nietzsche, Dostoevsky have done so each in his own way. There will be more even to our own time, when science has grown a trifle less certain of its own orthodoxy. But there will be some who will be as outspoken in their advocacy of the creed of the new science as the scientific philosophers themselves. There will be others, we may call them the hurt souls, who can neither wholeheartedly affirm, though the logic of the evidence seems irrefutable;

and cannot wholeheartedly deny, though the moral conscience and the deepest human instincts call out in painful
protest. These will try to discover some form of compromise; for the thought of a divided human nature, or
of a world without some values other than natural law,
is like a sentence of perpetual exile.

But this new age of science has at least one note in
common with the creed of Rousseau, a belief in the high
position of humanity, though the position is no longer
unique. The highest sciences concern themselves with his
mind and his institutions. All in a way are meliorists,
that is, are inspired by the hope that with the new weapon
of science man's place in society and his institutions can
be improved. No group of people ever appeared with
better intentions for human welfare than the sociologists,
though some are said no longer to share their confidence.
Comte became himself a worshipper of Mankind, like the
disciples of Rousseau in the French Revolution. Karl
Marx looked for the Age of Gold in the triumph of the
unspoiled proletariat—as Rousseau did in the life of primitive savages.

In consequence the social problem novel and the social
problem play, as though literature were a species of glori-
fied journalism, are going to dominate more and more the
purpose of thoughtful authors. They may be diligent
reformers with a moral in their pockets, and the names
of these hang thick on the leaves of all histories of the
literature of the later nineteenth century. Or they may
be purely descriptive, waiting for others with more evidence later, to draw the moral. Of these, too, there are
hundreds.

But because, perhaps, he was the most influential, and
in himself showed more of all these combined tendencies
I have tried to describe, than any other; because he was

both an advocate for more knowledge and yet could not go the whole road of science; because he saw the social problems, but could not take on him the rôle of reformer; because he felt the call to worship humanity, and yet knew its inescapable weaknesses and limitations; in short, because he was what he was, and therefore could not wholeheartedly love the world; because of all this, it is well to begin with Henrik Ibsen.

XIII. THE MASTER BUILDER

IBSEN

"I have made a great discovery.—It is this, let me tell you—that the strongest man in the world is he who stands most alone."

An Enemy of the People

THERE are two excellent and illuminating stories told of Ibsen when in self-imposed exile in Rome. Some members of the Scandinavian Club had insisted on proposing him for the presidency. He angrily retorted: "I tell you, I tell you I *must* belong to the opposition." The remark explains much in his life and his plays, for we know beforehand what most of his actions and ideas are not going to be. He will never be popular. Then, again in Rome, when one of his friends, on his protest that he was not writing for the immediate future but for all eternity, answered that in a thousand years even the greatest would be forgotten, Ibsen was quite beside himself. "Get away from me with your metaphysics. If you rob me of eternity, you rob me of everything." But it is a serious question now, after the War and the first quarter of the twentieth century, whether Ibsen any longer belongs, if most of the ideas he fought for are not almost out of date, and his revivals not more literary curiosities than vital events.

256

The truth is, the time has come to revise our studies of his plays, and to see him now, not from the corner of the nineteenth century where he was angel to some, devil to others, always the object of dangerous interest, but from a more nearly universal point of view. And above all it is necessary to ask the question, what have his incessant "oppositions" to do with the contemporary problem. Yet in venturing the sketch of an answer, it will be impossible ever to divorce him from Scandinavia, the home he never so completely belonged to as when he drove himself into exile, or from the complacent nineteenth century he so magisterially castigates.

It is true that Ibsen gave Europe and America a new drama, and gave tragedy a new definition. But this was due more to the dour seriousness of his own personality, and to the scientific prejudice of the age than to insight of transcendent genius. Really he belongs more to the tradition of serious comedy of Aristophanes and Molière, than to orthodox tragedy of Sophocles and Shakespeare. He is the conscientious social prophet censuring society for its offences against justice, and individuals for their presumption and folly; but he never can see folly and presumption and obstruction of justice as a grotesque theme for laughter. The nineteenth century with its large and alert social consciousness is equally unable to discover laughter in social maladjustments. The result is Ibsen the poet and prophet, writing *Dolls Houses* and *Wild Ducks* and *Pillars of Society*, as the new tragedy, and readers and audiences acclaiming the master, and New Theatres being formally opened with his daring plays.

It is for the same reason that he must be always a minority in opposition. It is orthodoxy he is challenging, the entrenched beliefs and creeds of the past, and nowhere in Western Europe in his day more powerful than in his own country. He is armed with the new science, "an artistic temperament endowed with a scientific brain," and conscientiously devoting himself, like Dr. Stockmann in *An Enemy of the People*, to the education of the human race in general and besotted, complacent, orthodoxy in particular. The school master, the prophet, even the physician, must always be in the minority, else his profession is endangered. And Ibsen is the professional. It is all this that makes him the central figure in the modern European drama. It was his serious technique that was the source and inspiration for most of the leading ideas and manners of the drama in the half-century to come.

One thing more, like the nineteenth century Ibsen is interested in the "average man," the you and me that make up the warp and woof of society. To be sure there are some figures of commanding stature, Hedda Gabler, Brand, Peer Gynt, who for a time play the rôle of the superman, only to discover that they haven't the fortitude, or its impossible cost. Others are outstanding, like Rosmer or the Master Builder, but even they find their lines hard to read. The characters are all average human men and women, a little better or a trifle worse, just suited to illustrate the way things go in the average human world. It is the problems in such a world that interest and inflame him, the situations where character and motives cannot, and perhaps forever cannot, compete with other characters and other motives, where tradition and the new ideas come into conflict, where convention has masked selfishness, or where conventional virtue has become an agent of destruction. It is the average world we all know, and to which we all somehow reconcile ourselves, but in which the man with Ibsen's convictions must find himself in a minority, and which one with Ibsen's artistic power must write into novels and dramas. So this Norwegian poet became the purveyor of problems, to shock those of delicate complacency, and to delight the restless taste for the vigorous new.

"An artistic temperament endowed with a scientific brain." The artistic temperament loves life and seeks to express its meaning; the scientific brain analyzes life and its forces and its conflicts to discover and formulate its laws. To combine thus knowledge and understanding, to be instructive and at the same time moving, this is at best a difficult task. And it will be increasingly difficult as the problem for the scientist becomes more and more specific. Goethe tried it in his prose novel the *Elective Affinities* with only moderate success. He was saved from failure only because at times he forgot the problem and went quite aside to larger issues of conduct and character. For life itself is infinitely more interesting than any single one of its problems, and will, unless we do as the scientist, confine it to the laboratory and test tube, overflow into apparent irrelevancies and actions quite beside the mark. All great fiction and drama abundantly proves that it can't be captured and made to behave as the sample in the chemist's laboratory. And it is this irrepressibility of life that gives it its unexpectedness and charm and also its convincingness. How far will Ibsen be able to meet this test, especially now after a half-century, when the eager interest in the specific problem has perhaps waned a little, or when much of his radicalism has become accepted social dogma? Jonah had his bitter quarter of an hour when after his denunciation of its sins the city of Ninevah repented in sackcloth and ashes. He became a prophet without a mission.

Ibsen is never more the scientist than in the method of his portrayal of life. He never sets it forth realistically, as do the novelists, Tolstoi or Dostoevsky, for example; his dramatic tableaux are too brief for that; but neither does he have the dramatic convincingness of Hebbel's *Maria Magdalene.* The dramatic form with him has the economy of the apparatus in a laboratory. There his technique, borrowed from the most approved French sources, is as direct and as assured and as deft as the manipulations of a skilful chemist or physicist, and almost as removed from the way things go in nature. He, like the scientist, is asking the right question in the right manner, and nature is manipulated or coaxed to return the directest answer. Is this artificial? Quite. So is science artificial; but the answers it receives have nevertheless the most impressive and edifying values. We ignore them at our peril.

He is artist in the manner in which he "illuminates" the questions and the answers. It is this illumination that is the quintessence of Ibsen, his downright significance, the thing that made each of his plays almost a major success in the new theatres, the thing that made him the beginner of a new tradition, and is the secret of his power after his themes have become a commonplace. It is not his dexterity, nor the daring themes, nor the plots and directness of dialogue; it is the spirit of frank interest in life with which every play is inspired. Though the artist's hand is always discernible, it radiates life and power. The pictures are like the anatomical cartoons of a great artist, they are not copies of life, they are life itself charged with a special and quite intelligible meaning. So it is with as fantastic a thing as *Peer Gynt,* an obvious imitation we can say of this greater author or that, and an allegory or moral tale; but it is not quite the allegory that carries the conviction, nor does the author imitated come to mind until later. It is the manner of illuminating a story, that might be so easily only an allegory, that sets it apart, that lifts us quite, for the moment, out of the laboratory of the scientist.

He sees life, as does the social or biological scientist, as a conflict, the new forces against the consistency of acquired habit, of the individual against the orthodoxy of society, or the revenge of the herd against the eccentricity of the individual. Or to put it in another way, he sees life as a contest in which there are joined the forces of the past, the present, and the future. Each has its claims, and each sincerely is urging its cause; a reconciliation among them seems impossible, and the result problematical. He dramatizes this conflict in the characters and situations of the play; and as it proceeds makes us forget that we are in the scientist's laboratory by the means of his "penetrative interpretation." For the characters themselves and the situations as they unfold are the questions and answers. So vital are they, they carry full conviction.

He asks a very large variety of questions, showing how many of the problems of the socially minded nineteenth century Ibsen touched. But nothing is more like Ibsen than the fact that none of these problems, even the simplest, is quite as simple as it seems, even when isolated in his laboratory. Take *Ghosts*, for example, the question of heredity; here it is bound up with all manner of subsidiary questions. Mrs. Alving had married an impossible rake. They had a child Oswald, and upon him are visited the sins of his father in the form of inherited disease, paresis. But one can't quite isolate these three individuals and keep them to the one motive, that is, to the chief question. Each lives a life also of his own, quite apart from this central motive. Mrs. Alving had loved another man and after discovering her husband's true character had thought of escape; but had been dissuaded, for the man, Pastor Manders, was rigidly orthodox in his conception of marriage: Question number two. Then Alving left another child, illegitimate, to be sure, but his. Mrs. Alving to do her wifely duty took her into the household, as a maid; and she, not knowing, on Oswald's return broken in health from school, is attracted to him as he to her, half-brother and half-sister: Question number three. And to crown it all, Mrs. Alving, on the death of her husband sought to atone for his evil life by building up for him after death a splendid tribute as a memorial: Question number four. There are others, but these will do for illustration. It is as though in the laboratory when the scientist wishes to decompose a molecule he suddenly discovers that each of the atoms has affairs of its own quite outside the molecule, and that it won't answer the scientist's question until the bearing of its other liasons has been given full attention. Such wilfulness in chemistry would destroy the science and drive the scientist into insanity. But with Ibsen, it is a very valuable part of his art, and as necessary.

The result is that the answers are never as clear as the scientist would want them, nor as convincing. To take again the play of the *Ghosts*. It is easy to say that the marriage was one that should have been dissolved. But against this easy solution there were two powerful objections. The one, the prejudice against divorce, has in our day been lifted in many western countries. But the other, the conscience of Pastor Manders, who was himself both spiritual physician and lover and beloved, is not quite so easy to remove even in these unchivalric days. How could he advise otherwise when he stood as an interested party? Here both answers to the problem are right, and the thing as bewildering as the solution of an algebraic equation to some beginners when x can equal plus or minus one. The alternative doesn't fit in with any logical and absolute moral code.

Again should Mrs. Alving have persisted then in building up the beautiful lie as a tribute to her husband's memory and passed the myth of his goodness on to her son? Awkward domestic truths are in ordinary life, except in screendom, not blurted out to strangers and not talked about even at home. And again did Mrs. Alving do wrong in the case of Regina? We know the motives for her actions both toward her son and toward her husband's natural daughter, though prompted by the best of conventional motives, like her action in shielding her husband and sticking it out for the sake of her son, were the immediate cause of tragedy. But can we from her tragedy argue, as can the scientist, that the same experiment repeated with another human group will, as in chemistry with another chemical molecule, produce the same result?

This precise difficulty is illustrated in *The Wild Duck*, and offered to those who look for formulas for conduct and impose ideals for others from without. Here is the family of the Ekdals where each member is living a lie. The daughter is not the child of Ekdal, and does not know it. Ekdal does not know the past of his wife, and that she had been his benefactor's mistress. But the family is happy and contented, and all would have gone well, had the single-minded idealist reformer Gregers not come upon the scene. "Tell the truth, the whole truth, and nothing but the truth," he preaches. And the result of his meddling is a cloud of unhappiness. Poor little Hedwig, the child, to sacrifice "the dearest treasure in the world," to win her supposed father's love, sacrifices her own life. A family's peace is destroyed. And Gregers comforts himself with the lofty phrase: "Hedwig has not died in vain. Did you not see how sorrow set free what is noble in him?" If this is not true, then to him "life is not worth the living."

And there we have it. The artist in Ibsen checks the scientist from drawing scientific conclusions, and giving laws, instead of "illumination," from his treatment of the problem. Life has its way of meeting the various factors, and giving its own direction to situations, which even the finest sociological technique and logic cannot generalize into laws like those of the natural sciences. Mrs. Alving was wrong only in the pragmatic test, her painful self-renunciation and her pious fraud led to tragedy. Where people should have applauded her as a martyr, they are shocked by the immoral course of the event. It is no wonder when the play was produced it shocked tender consciences. But the play is an excellent problem.

A problem in morals. For whether we are conscious of it or not we all of us, even today, prefer to speak of morals as something fairly definite and subject to definition. At one time they may have been given a transcendental origin and been proclaimed from the mountain wrapped in thunder, and have been engraved on tables of stone. At another they may have been thought to be the expression of the unalterable nature of the reasonable human in man. The new science, even, was prepared to explore human relations, as it did relations in physical and biological nature, and describe these in the codes of natural law. And it is precisely in this spirit of pertinent enquiry that Ibsen stated his problems in human relations. Morals in the concrete; and life gave the illuminating answer, often to the shocked bewilderment of his contemporaries.

For he found, as in the *Ghosts*, that the answer is not straightforward, but relative, for the reason that it is impossible to put a straightforward question. Thus the artist strove to bridge the gap between life and science, but nearly always life had the last word.

He takes the problem of the superman, or the individual that fancies he is impelled by an inner motive that will brook no restraint. It was his favorite theme, for he was something of a despiser of restraint himself, and he used it at least three times, twice in his early years and once near the end of his life. The answers he finds will be an interesting retort to the rhapsodies of Nietzsche's Zarathustra.

Everyone ought to enjoy hugely the fantasy and yet the serious allegory of *Peer Gynt*. The critic who tries to classify it has his work cut out for him. The thing suggests opera; and the music that has been composed for it by Grieg is for some an excellent introduction, but to me in places also quite misses the mark. For though Peer is a lovable buffoon he has about him a great deal of that good-natured, bewildered, and yet self-assertive old morality figure Everyman. And so one must take him seriously unless one is willing to ridicule oneself. Like most, his desire for self-assertion is purely one of emotional gratification, of the desire to pose as one's own hero. He has spoiled his doting mother, and his mother has spoiled him. He shines in speech and manner, and takes in the unwary by easy plausibility. Above all he is resourceful with witty cleverness, but utterly irresponsible and unwilling to pay the price, for he lacks utterly moral scruples and will. Here is the hero who would be a Napoleon.

His adventures carry him all over the world and involve all motives for distinction. First he upsets a village wedding, by running away with the bride, who sincerely has fallen in love with his impetuous wooing. Pursued by the outraged villagers, he takes to the mountains, abandons the girl, who must now in lonely faithfulness wait for his return. Faithful and responsible affection is not for him, yet. He sojourns among the Trolls, the symbols of pure animal lust, until even he discovers that life has its responsibilities; and some of these have hideous implications. Always he seeks the "way around," to take experience in the flank, to surprise it by his easy obliquity, and dodge the difficult frontal attack. So he seeks romantic adventure, in the manner of a Chateaubriand, or wealth in the manner of the romantic exploiter of distant regions. Each adventure leaves him weakened, but as hopeful, a more and more sinister Don Quixote seeking the throne from where he may claim his own adulation.

It is only his mother's death that brings out any spark of genuine affection. He returns to her cottage demolished by angry neighbors, sings in her last hours of a fantastic journey to a happier region, and she dies in his arms, comforted by the ecstasy of his affectionate folly. An uncomfortable creature he had been to live with, but he gave her a dying filled with rainbows of illusion. His one good deed, and more unreal even than his worst folly.

A return home from adventures all gone wrong, and a tempest where at last a word of sound sense is heard from his conscience above the roar of wind and wave. A questionable saving of his own skin; he is back where he began, as lonely, and life now all behind him, and it an empty panorama. It is here that death meets him in the forest in the form of the Button Maker. He must be recast in a new mould, for there is not one positive act to his credit, neither one good nor one evil. His assets and liabilities balance each at zero. Instead of a superman, as he fancied, he has been a cipher. But yes, there is one thing to his credit, the unselfish love of the woman who has waited all these years in the forest alone; and to her the Button Maker relinquishes the waif of his fancies. She may be able to transform him into something positive. *Peer Gynt* is a satire on the romantic cult of self and emotional hero worship by one fatally defective in will, but, lacking that ingredient, fit only for the crucible.

Brand, written at about the same time as *Peer Gynt*, is the effort at supermanhood through self-forgetful devotion to duty and ascetic self-denial. Appropriately he is a clergyman, and his mission in a region forbidding like the "all or nothing" of his own creed. But it is not only himself that he will sacrifice to his sense of duty, but even those who are dear to him; his "all or nothing" includes wife, child, mother, and every trace of affection these may have for anything except duty. His child is suffering, and to save its life a removal to some more genial climate is necessary; but this is to swerve from the God-given principle of duty. The child dies and its little grave in the Christmas snow is just outside the living room window. To comfort herself and to light the cold grave the wife decorates the room and opens the blinds. He chides the sinful thought as rebellion, closes the blinds and extinguishes the lights. We must serve God with single heart, and not show grief at His doing.

The sorrowing wife treasures the child's little possessions, its frocks and shoes; but when a trampwoman appears these must all be given up, even to the little cap the forlorn mother had hidden away in her bosom. "All or nothing." "Sacrifice what is dearest to you." He refuses to go to his own dying mother, because she has not rendered up her little property to the God that demands abject surrender. His mother dies, his wife dies brokenhearted, following her child; but his faith remains un-shaken.

Finally even his congregation deserts him, and he sets out on a mystical mission of his own to found a new church. An avalanche overwhelms him, but not before he has caught a vision. Has he understood the infinite will? Here is another type. Excess of will and devotion to duty, an ideal as unwholesome for life and as ineffective as the imagination of Peer Gynt shorn of will and moral purpose. If the superman is but an exaggeration of one faculty, an elephantiasis as it were, it is as destructive as any moral vice.

One more play on this theme of the superman, or on those that for a time fancy themselves such, that Ibsen's range of thought may be clearly seen. Of all of his plays the one that holds most of biographical significance is *The Master Builder*. It was written in his last period of literary activity, when he was thinking again of the more fundamental issues of conduct and less of the specific sociological problems of the period of the *Ghosts*, and more and more he was using the aid of symbolism to clothe and illuminate his ideas. And more and more he is using his command of poetry and its imagery. This is not an easy play to act; nor for that matter are *Brand* and *Peer Gynt*; but it is only because so much of the action is internal, and the poetic lines are its clue.

Halvard Solness, the Masterbuilder, has become what he is by sheer force of will. He began as a poor boy from the country in the employ of Knut Brovik. Gradually he broke his employer, and now when the play opens Brovik and his son Ragnar are in his employment. The son, who has exceptional talent, he holds by willing and winning the complete love of Kaia Fosli to whom the young man is engaged. Through her now in his office as secretary and bookkeeper he keeps a tight rein on the aspiring young architect. For he fears the younger generation, and he will shy at nothing to keep it down.

"*Solness.* It terrifies me—terrifies me every hour of the day. For sooner or later the luck must turn, you see.

Dr. Herdal. Oh, nonsense! What should make the luck turn?

Solness (*with firm assurance*). The younger generation.

Dr. Herdal. Pooh! The younger generation! You are not laid on the shelf yet, I should hope. Oh, no—your position here is probably firmer now than it has ever been.

Solness. The luck will turn. I know it—I feel the day approaching. Some one or other will take it into his head to say: Give me a chance! And then all the rest will come clamouring after him, and shake their fists at me and shout: Make room—make room—make room! Yes, just you see, doctor—presently the younger generation will come, knock at my door . . ."

This is one side of the difficulty that faces his will to power. Fear.

On the other side is a "sickly conscience." For he had been early married to Aline, whose genius for motherhood had been as great as his for building. After the marriage they lived in her ancestral home a gloomy half-castle, austere and ugly, that he detested; but to her it was home. He had detected a flaw in the chimney and *willed* the house's destruction by fire. It burned, not as he had wished, from the crack in the chimney he had failed to mend, but quite by accident. But as his will had triumphed in business, so he came to feel that his wife's exile from her family tradition had been due solely to him. And tragically it had killed her power, as it had given him his opportunity in his profession. He rose on the ashes of her life. For her two little boys had died as a result of exposure in the calamity. Now her mother instinct is forever denied.

The rest of his life was an act of expiation of this his

deed, and a "salutary self-torture." For he felt a "crushing debt" rested upon him and weighed him down. And he built now only homes, places where husbands and wives and children could be happy. He had prospered, but with added prestige came an added sense of guilt, and added estrangement between this husband and wife. How will it end?

The answer is the swiftly moving symbolism of the action that centers on a sprightly young woman, Hilda, that slips out of his own youthful conscience-free past and faces him with the enthusiasm and conscience-free joy of youth. Hilda, the unscrupulous urge of life itself, whispering now in the ears of weighted middle age, urging the ugliness and uselessness of duty,

> "*Solness.* Her duty?
> *Hilda.* She said that she would go out and buy something for me, because it was her duty. Oh, I can't bear that ugly, horrid word!
> *Solness.* Why not?
> *Hilda.* It sounds so cold, and sharp, and stinging. Duty—duty—duty. Don't you think so, too? Doesn't it seem to sting you?"

It chides the sickness of conscience

> "*Hilda.* I wonder whether you were not sent into the world with a sickly conscience.
> *Solness.* A sickly conscience? What deviltry is that?
> *Hilda.* I mean that your conscience is feeble—too delicately built, as it were—hasn't strength to take a grip of things—to lift and bear what is heavy."

It urges one more deed of grand endeavor that will restore health to the mind, power to the will, freedom and security.

He has built a home for himself, with three nurseries as a memorial tribute to his conscience for the family that will never again have children's voices of its own. On it is a tower, as a symbol of aspiration. And following the old tradition, a deed he had performed once in his youth, Hilda persuades him to climb the scaffolding, and there on the summit of the tower plant a wreath, as a symbol of his victory. Then he can afford to be generous to Ragnar, he can let Kaia go and wed the man she had chosen. He can let old Brovik die in peace. For with youth on his side, and its fresh enthusiasm inspiring his act, he will again be the nonchalant Solness, the Master-builder.

But can he? Fear and conscience, when they have become habitual, cannot be blown away by a transient enthusiasm. Will, though still potent, that has become sinister and morbid, cannot be restored to generosity in a moment. And above all is the handicap of age. He climbs the tower, against the advice of all, but with the admiring cries of Hilda, plants the wreath, and totters to his fall.

Such is the urge to life; and Hilda, the irrepressible spirit of life, who would love and live with a ruffian, "if it were a ruffian I had come to love." But Halvard Solness is no ruffian, nor was Brand when he saw the last vision, nor was poor deluded Peer Gynt. And even the righteous near-ruffian Brand suffers quite as intensely as his innocent victims. Such is Ibsen's comment on the superman. The claims of others, of society, or of tradition, cannot be ignored, in the final assessment of morals.

But this last play has also an allegorical meaning we cannot here allow to go untouched. It is a survey by Ibsen of his own life. He broke from tradition, and the past, and old social codes, as Solness when he willed the firing of his wife's old home. Like Solness, it touched him closer than he had imagined it could, for it meant misunderstandings and breaks with friends. The secret atonement he strove to offer, like Solness' efforts to make others happy with new homes, were Ibsen's social dramas demanding more light and a franker understanding of social problems. And Solness' final disgust is Ibsen's: does it matter?

> "*Solness.* . . . Men have no use for these homes of theirs—to be happy in. And I should not have had any use for such a home, if I had had one. (*With a quiet, bitter laugh.*) See, that is the upshot of the whole affair, however far back I look. Nothing really built; nor anything sacrificed for the chance of building. Nothing, nothing! the whole is nothing."

There is more than a little tragedy in this renunciation of a life's work.

But it is by this life's work that Ibsen gains his fame as a pleader for social reform and a critic of all social dogma. For a half-century he was to make the problem play a favorite of all dramatic writers, and give the *pièce à thèse* a constantly recurring popular interest. But social reform to him does not mean the substitution of one epidemic of orthodoxy for another. His desire is for individual emancipation, freedom of thought, with discipline, and intelligent conduct with an intelligent sense of values. If Ibsen is always a minority in opposition, it is the unreasoned orthodoxy of tradition that he opposes, the instinctive conservative (or radical) will of the "compact majority," the thing he calls with a savage gesture "public opinion." In one form or another, this theme runs through all of his plays of his middle period.

I select more or less arbitrarily *An Enemy of the People.* The title is well chosen, for every one, he felt, who tried to open the eyes of the community was to them a public enemy, and he himself and some of his friends had shared the public's dislike. The hero is a Doctor Stockmann who has come down from his practice in the north to be official physician for a cure opened in a little city, of which his brother is mayor and chairman of the bath committee. It is a typical, bustling little town, now beginning to feel the "boom" of a popular resort. There is Hovstad the editor of a liberal, semi-radical journal, his master printer who is head of the house-holders' association, good conservative property holders, and Morten Kiil, the doctor's father-in-law, the owner of the local tanneries, the representative of capital. Politics and big business are combined in the person of the doctor's brother Peter Stockmann. The picture is complete.

There had been an epidemic the year before and the doctor is suspicious. He sends a sample of the water to the university for analysis. The play opens with its report. The water is contaminated. Instead of a health resort the place is a menace. And Doctor Stockmann instantly proclaims the alarming discovery. In his own mind he is the savior of the community. The baths have been polluted by the tanneries. The company will either have to abandon the new enterprise, or raise large sums of money to purify the water. Hovstad hails him as a hero and rushes off to sound his praises in the press. The president of the householders' association promises the aid of the good property holders. The doctor must have the support of the "compact majority" in his praiseworthy effort to safeguard health.

But big business has not yet been heard from, for it holds the financial stakes, and stands to lose heavily on account of the new discovery. And the play goes the road of many such situations even in these more enlightened days. The financial integrity of the booming little city must not be endangered. Summer visitors must not be warned away by alarmist reports in the press. Property holders must be protected against any shrinkage in the already risen values

of their holdings. And anyway the alarm is in all probability quite baseless. Thus the first glad acclaim of the
city's hero turns into sullen resentment and open hostility
and active persecution. The public hero is a public enemy.
The town's integrity has been threatened by ill-advised
enthusiasm and a busy-body.

The reaction begins slowly. First it is his brother who
comes, suave and placating. Surely Thomas, the doctor,
can see that he has been precipitate in his public manifesto.
Surely a bit of tinkering could be quietly done at slight
cost, to patch up the difficulty. Such things ought not to get
into the press. The public might be alarmed. Why it can't
be so bad as the doctor fancies. But Thomas has scientific
facts on his side; he knows and will not compromise nor
remain silent. He has made a discovery and will not be
robbed of the reward of a public benefactor. People's lives
are at stake, and truth. Patching up, tinkering with the
water works won't touch the sources of the poison. The
whole thing will have to be overhauled. You can't compromise with an epidemic.

Then it is Morten Kiil that has his word. It is his tanneries, is it, that are causing the trouble? But Stockmann's
wife has an interest in these tanneries. The doctor surely
would not want to hurt his own family. He will see to
that. As the rumor spreads and the value of the bath
shares drops he buys them up to hold as a club over the
recalcitrant son-in-law.

Gradually the people are alarmed and see that their
purses may be touched, and, actively fanned, the resentment flames into bitter hatred. The public savior tries to
address a mass meeting, but is cried down. His home is
stoned, his boys ostracised from school, his daughter
loses her place as teacher. His job as physician is taken
away from him; and then as an ironical final jest, when

it is known that his father-in-law stands to win a great deal of money by cornering the depreciated shares, he is complimented on his financial astuteness. Such was the result of his efforts to educate his city to a moral sense of values. At the end he stands quite alone. But his enthusiasm for the truth does not falter, for he alone is free.

"*Dr. Stockmann* (lowering his voice). Hush! You mustn't say anything about it yet; but I have made a great discovery.

Mrs. Stockmann. Another one?

Dr. Stockmann. Yes (gathers them round him, and says confidentially:) It is this, let me tell you—that the strongest man in the world is he who stands most alone.

Mrs. Stockmann (smiling and shaking her head). Oh, Thomas, Thomas!

Petra (encouragingly, as she grasps her father's hands). Father!"

Really this play is a grim comedy, and its satire is double-edged. Its comment on "compact majorities" is painfully obvious. Ibsen is least of all a believer in democracy and the reasonableness of all sorts and conditions of people. More often they are a compact herd and led by the nose by the latest prejudice. It is a satire on the ethics of business, but this in these latter days has become so easy that Ibsen's words have lost any trace of novelty. But it is a satire also directed against the hero and his well-meaning want of tact. There is something also of the Gregers Werle about him, the obvious inability to see the other fellow.

And in these social dramas, like *Ghosts*, *The Wild Duck* and *An Enemy of the People* we see most clearly the weakness as well as the strength of Ibsen. He is interested in ideas, and their clash, the old and the new, the fixed and the changing, their dynamic movement that makes for change and also progress, the radicalism of today that becomes the crystallized orthodoxy of tomorrow. Again this is the scientist in Ibsen, the student of social unrest, change and stabilization. "The ideal is dead, long live the ideal." "The old beauty is no longer beautiful, the new truth is no longer true." Hence he is not interested in persons save as they personify ideas. So his heroes, Mrs. Alving, Doctor Stockmann, Gregers Werle and even Halvard Solness are not people, much less the lesser characters Manders, Hovstad, Ekdal, or Hilda. We don't watch them develop out of situations, but the situations develop out of them. The plays are tailor made, to illuminate a social problem which has as its factors such and such ideas.

Great and enduring drama cannot be created thus out of a chemical formula, or a sociologist's note book. When the ideas are vital, and their significance to an epoch very great, the plays will be acclaimed as masterpieces, and their characters recognized. But when the ideas have become commonplace or out of date, then interest flags, the characters appear for what they are; and it is only the peculiar character of the situation that remains. It is only for this reason, I suspect, that *The Ghosts* is available today, as a slightly melodramatic story of the stages in inherited syphilis leading to paresis. Certainly it is impossible to grow enthusiastic over Nora's rebellion in *A Doll's House*. But to say this is by no means to detract from Ibsen's importance to his own age. To be a prophet for all time one must undertake a universal message.

It was precisely this that Ibsen succeeded in doing in *Rosmersholm*. The play begins as do most of his social dramas as a contest between the old and the new, between tradition and fresh youth and life. But before it has gone far the characters become personalities, with lives and wills of their own. They leave the test tubes and laboratory and go into experiences of their own making. And we have a drama, though not great, which is universal. The artist Ibsen here is quite unconscious of his scientific brain, and the result is his masterpiece. There are ideas, but they are human, and they never obtrude.

As the play was planned there were the same carefully selected characters who would represent the clash of ideas. Rosmer is Everyman, of old and conservative stock, but now touched by the new ideas and wavering in his allegiance. His wife Beata, who has recently died, belonged to the past tradition. Her brother, the clergyman Kroll, is aggressively of the orthodox old in religion and social politics. But there is on the other side Rebecca West, the spirit of emancipated youth and the joy in life and its free acceptance. Then there is a radical journalist, Kroll's pest, who is sowing the countryside with horrible social and political and even religious unrest. Rosmer must come back to life and activity and combat this new foe of all that his family and his once profession of clergyman had detested. Who will gain the victory, family tradition and Kroll, or life and Rebecca West? Or is a victory possible? Hidden at first also, there are seeds of tragedy.

And it is as these seeds sprout and show their power that the play flies out of the window of the laboratory and we forget Kroll, forget the lay figure of the journalist, forget the problem of the old and the new, and begin the entirely human tragedy of a sensitive man and a sensitive woman, who love, but between whom lies the shadow of the woman who loved even to self-sacrifice. Sociology can find no formula which will plot the curve of life when it grips the fortunes of three people and sets them on the path of tragedy.

Rebecca West is a stray. She has come into the family

of Rosmer as companion to the invalid Beata. She is ardent, she is beautiful, she is just what the austere home of the clergyman had never known; and her coming was to him the breath of life from a mountain peak. She falls in love with him, and he innocently, without knowing it for a time, with her. She is emancipated, has no scruples, but knows the ailing wife is a barrier, and hastens its removal. For Beata guesses the truth, and for the sake of her husband drowns herself. No one has a hint of the truth except Rebecca.

But now when the game is in her own hands Rebecca falters. It is the generous, unsuspecting, noble character of Rosmer that awakens in her also the knowledge that in perfect love there must be also generous truth. And when she openly wins his love and he would accept hers, she suddenly learns that sacrifice demands sacrifice. She reveals to him the cause of Beata's death.

> "*Rebecca.* She had conceived a fixed idea that she, as a childless wife, had no right to be here. And then she imagined that it was her duty to efface herself.
> *Rosmer.* And you—you did nothing to disabuse her of the idea?
> *Rebecca.* No. . . .
> *Rebecca* (vehemently). You think then that I was cool and calculating and self-possessed all the time! I was not the same woman then that I am now, as I stand here telling it all. Besides, there are two sorts of will in us I believe! I wanted Beata away, by one means or another; but I never really believed that it would come to pass. As I felt my way forward, at each step I ventured, I seemed to hear something within me cry out: No farther! Not a step farther! And yet I could not stop. I had to venture the least little bit farther. Only one hair's-breadth more. And then one more—and always one more.— And then it happened.—That is the way such things come about."

This is a very different spirit from Brand's "sacrifice of what is dearest to you," an oblation to an external idol of duty that demands "all or nothing." It is the genuine prompting of one's own heart, the transformed Rebecca could do no less. And Rosmer? He stands utterly bewildered by the revelation. "The cause that is to win a lasting victory must have for its champion a happy, innocent man."

"*Rosmer.* Oh, Rebecca—I no longer believe in my power of transforming any one. My faith in myself is utterly dead. I believe neither in myself nor in you.

Rebecca (looks darkly at him). Then how will you be able to live your life?

Rosmer. That I don't know. I cannot imagine how. I don't think I can live it.—And I know of nothing in the world that is worth living for.

Rebecca. Oh, life—life will renew itself. Let us hold fast to it, Rosmer.—We shall leave it soon enough.

Rosmer (springs up restlessly). Then give me my faith again! My faith in you, Rebecca! My faith in your love! Proof! I must have proof!

Rebecca. Proof? How can I give you proof—?

Rosmer. You must! (Walks across the room.) I cannot bear this desolation—this horrible emptiness—this—this—"

To him there is only one way to the proof he longs for. The test is the path that Beata had taken.

"*Rosmer.* We go with each other, Rebecca—I with you, and you with me.

Rebecca. I almost think that is the truth.

Rosmer. For now we two are one.

Rebecca. Yes. We are one. Come! We go gladly."

Conscience, tradition, the will for life and happiness are in this play in hopeless conflict, social morality, individual morality, and the disposition of all to carry on as conscience or morality or the best of intentions dictate. But these are no longer ideas, but vivid impulses of vivid personalities, who grow and wither before our eyes as the action progresses. These are motives transferred from the sociological-minded nineteenth century to the panorama of life in any age, when duty and conscience urge their claim against the instinctive will to live and be happy. And the play that began as just another effort of the Master-builder to build a house in which happy people could live, became his masterpiece, his gift to world tragedy.

A paradoxical spirit of the nineteenth century this aus-tere Scandinavian. He belongs to the century and yet is a spirit in rebellion. The new sciences were in danger of overlooking the uniqueness of the individual, interested as they were in "natural law." He sees the vital neces-sity of keeping the claims of the individual in the fore-ground, his relation to society and society's to him. But frequently these are in conflict. Who is wrong? Per-haps neither; for right and wrong after all are only rela-tive terms in Ibsen's evolutionary view of morals—again another gift of the age of science to the dramatist.

And so he asks questions, pertinent and often unan-swerable, questions that puzzled the complacent accept-ers of an external code, and the partisans as well of the new science. How can one, where can one, seek for the regeneration of the fatigued individual like Solness or Rosmer? Hilda and Rebecca West—are motives like theirs blessings or tragic curses? Is there any room for moral freedom in human nature? Was Oswald in *Ghosts* only a helpless victim of heredity? Or was his inner con-flict in spite of his psychological and pathological chains a sign of an inner moral nature beyond the limitation of his inheritance? Ibsen is interested in the new brutalities committed in the name of the struggle for existence; the Knut and Ragnar Broviks kept under by remorseless suc-cess, not quite fit to survive, and yet having many quali-ties superior to their oppressors. Is the law of survival moral? Can its moral implications be discovered? The new interest in woman's place in the social code; is there a double standard, one for man and another and less compromising for woman? What about the recalcitrant individual, the one, whether a Peer Gynt, Brand, or a Hedda Gabler, who would be a law unto himself? He finds the answer is not nearly so easy as the reformer or the scientist might fancy. But the posing sometimes of even an impossible question has its place. It may bewilder and also annoy, but it leaves the questioner and those that follow humble. And in that sense, if in no other, Ibsen has been of great significance to his time. The virtue of humility is none too easy to cultivate.

Above all Ibsen is refreshing to our thought, even to-day, in that he sees that morality, if it is to mean anything, is not an external matter. Nietzsche says much the same thing, but in a way that leads to abundant misunderstanding. It must be a living motive, but one to be judged only by its effects. It must have survival value, that is, contribute to the well being, whether of the individual or of society as a whole. But of it no formula has as yet been devised, for its mathematics has not been invented. It is as elusive as human nature, and depends for its vitality on human freedom, and on discipline. It is the value of this last even in his best that Ibsen seems to miss.

XIV. THE NATURALIST'S CREED

ZOLA

"He felt the need of glorifying these workers, whose odor of wretchedness was now unpleasant to him; he would show that they alone were great and stainless, the only nobility and the only strength in which humanity could be dipped afresh."

Germinal

"J'accuse"—Even now many of us recall the tumult this little phrase produced in 1898. It was the celebrated Dreyfus affair, a country gone mad over a spy scare; a scandal that even yet gives the French imagination its bad quarter of an hour. A series of farcical trials, the perplexity of all lovers of justice and fair play, and then the long letter *"J'accuse,"* and the long list of officers small and great who had played a part in the game, ending with the President himself of France. All the presses of the world from Melbourne to Bombay to Boston carried the challenge.

It was Émile Zola at the climax of his career, risking his future and perhaps even his life with this appeal for justice. But it is only the supreme moment of a life time devoted to warfare. "Ah! to live indignant, to live enraged at treacherous arts, at false honor, at universal mediocrity! To be unable to read a newspaper without paling in anger! To feel the continual and irresistible need of

282

crying aloud what one thinks, above all when one is alone
in thinking it, and to be ready to abandon all the sweets of
life for it!" This was written in the eighties. The militant
Zola. Of course there is always something theatrical about
his militancy; he was French one must remember, and he
loved a pose as much as did Napoleon—and some dictators
today who are not literary. At times it brought him popularity. But this his last challenge endangered his life
and fortune, and brought exile.

There is the same downright conviction, and will to
express it uncompromisingly, in his whole literary career.
And as on the occasion of his open challenge to all comers
in *L'Affaire Dreyfus*, so on the occasion of each and all of
his novels, he had noisy partisans not a few among the
young and ardent, but also the unnumbered majority
of the many who stopped their ears at the scandal. It is
only in recent years that attempts have been made to see
this speaker of plain, unwelcome fact aright. Even yet
there are large numbers to whom his books are forbidden
and his name a reproach to humanity. It is high time to
attempt to see him in a true perspective, for Zola has
been a potent influence in Europe and America; and his
literary doctrine of Naturalism, in one form or another,
has had a leading influence on the novel and drama.

Naturalism. This is nothing more than to say that
Zola was a devotee of the Comtist doctrine of science, that
"science alone would ensure the happiness and pacification
of all the nations." And, as a corollary, it was added that
literature in its effort to assist in this happiness and purification must become a hand-maid to science, utilizing all
its powers to make the discoveries of science prevail, ever
alert to the significance of new discoveries and ever ready
to widen men's knowledge of its resources. Literature can

thus herald the grand triumph, when outworn theories of life will be abandoned, and in their place science will rule the world.

But literature and science to Zola are even yet more closely related. As naturalism thinks of its aim, literature is as scientific as science itself, and a novel or drama quite as much a thing of accurate observation and record as the biologist's experiment in the laboratory. The form of the novel in particular, because of its convenient length, is a frame like a laboratory, biological and sociological, into which characters and situations are introduced and isolated, that their mutual dependence may be checked and ticketed, and general laws arrived at by induction in the orthodox manner. This can be done, Zola insists, if the artist becomes the sincere and dispassionate observer, and records with perfect objectivity the results of his observation. These will be the novel or drama.

In a manifesto he published in the seventies—Zola never did anything without a proclamation—*Le Roman Expérimental*, or the novel founded on experience, he laid down with such precision as the theory admits the *procédé* of all future fiction. The new novel will be no more than the *"procès-verbal,"* the formal report, of the author's observation. His master Claude Bernard had given him the clue: "In all living things, as in dead matter, the conditions of existence of all phenomena are determined in a manner that is absolute." These in biology are heredity and environment. "I come therefore," Zola adds, "to this conclusion: the novel based on experience is a consequence of the evolution in science of the century; it continues and completes physiology, which itself is founded upon chemistry and physics; it substitutes for the study of man in the abstract, the man of metaphysics, the natural man, obeying the laws of physics and chemistry and determined by the influence of his environment; it is in a word the literature of our age of science, as the classic and romantic literature have corresponded to the age of scholasticism and theology."

So much for the scientific nature of all new fiction. Now for the aid that such fiction will be for the rediscovery of the happiness and welfare of society. Here the analogy of the scientist and the physician will serve admirably. The successful artist must be both; he must detect the symptoms, whether in heredity or in environment, and then point out the necessary remedies. "Within society as in the human body there exists a bond which unites its several members, the different organs, to each other, in such a manner that if one organ is diseased, many of the others are affected, and a complex malady is set up. So in our novels, when we study an inflammation which infects society, we proceed in the manner of the clinical physician, we seek to find the simple and original source of the infection, to arrive in the sequel to the complex effect which has followed."

This is superb, in theory, the wonder would seem to be that no one had practiced it before. I am not so sure that even Zola is convinced of its newness. What is new perhaps is the zeal of this late practitioner and his use of scientific terminology. We in these later days have called the resulting picture of situations "a slice of life," and that was what Zola strove to exhibit in its natural rawness, without apology and without ornament. His definition came just at the time when others were at work in much the same manner. Balzac had done a great deal in this manner, see his *Country Doctor* and the study of cretinism. Stendahl, Flaubert and Maupassant were contemporaries using a not different method; and the end of the century and the beginning of the twentieth were to see a host of followers like Hauptmann in Germany and Dreiser in America.

A "slice of life," a particular series of situations as they are in nature with a set of carefully studied characters, moulded into what they are by their past, their ancestors, and their environment. How will these comport themselves in their habitual and in other and novel situations? The novel or drama that is the result of this study will have no more plot than the laboratory notebook of a physiologist or biologist. For plot in the ordinary sense represents the deliberate liberties the artist takes with the course of the action, giving it in Aristotle's phrase, "a beginning, middle, and an ending." But living situations flow according to the laws of their own nature, and the scientific artist must never interrupt the natural course. In any case, according to Zola, "if one wishes to have my opinion in a word, it is that people attach entirely too much importance to plot."

So Zola, who in his youth had been a journalist, armed himself with a notebook and went to the life of France to study it first hand, getting the facts that, when he had put them together, made his novels. In this sense it is true that naturalism is a species of extended and literary journalism. It is not at all to be wondered at that a very large number of its school should once have been, like Zola, journalists in their careers. And just as journalism of the higher variety has served excellently as a means for reform, so Zola and naturalism can be credited with the serious purpose of social reform. He painted with objective fidelity the ills of contemporary French society, roused the popular conscience, and when it was possible remedial legislation followed. But again this is not quite the novelty the manifestoes of its partisans have asserted. Dickens and *Nicholas Nickleby* and *Oliver Twist* come to mind, and long before that De Foe and *Moll Flanders*, and I have no doubt that Homer's Thersites in the *Iliad* had some ulterior journalistic purpose of beneficial reform.

But Zola made novel writing a serious profession, with laborious study of his clinical notebooks for each novel, which might have taken the heart out of the more spontaneous manner of a Scott or Fielding. They observed, studied, read; but Zola never left behind his stethoscope and clinical thermometer, and looked up case histories, in the modern approved manner of social workers, unto the third and fourth line of ancestry. To look at the chart he drew of the Rougon-Macquart family reminds me of the charts of the kings of England which I studied as a boy. But there one had only dates of birth, death, and marriage; here on these leaves of the family tree are inscribed the inherited assets and liabilities of body and mind. They are a genealogy of case histories that should delight a sociologist.

The Rougon-Macquart chronicles are a score of volumes dealing with the criss-cross of heredity in four and more generations, with each novel devoted to one specific member placed in a situation where his study will be edifying as a sociological "case." There are twenty volumes in all, I am told—I haven't read them all. They are entitled, *The Rougon-Macquart, natural and social history of a family under the Second Empire.* "If I accept a historical frame it is solely to have a milieu which reacts. . . . Instead of having principles (royalty, Catholicism) I shall have laws (heredity, atavism). I do not wish like Balzac to come to decisions on the affairs of men, to be political, philosophical, or moral. I am satisfied to be a scientist, to tell of that which exists, while seeking underlying reasons. Furthermore no conclusions.

A simple exposé of the facts of a family by showing the interior mechanism which directs them."

But science may be said to have also a higher purpose, to lay the foundations of a better state. So Zola could not rest merely with the discovery of the mechanisms of social life. Like the applied scientist he will suggest ways by which the mechanism may be employed to bring the happiness and welfare of society. "I have said that there is an urge toward liberty and justice. I believe that it will be long in arriving, while holding that we may be led to a better state. But I believe above all in a constant march toward truth. It is only from the knowledge of virtue that a better state can be born." And finally, "If my characters do not arrive at good it is because we are only beginning in perfectibility. . . . To describe my work in a sentence: I wish to paint, at the beginning of a century of truth and liberty, a family which throws itself toward the immediate good, and which is overcome by its own *élan,* by the fatal convulsions of a new world in travail. Thus, two elements: (1) the purely human and physiological element, with its relationships and its fatal descent; (2) the effects of the modern day on such a family; its derangement by the fevers of the time, the social and physical action of the *milieux.*"

I have quoted somewhat extensively from another of his manifestoes, the general plan for the series, in order that we might here at the beginning have a fairly clear idea of the scope of naturalism. That he adhered with remarkable consistency to this purpose in the larger number of the volumes of the series is a tribute to his self-effacement as a scientist; that as clearly in a few of the volumes near the end of the series he added something of his own is a tribute to Zola the artist. It is my sincere conviction that it is only on these last that Zola's claim for a large place in nineteenth century thought rests.

But Zola cannot be content with the impersonal and quite unobtrusive manner of the scientist working quietly in his laboratory and emerging quietly only after he has made his discovery. He must ballyhoo the performance and drag in the public to the exhibitions, and shock, even terrify them by the unexpectedness of his experiment. If his work has any social value he must startle his readers into thinking. "Never forget that a drama must take the public by the throat. They grow angry, but do not forget. Give them always, if not nightmares, at least excessive books which will stay in their memories. . . . No more epithets. A magisterial bearing. But always warmth and passion. A roaring torrent, but broad and of a majestic grace."

The "majestic grace" many at first could not discover, but they found plenty of nightmares, excess, and passion; so much that tender-minded readers amid the horrors of *La Débâcle* or *Germinal* or *L'Assommoir*, lose their way to the essential human situations, the vision of "humanity in the gross," the "masses and volumes" of humanity acting under pressure of social or animal law. But Henry James, an author of a very different sphere, wrote admiringly of his plan: "No finer act in the history of letters. . . . Entertained and carried out from the threshold of manhood, the high project announces beforehand its inevitable weakness and yet speaks in the same voice for its admirable, its almost unimaginable strength." The "majestic grace" perhaps is better called scope and power, the vision that can see masses of men joined in common action, the panorama of the *bête humaine*, and the ability to tell its story. And into this massed movement is projected the character who is prepared, by the scientist, for the experiment. If it is a nightmare, it is one created for a definite purpose.

This "nightmare," if one wishes the phrase, is a thing to Zola not wholly different from the horror of the ancient myth that became the theme of great tragedy. The Nemesis, the family curse, that brooded over the house of Agamemnon, that laid low the family of Oedipus, this the ancient poet strove to humanize in his tragedy, losing in the process none of its malignant potency. In doing so Greek tragedy became moral. But in the nineteenth century when the old bases of morals are in question, the new tragedy must become scientific. So the Rougon-Macquart novels are the new tragedy of mankind presided over by a new Nemesis, whose ways Zola would make intelligible, and its name would be Heredity. As implacable, as predetermined, as ironically malignant, he would have it as the moral bewilderment that drove Oedipus into blind exile and Antigone to virgin death. There is some justification then in Zola's pride of accomplishment. "This is my formula; and best of all it will be a new art, a new literature, which will be my own literature, my own art."

Perhaps the best known of his novels of pure naturalism are *L'Assommoir*, or, as it has been translated, *The Dram Shop*, and *Nana*. His notebooks tell us how scrupulously he studied the regions of Paris where he determined to place these stories, how he picked out houses and rooms for the scenes and photographed them on his memory, how he studied minutely the life of these regions, the topics of conversation, the most intimate habits and labor and pastimes of the people. For *Nana* he must learn the least of the little things that go into the lives of these *filles de joie* whose time is shared between the theatre and the men who support their extravagance. There is in this exactness to fact all the difference in the world between the horrors of the slums of Paris that Hugo gives in the *Hunchback of Notre Dame* and Zola's photographic accuracy, conscientiously avoiding exaggeration or melodrama, or between the sentimental charm of Dumas' *La Dame aux Camélias* and the purely physical call of sex in *Nana*.

Nor does the plot of either touch extravagance or horror or the ugly for the sake of any literary effect. The notebooks on *L'Assommoir* tell us not once how he deliberated over the turns in the situations which would be true to the lives of just such people, and the avoidance of Hugo melodrama not seldom makes the scene the more powerfully affecting. There are of course the grim ironies of coincidence, as when the once glorious Nana lies dying, gnawed by smallpox, while from her window she hears the shouting mobs, and the tramp of soldiers, "*À Berlin*," the light-hearted beginning of the Franco-Prussian War.

L'Assommoir is the story of the life and death of Gervaise Macquart "at forty-one, slowly, horribly, exhausted by pain and misery." All she has wanted was "work, bread, a clean home, children, not to be beaten." And all her hope is taken from her. She has been abandoned with her two children by her lover Lantier. Now she marries Coupeau. Her lover returns. A *ménage à trois* is arranged complaisantly. She supports the two men, as Coupeau after an accident slowly becomes a victim to drink, and so to the bitter end.

Zola calls it a drama of a "magnificent reality and a bold cruelty." The result was a tremendous success, and a literary battle whose reverberations are not yet stilled. Nana is her daughter, picked out of the dram shop and put on the stage, full of the sheer joy of living, and yet inheriting also the family Nemesis. She is the best of the Macquarts and yet by profession intolerable in any society; but, to Zola's creed of journalistic naturalism, necessary for the public to know, like her mother, if ever a cure is to be discovered for the social malady.

All this can be generously acknowledged when one today reads this naturalism at its naked best, and yet there persists unanswered one irritating question. Is this exactly the whole function of the novel that purports to be great? Has not something vital been overlooked by the author, even though he has with notebook and microscope picked up and arranged with perfect fidelity every relevant detail? It is this persistent question that arises after every work of this Zola's school, no matter how powerful, Gorky's *Foma*, Hauptmann's *Weavers*, Dreiser's *American Tragedy*. The question we shall see will worry the mature Zola; and he will write also *La Débâcle*, *Germinal* and *The Three Cities*.

To be sure in *L'Assommoir*, in *Nana*, in *La Terre* (*The Land*), he is describing the canker that eats the heart of civilization, the discrepancies seen between the lots of the classes, the brutalizing of the poor, the selfish aimlessness of the rich, the *bête humaine*, masked by the veneer of civilization, or naked and shameless, yet at the close of a reading one puts the book away with a feeling of its aimless power. Brutal, overwhelming, a nightmare that "takes the reader by the throat," but in the way also of the brute who attacks for the lust of killing. One asks why? I do not mean to suggest that the ugliness is offensive and hence to be condemned, but should it not be employed for some end beyond itself and the mere sociological and journalist purpose of possible reform? If this last aim alone is allowed, then the moment slums are cleared away, or other reform secured, the power of the novel is gone, save as an interesting though unpleasant relic of once barbarous ugliness. And were there no more in Zola than the ability to paint with utter realism the social evil of his day, the power and influence of the artist would be, though of much salutary value to his own age, a thing of lesser significance. It is the universal Zola that I am trying to define for us today.

Zola never ceased to call himself a naturalist. But he learned in his maturity to use his naturalism as a means to an end, and discovered, through it perhaps, a philosophy of life that has less connection with Zola the man of science. To be sure it was impossible for him to turn his back on science, or renounce his faith in his method. But more and more science became to him the means to great social ends, and literature more the handmaid of science than a department of experimental biology and physiology. And above all, because of his minute social studies, he acquired a faith in human nature, a belief in its essential soundness, that will make him a defender of the oppressed, but for a reason that has in it nothing of the sentimental love of the lowly or the liberal belief in democracy.

Zola, too, is of the family of Rousseau, a belated arrival, like some of the descendants of his fictional family, almost unrecognizable after the generations of conflict. He believes with Rousseau that refinement and so-called culture has fatally ruined the moral health of the upper classes, and that their new weapon of economic power has utterly lost any hope of their aid being enlisted for the regeneration of humanity. Sick and avaricious they are past hope themselves, and unwilling by instinct now to cast their lot in any common human cause. There is more than a little of Karl Marx in this, though Zola is no Marxian. The lower classes, brutal though they are, and exploited, alone remain unspoiled, and when not aroused in self-defense are patient, good-natured, generous, and even on occasion sublime. In them Zola has a mystic faith. The virile and "tough" proletarian of Zola is thus related to the mystic "noble savage" of Rousseau, the simple peasant of Tolstoi, and from him alone can come the salvation of society.

It is interesting to see how after we pass into his work of the nineties that this idea comes more and more powerfully to be expressed. A revolution has taken place imperceptibly between *Nana* and *Germinal,* though the hero of the latter is a half-brother of Nana. Perhaps when we get to *La Débâcle* and *The Three Cities* the enthusiast with a mission to proclaim has somewhat obscured the realistic artist.

La Débâcle (The Downfall) is one of the most powerful war books ever written, and it was composed by one who had never smelt powder. Something like two hundred pages are given to the disaster of Sedan alone. Again following his custom he spends years getting his documents. He interviews soldiers, studies the battleground, consults all manner of records, to get not only the facts but also the "feel" of the whole action. It is not a novel of one or more heroes, but one in which the "mass" acts as one man, and its response to danger and death, to privation and discipline, and its explosion in anger in the Commune after the siege of Paris: these form the plot of the story. The hero, if he can be called a hero, is the average French soldier, misled and sacrificed to the stupidity of generals, politicians, and seekers after glory. It is his tragedy, for he is the one that suffered. There have been few indictments of war so powerful. Of course there was the outcry against the book. Even a German officer who had fought in the campaign protested that Zola had slandered the French army. But this was the book, on the other hand, that made him also an international figure.

But of all his books I think it is *Germinal* that is from all points of view his best, and at the same time with a theme that touches our times most closely. Like all his others it is fully documented, so fully that it can almost serve as a text-book on coal miners and mining. But with this precise background it is a study too of the lot of the miners, the curious impersonal way by which indifferent or even benevolent owners of mining stock and mine managers can become, without even being conscious of it, oppressors of great masses of people. And then it turns and describes with panorama-like sweep the masses and volumes of the workers, their families, the hereditary worker in the earth, his dangers always, and his little feelings even of loyalty to the mine that in turn consumes him.

"The family had worked for the Montsou Mining Company since it started, and that was long ago, a hundred and six years already. His grandfather, Guillaume Maheu, an urchin of fifteen then, had found the rich coal at Réquillart, the Company's first pit, an old abandoned pit today down below near the Fauvelle sugar works. All the country knew it, and as a proof, the discovered seam was called the "Guillaume," after his grandfather. He had not known him—a big fellow, it was said, very strong, who died of old age at sixty. Then his father, Nicolas Maheu, called the Rouge, when hardly forty years of age had died in the pit, which was being excavated at that time; a land-slip, a complete downfall, and the rocks drank his blood and swallowed his bones. Two of his uncles and his three brothers, later on, also left their skins there. He, Vincent Maheu, who had come out almost whole, except that his legs were rather shaky, was looked upon as a knowing fellow. But what could one do? One must work; one worked here from father to son, as one would work at anything else. His son, Toussaint Maheu, was being worked to death there now, and his grandsons, and all his people, who lived opposite in the settlement. A hundred and six years of mining, the youngsters after the old ones, for the same master. Eh? there were many *bourgeois* that could not give their history so well!"

In truth it is the epic of a class, its dawning class-conscious-
ness, driven finally to act, the horror of its deeds, when
passion has transformed even good-natured people to
savage brutes, and the calm of despair, when without
having gained one of their pleas they return uncomprehendingly to their old loyalty.

Here Zola has something more to maintain than the
war between the classes, and the plea for a more adequate
understanding between separated peoples. He is something more than the scientific sociologist painting the
squalor of the oppressed, and the hatreds that oppression
will always engender. For the novel as it develops is more
than an indictment of the capitalistic system, when one
party must be wrong and the other right. What remains
longest after reading is the humanity of the picture, and
Zola's essential faith in the soundness at heart of the
worker. He is not setting class against class, and passing
judgment on a social evil; but examining the humanity of
each of the warring classes, to see which fundamentally is
the better fitted to survive. He asks for justice, not because of injustice done to the workers, but because they are
better fitted to reorganize society. In this way, with this
moral justification, *Germinal* is the first great proletarian
novel, but with its faith based on no economic or sociological theory.

The plot is simplicity itself, an opportunity to see the
mines in northern France, to learn the ways and homes
of the miners, to see them at their work, to discover gradually the causes of their grievance, to see the minds of
their managers and of some of their stock holders, and the
mining problem, to watch for two hundred pages the
crescendo of the strike, and finally to feel the sinking of
the spirits of all at its futility and tragedy. The plot is
from one point of view as commonplace, and as harrowing,

too, as the journalistic accounts of any strike past or present, with its blind heroism, patient courage, famine and disaster, orgies of passion, and disillusioning conclusion. From this point of view the story is a novel only because it is among the first of a long series in journalism, fiction, and drama.

The hero is Étienne Lantier, the half-brother of Nana. He comes to the region in search of work and finding it becomes an inmate in the home of Maheu, his wife and innumerable family. (These miners have only one recreation after their long hours in the pit, sex and the resultant families. They begin before puberty, promiscuous like animals, and as unashamed. They continue, as in the cities the search for life takes to the intoxication of drink, until the impotence of age, and with its curtain comes death, unless as more often, death cuts them off in the ever-menacing pit.) Lantier is by temperament a student, and his hours of leisure are devoted to the social problems. He reads Darwin to understand the secret of survival. He knows Karl Marx, Saint Simon and Proudhon and Lassalle, and thinks of socialism, the rights of workers, and dreams of the International and the coming revolution.

With him is the Russian, once aristocrat, Souvarine, the Nihilist, who had seen the hanging in Russia of his sweetheart, and is now a refugee, ready against the day of reckoning. He has become cold and calculating, strikes for him are faint-hearted measures, predestined to fail. Only by wholesale destruction of property and life can the debris of the old be swept away to make room for the new.

"We were guilty to love each other. Yes, it is well that she is dead; heroes will be born from her blood, and I no longer have any cowardice at my heart. Ah! nothing, neither parents, nor wife, nor friend! Nothing to make my hand tremble on the day when I must take others' lives or give up my own." . . .

"To the primitive formless Commune, to a new world, to the renewal of everything."

After the destruction of the mine, coolly planned by him and as coolly executed.

"he threw down his last cigarette; he went away, without looking back, into the now dark night. Afar his shadow diminished and mingled with the darkness. He was going over there, to the unknown. He was going tranquilly to extermination, wherever there may be dynamite to blow up towns and men. He will be there, without doubt, when the middle class in agony shall hear the pavement of the streets bursting up beneath their feet."

Then there is the Christian Socialist, the Abbé Ranvier, thin with zeal and prophetic, who can offer the suffering miners in their distress nothing but a faith. The Abbé with eyes like red-hot coals.

"He found excuses for the atrocities of the strikers; he violently attacked the middle class, throwing on them the whole of responsibility. It was the middle class which, by dispossessing the Church of its ancient liberties in order to misuse them itself, had turned this world into a cursed place of injustice and suffering; it was the middle class which prolonged misunderstandings, which was pushing on towards a terrible catastrophe by its atheism, by its refusal to return to the old beliefs, to the fraternal of the early Christians. And he dared to threaten the rich. He warned them that if they obstinately persisted in refusing to listen to the voice of God, God would surely put Himself on the side of the poor. He would take back their fortunes from those who faithlessly enjoyed them; and would distribute them to the humble of the earth for the triumph of His glory."

Against all this is the picture of the mines, a haunting menace, the home of these people and the thing that gave them their poisoned life.

"Before him the Voreux was crouching, with its air of an evil beast, its dimness pricked with a few lantern lights. The three braziers of the bank were burning in the air, like bloody moons, now and then showing the vast silhouettes of Father Bonnemort and his yellow horse. And beyond, in the flat plain, shade had submerged everything, Montsou, Marchiennes, the forest of Vandame, the immense sea of beetroot and of wheat, in which there only shone, like distant lighthouses, the blue fires of the blast furnaces, and the red fires of the coke ovens. Gradually the night came on, the rain was now falling slowly, continuously, burying this void in its monotonous streaming. Only one voice was still heard, the thick, slow respiration of the pumping engine, breathing both by day and by night."

"Who was the guilty one?" Étienne asks, as mournfully he takes up his life again after the strike's failure. And to this question there is no answer. The miners? Patient they had been, then transformed by passion into brutes. They lacked intelligence, but their first pleas had been wholly reasonable. It is a miner speaking:

"Now that he had set out his words came by themselves. At times he listened to himself with surprise as though a stranger were speaking within him. It was the things amassed within his breast, things he did not even know were there, and which came out in an expansion of his heart. He described the wretchedness that was common to all of them, the hard toil, the brutal life, the wife and little ones crying from hunger in the house. He quoted the recent disastrous payments, the absurd fortnightly wages, eaten up by fines and rest days and brought back to their families in tears. Was it resolved to destroy them?"

The manager, was he guilty? But M. Hennebeau was only an official set up to carry out orders; in himself he is a patient, diligent, and even benevolent personage. There is irony in his own predicament; for as the savage rioters are calling for "bread, bread," he would change places even with them.

The stock holders? The good-natured and benevolent Grégoires were stock holders whose entire income came from the mines. They had prized it only for the happiness of their daughter Cécile; and she had been savagely

murdered by the harmless old man who had given his
life to the mines.

The answer to this question does not lie with any court.
The question must be erased by a new organization of
society. This is the conclusion that Lantier comes to as
mournfully he turns away from the scene of his tragic
failure as a leader of a cause. He has failed. But no
one could have succeeded. He has learned to hate the
miners, as he has also learned to love them. He hates
their sordid life, the odor of onions, the filth, the absence
of any spark of faith in themselves. He hates them. Nor
could success come by enrolling them in an army of rebellion "cutting cables, tearing up rails, breaking lamps.
What a useless task it was." No, rebellion and destruction could do nothing. Yet he thought of his Darwin.
Was the world only a battle field, "where the strong ate
the weak?" "If any class must be devoured, would not
the people, still new and full of life, devour the middle
class, exhausted by enjoyment?"

They were the people who were "great and stainless,
the only nobility and the only strength in which humanity could be dipped afresh." What an "awakening of
truth and justice," on the morning when these, using
lawful methods, more terrible by far than any wrecking
of mines, would take over the power and become masters.
Étienne Lantier has been speaking with more and more
insistent power in these later decades.

Such is one half of the faith of the later Zola. The
other half he proclaims at the end of his trilology, *The
Three Cities, Lourdes, Rome, Paris*. In a way these books
suggest Tolstoi's *Anna Karenina*, only that Zola had his
answer in his pocket before he began, and Tolstoi is not
sure at the end that the answer is an answer at all. *The*

Three Cities is a search for the way out, for a meaning for life in this day of perennial unrest and conflict, for a clue to the coming revolution that shall transform society and make it more just to all. In a way we go back again to the theme of Rousseau's *Social Contract,* how shall society be organized to give each individual his rightful due? And each of the three books by Zola suggests an answer. Which one is right?

The hero of the search in all three is the Abbé Froment. (Is the name a reminder of the parable of the sower of wheat?) His search is for the true way of life, the true motive that will enable him to live richly and devote himself richly to others. He goes first to Lourdes, the city of miracles, to find in the mystery of Christian love and faith and works the right motive. There he finds the Abbé Rose who has devoted himself to Christian loving service, a beautiful figure of devotion to others and idealized charity. But though charity can lead to the miracle of self-sacrifice and beautiful devotion, the ideal is empty of harvest. Wheat sown here cannot serve humanity, as Froment himself confesses later in the *Paris:* "Charity! . . . it is its nothingness and bankruptcy that has killed the priest that there was in me. . . . The sufferings of mankind are every whit as great and unjust as they were when Jesus came."

So the sower must go forth again to sow. This time the wheat falls in Rome, the capital of organized religion. Perhaps there the Abbé, so socially conscious, so desirous of discovering the formula for reform, for adjusting life to true motives, perhaps there he will in a new Christianity, a new Christian socialism, discover justice and the way. This book is in a way a criticism of the answer to life that Tolstoi announced in his later years when he turned peasant and cobbler. But again fact is against him. "The church can solve no social problems." It can give the ideal of absolute justice, but an ideal absolute gets nowhere in a real world. "But when your absolute ideas of justice come upon you, you lose both equilibrium and reason."

Again the sower went forth to sow and the seed fell on Paris; and there it found ground ready for it, and it sprang up bearing a rich harvest. Paris is to become the Eternal City, the City of Light whose radiance will illumine the whole earth. But to discover the fertile ground here we are shown also the whole picture of conflicting creeds and classes that make up the bustling city, and discover where hidden in all this confusion is the true soil. Again as in Tolstoi's *Anna Karenina*, but here with the rapid strokes of a brush that never lingers, we pass in review the varied life of a modern city and all its social ranks and creeds. He describes the decay of modern society, the varied proposals for reform, the false values, and false motives, and finally the gradual awakening of the Abbé to the true motive for living, life itself, and science the new weapon that will blow up the old order, or convert it to new values and new motives. In this, again, the book in spirit is not unlike the Vision of Dante of Hell and Purgatory as a discipline of man's intellect and will.

In this novel we pass in review the aristocracy, like Baron Duvillard, rich through illicit speculation, his wife having intrigues with the man her daughter is to marry; like the Princess Rosamund carousing all night that she may be ready in time in the morning for the guillotining of an anarchist. She is the vagrant caprice of aimless aristocracy: "And she mingled one thing with another; her cosmopolitan tastes, which had thrown her into Anarchism and the society of shady adventurers; her new passion for mysticism and symbolism; her belief that the ideal must triumph over base materialism; her taste for aesthetic verse; and her dream of some unimagined rapture when Hyacinthe should kiss her with his frigid lips in a realm of eternal snow."

There is the old royalist soldier General de Bozonnet, who deplores the democratizing even of war. "By democratizing warfare people have simply killed it . . . for, as soon as it became every man's duty to fight, none were willing to do so." The old general or Zola missed something here. But in the old days "rulers hesitated to throw a whole nation against another nation, for the loss both in life and treasure would be tremendous." There also is the old diplomat of the aristocratic church, itching again for power and prestige, Monseigneur Martha, as deft and sleek a schemer and as unscrupulous a religious politics can produce.

There are the newspapers, the conservative press, Massot, and the yellow, Sagnier, both busy-bodies like gnawing rats, consumed by diplomatically concealed greed, and generous only when it pays in power and publicity. There are the army of politicians, good, bad, indifferent; and the most indifferent is the socialist deputy Mège, who sleeps through the execution of the poor anarchist. There are pure Comtian scientists who proclaim that "science alone would ensure the happiness and pacification of all nations." But they lack all motive to put science into action. There are workers, paupers, reformers, and anarchists, like Salvat whose execution was society's revenge for his bombing a church. "At bottom he is simply a martyr who has followed the wrong track. And yet he has become the scapegoat, laden with the crimes of the whole nation, condemned to pay for one and all."

All of these are futile, for they have no motive that can lead to regeneration. So are all the creeds he passes in review: Fourierism, Socialism, Anarchism, Capitalism, Clericalism, Militarism, all equally futile. It is a picture of the motives for life in the nineties and not far out of perspective today.

The motive for living can come only in the joyous acceptance of life and work. The one gives the necessary will, and the other the object of will. The Abbé discovered one of these in Marie the girl he loved, and the other in his brother, the inventive scientist who devotes his science to human welfare. These three, and the brother's three sons, the genius of art, Antoine, of scholarship, François, and of industry, Thomas, are the family from which will radiate the new light that will illuminate the whole world. Love and intelligent, creative work will save society, and these only when creative work is directed by science. They will cure and rejuvenate the sick Abbé.

"I will cure you . . . simply by allowing life to do its work, for life alone can give you back your health and hope. . . . You will then see that when folks have allotted themselves a task and work together in unison, they escape unhappiness. A task of any kind— yes, that is what is wanted, together with some great passion and frank acceptance of life, so that it may be lived as it should be and loved."

It is with this spirit that the group see the vision of the future: "The sun is sowing Paris with grain. See how it casts the seed of light and health right away to the distant suburbs." Paris—"it is the only ground in the world where Ideas can germinate and bloom. . . . Golden ships, thousands of golden ships, setting forth from the ocean of Paris to enlighten and pacify the world."

There is an optimism and generosity in this picture

hard to associate with the Zola of the early naturalism. Perhaps the best thing I can select for the last word is the pious wish of Pope Leo XIII: "Zola was an enemy of the Church, but he was a frank and straightforward enemy. May his soul repose in Heaven."

XV. A NEW HUMANISM

MATTHEW ARNOLD

"And life ran gaily as the sparkling Thames;
  Before this strange disease of modern life,
  With its sick hurry, its divided aims,
  Its heads o'ertaxed, its palsied hearts, was rife."

Scholar—Gypsy

As one looks at it in retrospect—those perhaps who knew
it in childhood—the age of the great Victorians, Tennyson and Browning, Carlyle and Matthew Arnold, Gladstone and Lord Salisbury, seems a placid era, as placid
as its monumental queen. An age of hard work, wealth,
and honest respectability at home, and discipline and
responsible empire abroad. An age apostrophied by Kip-
ling in the *Recessional,* with a trust in God's providence
and the destiny of Britain to leaven the earth. An age
when the serious problems of today were yet unvocal
infants, when General Booth and the Salvation Army
and County Boards and Liberal laws could manage the
social evils at home, and missionaries and British-made
goods could carry the gospel to the benighted. It seems
the age of potent faith and solid accomplishment. How
different, we think, its placidity and naïve cock-sureness
from our contemporary disillusionment and doubt.

306

Yet Arnold, writing nearly seventy-five years ago with the perennial yearning for a lost joy of youth when life ran gaily, mourns the "strange disease of modern life," its "sick hurry," "its palsied heart." And the thoughtful Victorian, be he Carlyle or Tennyson, seldom allowed his heart to swell with youthful pride at the spectacle of "dominion over palm and pine." It was an age of great accomplishment, of splendid triumph in all fields of national endeavor, from the laboratory of science to the shop of industry, from the library of the scholar-poet to the hall of statesman and legislator, from the humble acres of the crofter to the far-flung battle-line of ever advancing conquest. *Civis Britannicus Sum* in those days of Disraeli's triumphs brought something not wholly different from the pride of the Imperial Roman in the days of Trajan and the Antonines. Yet England was seldom happy and never gay.

It was a time, as Arnold called it in one of his letters, "not profound, not ungrand, not unmoving; but unpoetical." And this in spite of the growing reputations of its chief poets, Tennyson and Browning, and its constellations of lesser poets—seldom in any age of the world's history were there as many—among whom Arnold himself is no unworthy star. There was, however, no Chaucer, no Shakespeare, no Milton, no Shelley, yes, and no Pope. To be sure the supreme genius like Shakespeare or Milton comes to a people as an unexpected gift of Providence, to make the nation blessed among all peoples. And many are there among the nations that have never been so signalled out by destiny. But even poets of a lesser stature come and express the thoughts and ideals and aspirations of their time to a nice perfection, crystallizing once and for all what otherwise had been left unuttered, bringing to a focus in their radiant personalities what otherwise would have been unintelligibly diffused. Such a poet was Pope.

But there is something of a groping after unreality even in the best of Tennyson, or something of a triumphant faith without real conviction in Browning, that suggests the effort to convince oneself by iteration of a creed to compensate for the lack of conviction by evidence. These perhaps seem hard sayings to some. Let me illustrate by examples. That it was an age that was striving after new values for life, and had been since Waterloo; that the old settled order, partly feudal with the upper middle, land owning class in large control, was giving way reluctantly and slowly to the new industrial democracy; that a new social conscience was emerging with a larger sympathy for the unfortunate debris of society; that the ethics of liberalism and its economics left much to be desired for the welfare of the nation as a whole; all this is pretty obvious if, for example, one has dipped ever so lightly into the prophecies of Carlyle. It is this coming of the new era that Tennyson sings in his well-known Song of the New Year in *In Memoriam*.

> "Ring out the old, ring in the new,
>   Ring happy bells across the snow:
>   The year is going, let him go;
>   Ring out the false, ring in the true."

But it is not a wholly joyous song, the joy is forced, or at best put on for the occasion as a festive garment, and not the sincere speech of one convinced. Compare it with Shelley whose faith was complete conviction in the closing lines of the *Prometheus*.

> "To love, and bear; to hope till Hope creates
>   From its own wreck the thing it contemplates."

Or, and perhaps better, take Tennyson's profession of faith, again in the *In Memoriam*.

> "Thou wilt not leave us in the dust;
>   Thou madest man, he knows not why,
>   He thinks he was not made to die;
> And thou hast made him: thou art just."

How often these lines have been repeated, and yet what slender conviction of faith they carry. It is faith against the overwhelming convictions of doubt, not the old faith that could maintain itself against mountains: the *credo quia impossibile est*, the ability to believe the impossible. Only Lewis Carroll's White Knight in the Victorian age could do that. Tennyson's faith is a *pis aller*, a grasping at a straw in a sea of doubt. And those of us who have quoted these lines, "Thou madest man, he knows not why," for comfort to our souls, have found only a shallow comfort. If that is all—?

Browning, though more vocal in his creed, and more given to say, "I know," than "I believe," has not much more genuine conviction to offer, when set beside a convinced poet, let us say Dante. As a boy I used to read with edification *Saul*, and my master, a Victorian with the Victorian faith, never ceased to underscore the conclusion of David's song to the distracted king.

> " 'Tis the weakness in strength, that I cry for! my flesh
>   that I seek
> In the Godhead! I seek and I find it. O Saul, it shall be
> A face like my face that receives thee; a man like to me,
> Thou shalt love and be loved by, forever: a Hand like
>   this hand
> Shall throw open the gates of new life to thee! See the
>   Christ stand!"

But do these lines carry faith to the point of intuitive knowledge that is forced even from an unwilling reader by the last vision of the great Florentine?

The Victorian age is the age of doubt, but a doubt that will not be honest to itself in the chief Victorian poets: "not unprofound, not ungrand, not unmoving; but unpoetical." Poetry must be utterly sincere, faithfully honest, if it is to approach greatness; and in this test the Victorians have, nearly all of them—there are great exceptions —left something much to be desired. As a sign of their part futility, how seldom are they read now for precisely the reason for which they wrote for their own age, their religion. It is chiefly this that we ignore in them. But with Dante, from an age utterly unlike ours in faith, it is his religious conviction that speaks to us with undiminished power.

The result is that Victorian prose, where the Victorian mind is honest and unafraid, has something for us quite different from Victorian poetry. There the conflict between Faith and Doubt, though it remains a conflict with issues undecided, is an honest conflict with no quarter asked and no victory confidently announced. The limitations of Victorian poetry are seen at their clearest in the series of narrative poems on which Tennyson labored from youth to age, *The Idylls of the King*. Splendid as they are as versions of the age-old stories of King Arthur and his knights, and the gradual breaking down of the edifice of chivalry founded upon truth and moral excellence, they seem utterly to miss the dominant issues of the nineteenth century in England, faith and doubt and the moral implications of the new order that was rising on the ruins of the old.

The doubt in the nineteenth century in England was the gift of science with its implications of man's place in nature; the new sciences of biology and sociology, and the narrowing horizon they seemed to be granting to

the ideal of moral freedom. The old faith was main-
taining that man was not "made to die" like the rest of
nature, and that

> "those first affections,
> Those shadowy recollections,
> Which, be they what they may,
> Are yet the fountain light of all our day,
> Are yet a master light of all our seeing."

This "master light" is the essence of faith. But in *The
Idylls of the King* where is the allegory of this conflict?
Tristram, Mordred, Guinevere and Lancelot whose mis-
deeds broke up the Round Table, or Galahad and Perci-
val who journeyed for the Holy Grail? The spiritual
mysticism of the one, the spiritual blindness of the other,
suggest problems in conduct to be sure, but not problems
of deep significance for the practical nineteenth century.
And King Arthur's climax in his last speech with Guinevere describes the conflict between an ideal and the real
which even to Tennyson's own age must have been purely
visionary:

> "Lo, I forgive thee, as Eternal God
> Forgives! do thou for thine own soul the rest.
> But how to take last leave of all I loved?—
> Let no man dream but that I love thee still.
> Perchance, and so thou purify thy soul,
> And so thou lean on our fair father Christ,
> Hereafter in that world where all are pure
> We two may meet before high God, and thou
> Wilt spring to me, and claim me thine, and know
> I am thine husband.—Leave me that,
> I charge thee, my last hope."

Here we have something much nearer to the Calvin-
istic quarrel with humanity on the ground of original sin,
than the nineteenth century quarrel on the ground of a

division between reason and faith. I suspect Saint Paul, had he been less the misogynist he was, might have written these same *Idylls*. And where in their beautiful romance is there suggested even the larger social issues that were bewildering thoughtful people?

But the prose of the same age is completely in accord with the new currents of thought. Dickens and Thackeray, even Anthony Trollope, are never out of touch with its perplexities. George Eliot plunges toward an attempted solution with the eagerness of a crusader. And at the end of the century Samuel Butler and George Meredith can well be said, as poets of ages gone by, to be the master spirits of an age, and this a troubled one.

It is this insufficiency of the chief poets, before the chief moral and mental conflict of the age, that called forth the criticism not long ago, from a contemporary, that doubt and bewilderment then was not as painful as it is today; that Tennyson and Browning wore their melancholy as a not unpleasant poetic exercise, as the chronic invalid enjoys the exercise of frail health when it is accompanied with attention and flowers. On Arnold he is a bit more severe. He "filled our gardens with a scent of nice crushed fundamentalism in an age when the redoubtable word was yet unborn." Not quite fair to the first two, and quite wrong about the third. Arnold's faith in ruins, and his poetry proclaiming his doubt, is not a thing of fragrance and gardens. It is an honest man's honest conviction that without faith a people perish, and an attempt to find a substitute for the old religious convictions. But more of this later.

For the new philosophy of science fell upon the conscience of England about the middle of the century with the same crushing weight that the guilt of slavery carried for the conscience of Whitman's and Emerson's America.

"So near is grandeur to our dust
So near is God to man;
When duty whispers low thou must,
The youth replies, 'I can.'"

The appearance of Darwin's *Origin of Species* divided long friendships. It was regarded not as a book on biological theory, but as an assault delivered from a new quarter on the rock of the Holy Scriptures, and its adherents were seen not as sincere searchers for the truth, but as advocates of the Anti-Christ. It seemed deliberately announced only to degrade the creature into whose nostrils God had breathed the breath of life. Carlyle called it the "monkey damnification of mankind," and was never able to forgive its advocates. Even near the end of his life one day Huxley saw him solitary, walking on the opposite side of the street, and crossed over. Carlyle raised his eyes and said simply, "You are Huxley who thinks we are descended from monkeys," and passed on.

The weapons of theology and of statesmanship were polished for the fray. The debate at the meeting of the British Association in 1860 is a classic, the spectacle of one side having not the slightest idea of the scientific issues involved. Bishop Samuel Wilberforce, otherwise a mild, unexceptionable man, went at the thing as a mediaeval inquisitor before a new and dangerous heresy. Gladstone, an authority on the British budget, and a lover of Homer, wrote a stupendous volume of biblical criticism. And in my young boyhood when I had read Mrs. Humphry Ward's *Robert Elsmere,* a timely novel expressing much of her father Arnold's doubts, an instructor, worried over its possible consequences, put into my hands Gladstone's *Impregnable Rock of the Holy Scripture.* The effect was overwhelming. No Goliath ever came out more terribly panoplied. But he was a stuffed Goliath, like Wagner's dragon.

Naturally there were those who made the effort at a "compromise," a word that has come to describe the age. Tennyson welcomes the science, but will not receive it into the secret places of his mind where it can give its contagion to his faith. Browning tries to discover a spiritual process in evolution, much as Goethe had done a half-century before. Tennyson's *Locksley Hall*, though written much earlier, became a favorite with those of tender conscience. "Yet I doubt not through the ages one enduring purpose runs." The line has a pleasing emotional promise. It is impossible for faith to reject the thought. And there are many yet today who will recall that book, planned with something that resembles the logic of science, enormously popular and rich with unexpected meaning, Dr. Drummond's *Natural Law in the Spiritual World*. Yes, there were efforts aplenty at a compromise; but it is unfair again to speak of the Victorian compromise as something describing a shrinking by the Victorians from the full import of the new scientific discoveries. They accepted them, mournfully perhaps or gladly, or fought them savagely and unscientifically; as we today do the philosophical implications of relativity in physics and the sex obsession of some psychologists, but we do not call our quarter century the Age of the Freudian Compromise,—perhaps we should.

For these Victorians, Arnold was a sturdy man-at-arms, training himself from youth in the exercise of his intellectual sword and spear. The son of the famous headmaster of Rugby, he had the best that England and the Continent had to offer. Better than Tennyson, better than Browning, better than Carlyle, he is the man—

though never the genius—to represent as nearly as it could be represented by any one individual the best of the age. It was an age of reflection and prose rather than poetry, as he himself said, and his poetry even is reflective. It was an age of new ideas coming too rapidly for complete assimilation, hence better for the discursive essay than even the technique then of the novel. And Arnold next to his rare poetry is seen at his best in his many-sided essays.

Early in his career this young man is afflicted with doubt, and a conviction; doubt of the prevailing order, and a conviction that without an abiding and genuine faith a people perish. He as resolutely faces the bleak emptiness of a world without a faith, as he resolutely faces the problem of discovering a faith that will transcend the more intellectual formulas of science, and give poetry to life and illuminate conduct. Here is an ambitious program, but thoroughgoing. It inspires his criticism, it gives his definition of poetry and its place in human life, it turns in his essays to a critical examination of the life of the time and to the search for a substitute for the outgrown religion and social creeds.

For a serene wholesome philosophy of life can only be discovered if one can see life whole, with all its motives for living, intellectual as well as moral, in perfect accord. Hebbel in his tragedies attempted to discover a metaphysical formula for this, and condemned the ingrained habit of partiality, *Einigseitigkeit* as the source of all evil in the world. Arnold, the practical Englishman, avoids the metaphysical road. Dostoevsky, too, in his novels seeks for the same wholesomeness through psychology, in much the contemporary manner. From Arnold this power of psychological analysis is largely withheld; and I suspect the moral disturbances of the

Karamazov brothers would have appeared to his English reticence as sheer moral anarchy. He early sees his model for the good life in the figure of the old Greek poet Sophocles,

> "whose even-balanced soul,
> From first youth tested up to extreme old age,
> Business could not make dull, nor passion wild;
>
> Who saw life steadily, and saw it whole;
> The mellow glory of the Attic stage,
> Singer of sweet Colonus, and its child."

It is this lack of balance, this lack of wholesome moral purpose, and moral faith, that makes Arnold's age unpoetic, shakes its heart with palsy, and divides its aims. In what is one of his best poems he describes the symptoms and their cause. Even a wandering gypsy, who has a motive for life, is better than those dwelling amid the ruins of their faiths.

> "And we
> Light half-believers of our casual creeds,
> Who never deeply felt, nor clearly will'd,
> Whose insight never has borne fruit in deeds,
> Whose vague resolves never have been fulfill'd;
> For whom each year we see
> Breeds new beginnings, disappointments new;
> Who hesitate and falter life away,
> And lose to-morrow the ground won to-day."

Loss of the old faith and no substitute that can supply a motive for life, and in the meanwhile the new world of knowledge, science, that is building a new external world now quite unfamiliar to the wandering, lost soul. It is the old parable of the soul, with the devil banished, swept and garnished and made ready, only to receive seven other devils, with its later state more evil and unhappy than its former. The old theology with its moral faith was dead, and the mind cleansed of its decayed beliefs; in their place can the new intellectual faith of science supply a motive for moral conduct? The question was, and still is a hard one.

In the *Dover Beach* Arnold asks this very question:

> "The Sea of Faith
> Was once, too, at the full, and round earth's shore
> Lay like the folds of a bright girdle furl'd.
> But now I only hear
> Its melancholy, long, withdrawing roar,
> Retreating to the breath
> Of the night-wind, down the vast edges drear
> And naked shingles of the world.
>
> "Ah, love, let us be true
> To one another! for the world, which seems
> To lie before us like a land of dreams,
> So various, so beautiful, so new,
> Hath really neither joy, nor love, nor light,
> Nor certitude, nor peace, nor help for pain;
> And we are here as on a darkling plain
> Swept with confused alarms of struggle and flight,
> Where ignorant armies clash by night."

The "naked shingles of the world," "we are here as on a darkling plain," "where ignorant armies clash by night," the absence of joy, and love and light, it is a dreary picture. And the compensation the poet finds is only that of a seeming beauty, a seeming newness, "a land of dreams." These are all that the new age with its new knowledge has to offer; for science has never pretended to offer certainties for the old certainties it displaced. For the old faith in God, immortality, and happiness, it offers only cold formulas, and these only hypotheses, with the promise of ceaseless search and no prospect of verification: the law of selection and survival, the formulas of physics and chemistry, and the economic law of supply and demand. All of reality that the poet now can cling to for motives for conduct is the shivering of naked helpless creatures that cling together in their misery: "Ah, love, let us be true to one another." Human love, and truth in human dealings, slender fare for the soul that once was satisfied with nothing less than God and Heaven.

Such was Arnold, the doubter, not unflinching but sensitive, never able quite, like Montaigne who went even farther and was unafraid, to see that man must learn to trust only in the qualities he possesses, and to trust wisely, carefully exploring those qualities; never able quite with the ancient Greek to carry out the old injunction that to know oneself is the highest attainable wisdom. There is in this attitude of desolation none of the garden "fragrance of nice crushed fundamentalism." The pain is too acute, though the Stoic repression reminds one of Arnold's chief hero, the Emperor Marcus Aurelius. Above all there is here none of that sneered at "Victorian compromise." It is only the cold intellectual to whom faith means nothing that can sneer.

To show the lengths to which this mental malady can go, when honest and uncompromising, he wrote the *Empedocles on Etna*. Here is a poem that deserves to be set beside Shelley's *Prometheus* to show how in the years that had intervened optimism was gradually replaced by its opposite. Both poems lean heavily on the Greek, both are founded upon Greek story, only Empedocles was a well known philosopher, some of whose ideas have come down through his successors and in fragments of his own poems. Myths gathered about his life, especially of his sojourn in Sicily where he was greatly honored with garlands and wreaths. He is said to have restored a woman to life, to have controlled the seasons, and finally to have leaped into Etna, but with a motive quite the opposite to that Arnold gives.

But Arnold's story is the more consistent for the sake of the English poet's moral. Empedocles was in a way one of the forerunners of what has been called materialistic philosophy. He found no difference between man and the rest of nature, holding one destiny for both. Lucretius was later to celebrate him with enthusiasm in his great poem *On the Nature of Things*. To Arnold, Empedocles is the thorough-going scientific mind that has explored all knowledge and is now without illusion and without faith, and without a motive for love.

In the poem the hero, heart-sick and hating humanity, forsakes the crowd that, though they throng his path, will not follow his counsel, resentful after reviving a dead woman, because they demand an explanation of the miracle, and makes his way up the sides of Etna. He is accompanied by Pausanias, a disciple, and at a distance by Callicles, a joyous harp player. Pausanias is eager with inquiry. Callicles, affectionate youth, wishes to charm with music and poetry the wasted heart of his idolized philosopher. The dialogue with interludes of music, which are a call back to the joy of living, gives its dramatic form to the poem.

Pausanias pleads for the master's return, and asks for an explanation of the miracle. The first request is unanswered by the philosopher, for the second he suggests instead a recipe for meeting life bravely: neither ask nor expect more than nature can give. The fault with humanity is that it mistakes its desires for the order of nature, and its *wishes* for its *rights*.

> "And why is it, that still
> Man with his lot thus fights?—
> 'Tis that he makes this *will*
> The measure of his *rights*,
> And believes Nature outraged if his will's gainsaid.

> "Couldst thou, Pausanias, learn
> How deep a fault is this;
> Couldst thou but once discern
> Thou hast no *right* to bliss,
> No title from the Gods to welfare and repose."

Man's attitude leads to a multitude of evils; for first, who knows whether nature has any thought for human welfare?

> "Nor is the thirst to blame.
> Man errs not that he deems
> His welfare his true aim,
> He errs because he dreams
> The world does but exist that welfare to bestow."

Man acts as an impolite guest entertained by nature, the host, and desirous of prescribing the manner of his entertainment.

> "But we—as some rude guest
> Would change, where'er he roam,
> The manners there profess'd
> To those he brings from home—
> We mark not the world's course, but would have *it* take *ours*."

But this evil state goes even deeper; when man suffers for his impertinence in going against nature, he ascribes his evil to gods whom he invents for the purpose.

> "So, loath to suffer mute,
> We, peopling the void air,
> Make Gods to whom to impute
> The ills we ought to bear;
> With God and Fate to rail at, suffering easily."

Because his knowledge is imperfect, he postulates perfection, and again invents gods who know all.

> "Fools! That in man's brief term
> He cannot all things view,
> Affords no ground to affirm
> That there are Gods who do;
> Nor does being weary prove that he has where to rest."

And finally as his most impertinent gesture of all, he discovers a heaven, where he will attain the peace impossible for such as he here on earth.

> "That we must feign a bliss
> Of doubtful future date,
> And, while we dream on this,
> Lose all our present state,
> And relegate to *worlds yet distant* our repose?"

Then, that his final words may give the sum of wisdom, he utters the familiar sceptic's injunction, live within your means.

> "I say: Fear not! Life still
> Leaves human effort scope.
> But since life teems with ill,
> Nurse no extravagant hope;
> Because thou must not dream, thou need'st not then despair!"

Wordly wisdom can go no farther, without faith. But here also is no motive for action. "Nurse no extravagant hope." Compared with Callicles' carefree joy in life for its own sake, this is no hope at all. And Empedocles has learned to hate human nature. Doubt has bred hatred, and hatred loneliness. "And being lonely thou art miserable."

> "For something has impair'd thy spirit's strength,
> And dried its self-sufficing fount of joy.
> Thou canst not live with men nor with thyself—.

"Then we could still enjoy, then neither thought
Nor outward things were closed and dead to us;
But we received the shock of mighty thoughts
On simple minds with a pure natural joy;
And if the sacred load oppress'd our brain,
We had the power to feel the pressure eased,
The brow unbound, the thoughts flow free again,
In the delightful commerce of the world."

There is nothing left now to him but intellect and knowledge, and this has destroyed peace of mind and joy of living. For knowledge is nothing, and nothing will come of nothing. The thought is maddening.

"But mind, but thought—
If these have been the master part of us—
Where will *they* find their parent element?
What will receive *them*, who will call *them* home?
But we shall still be in them, and they in us,
And we shall be the strangers of the world,
And they will be our lords, as they are now;
And keep us prisoners of our consciousness,
And never let us clasp and feel the All
But through their forms, and modes and stifling veils.
And we shall be unsatisfied as now;
And we shall feel the agony of thirst,
The ineffable longing for the life of life
Baffled for ever; and still thought and mind
Will hurry us with them on their homeless march,
Over the unallied unopening earth,
Over the unrecognizing sea; while air
Will blow us fiercely back to sea and earth."

And fearless searcher that he is and eager for truth, he plunges into the fiery crater. The nihilism of pure intellect, the hopelessness of a purely scientific creed. We have seen the same theme, in a different setting in Goethe's Faust, when the man, who had pursued all knowledge to the final blank wall, lifts the chalice of poison. Faust is saved by the temptation of the Devil for a new assault on life. Callicles with his poetry was not as potent as Mephistopheles.

But to Arnold it is only the poetry of life that can save man from the nihilism of intellect. It is the only means that will, with its illumination, give a new motive to conduct. Its imaginative insight alone can privilege the poet to discover, what the scientist-philosopher, Empedocles, with all his wisdom, never discovered, the view of life steady and whole. "Modern poetry," he wrote in a letter to Clough, "can only subsist by its contents: by becoming a complete *magister vitae* [master of life] as the poetry of the ancients did: by including, as theirs did, religion with poetry, instead of existing as poetry only, and leaving religious wants to be supplied by the Christian religion." And he might again have added his comment on contemporary poets and poetry. In effect, this is to say in one word, that poetry somehow must supply the new faith for the old that the intellect alone had so painfully destroyed. Poetry, a substitute for religion, or a new religion, adding richness and completeness to life, and illuminating and giving values to conduct. Shelley had once, a half-century and more before him, said something not wholly different, and written a great poem as a monument to his faith. Arnold did not write his monument in poetry— he was no poet of the stature of Shelley—but he wrote his essays, many of them controversial in those days of controversy, but some of them models of lucid and genial persuasion.

Arnold was not an Empedocles. It really is not necessary to prove that Arnold had at heart a deep craving for religion or at least for the thing he called "righteousness and the will of God." This was his good English inheritance fed for centuries on the moving and poetic liturgies of the church. But if a religion it must rest "on what can be verified"; the foundations can no longer be the pillars of dogmatic theology, for its language, unlike the poetry of the liturgies, is "scholastic and scientific." Nor is his idea of religion, as with Rousseau and Chateaubriand, a thing purely of poetic imagination and feelings, for these are only a fraction and a small fraction of life. "And so, when we are asked, what is the object of religion? let us reply: Conduct. And when we are further asked, what is conduct? Let us answer: Three-fourths of life." This is his central idea for the new humanism, an ethical idea sustained by poetry. Conduct touched by emotion, illuminated with inspiration, giving the joy in life and its activities that Empedocles lost, and truth to human relations the poet longed for in *Dover Beach*.

> "The noblest souls of whatever creed, the pagan Empedocles as well as the Christian Paul, have insisted on the necessity of an inspiration, a joyful emotion, to make moral action perfect.—The paramount virtue of religion is, that it has *lighted up* morality, that it has supplied the emotion and inspiration needful for carrying the Sage along the narrow way perfectly, for carrying the ordinary man along it at all."

An "inspiration for conduct," "morality touched by emotion," "the object of religion is conduct," "so much is there incalculable, so much that belongs to *not ourselves*, in conduct": I select chance phrases, from here and there, but all significant of a source beyond the individual from which these religious yearnings and values spring. Religion is not then the outpouring of the single human heart, but the response of the mind and the heart to something higher than the individual whose influence is felt on the whole of human life, and above all on the meaning of conduct. Though Arnold had turned his back on the throne of the theological Jehovah, he cannot stand alone in a world without Deity, the "Eternal, not ourselves, that makes for righteousness." It may be an ethical creed, but it must be tinged with emotion, the God may be an abstract idea, but he makes for illumined conduct, it must be verifiable by the tests of science, but it must meet the imaginative requirement also of poetry; more than this it must supply the only available motive for life. For the total man, therefore, the truer conception of God is "as the Eternal Power, not ourselves, by which all things fulfill the law of our being: by which, therefore, we fulfill the law of our being so far as our being is aesthetic and intellective, as well as so far as it is moral." Such in a word is Arnold's definition of the needs and formula of the new religion.

Education and discipline, therefore, of the will, and education and discipline of the intellect, the ideals of the two great forces that have dominated history, Hebraism and Hellenism as he calls them, conscience and intelligence. Each has its special function, but alone each results in a disproportioned and even grotesque man. Only when these two work jointly and in perfect harmony does man come to perfect stature, as once he did in classical Greece. How often Arnold turns for comfort to the days of Sophocles and Pericles, that bright day of the great triumph of human nature. One wonders if the old classical poet would have recognized himself in the idol that Arnold and the new classicists set up to worship afar. "But the grace and serenity"—how Arnold loves this word—"is that of which Greece and Greek art suggest the admirable ideals of perfection,—a serenity which comes from having made order among ideas and harmonized them."

Hellenism, Hebraism, these two motives of life—intelligence and conscience.

"The uppermost idea with Hellenism is to see things as they really are; the uppermost idea with Hebraism is conduct and obedience.— The Greek quarrel with the body and its desires is, that they hinder right thinking, the Hebrew quarrel with them is, that they hinder right acting.—The governing ideal of Hellenism is *spontaneity of consciousness;* that of Hebraism, *strictness of conscience.*

"To get rid of one's ignorance, to see things as they are, and by seeing them as they are to see them in their beauty, is the simple and attractive ideal which Hellenism holds out before human nature"— [quoting Xenophon] " 'The best man is he who most feels that he *is* perfecting himself.'—As Hellenism speaks of thinking clearly, seeing things in their essence and beauty, as a grand and precious feat for man to achieve, so Hebraism speaks of becoming conscious of sin, of awakening to a sense of sin, as a feat of this kind."

These two factors in human conduct have nearly always worked at cross purposes. The decline of Greece was because of the over-cultivation of the pure intellect; and the wilful destruction of Empedocles is a warning of the aridity and loneliness of the intellect that has only itself to feed upon. The Middle Ages and the later fires of Puritanism were the triumph of the consciousness of sin and the denial of the intellect. The moral sense, too, can be sombrely self-destructive and grotesquely ugly. Its excesses can be seen in the Inquisitor who condemned Galileo, the puritan that destroyed beauty in religion, the saint that condemned himself to prayer and asceticism. Without character, Hellenism is "something frivolous, vain and weak," or arid and cynical; without true intelligence, character is on the other hand "something raw, blind and dangerous."

But in their perfect and serene harmony they are Culture, the Tradition of Human Excellence, the Ideal of Humanity. And, here, as near as we can get it, is Arnold's idea of a God, "the eternal, not ourselves, that makes for righteousness." It is the belief in and pursuit of excel-

lence, of perfection. It looks for the humanization of man.
It is the motive for human civilization and progress.
"Power of conduct, power of intellect and knowledge,
the power of beauty, the power of social life and manners. Expansion, conduct, science, beauty, manners,—
here are the conditions of civilization, the claimants which
man must satisfy before he can be humanized." Culture,
the tradition becomes a motive for life of "a finely tempered nature . . . a harmonious perfection, a perfection
in which the characters of beauty and intelligence are
both present. . . . 'the two noblest of things, *sweetness*
and *light.*' "

And Arnold describes culture with a persuasiveness
that reminds of the pleading of the first great missionary
of Christianity: "Culture lies beyond machinery, culture
hates hatred; culture has one great passion, the passion
for sweetness and light. It has one even greater!—the
passion for making them prevail. It is not satisfied till
we *all* come to a perfect man; it knows that the sweetness and light of the few must be imperfect until the raw
and unkindled masses of humanity are touched with
sweetness and light." Culture "does not try to reach
down to the level of inferior classes; it does not try to
win them for this or that sect of its own, with ready-made
judgments and watchwords. It seeks to do away with
classes and sects.—This is the *social idea;* and the men of
culture are true apostles of equality."

But this is poetry, and also a description in Shelley's
words almost of its office; ethical culture through poetry,
with its altars now dedicated to an Idea. The personal
God, no longer verifiable, is displaced and into his temple
now swept and garnished comes the abstract God whose
ministers must be, not theologians and scholastic phrase
makers, but poets with the wealth of their imaginations.

So poetry assumes for Arnold—or should reassume—its high office of an inspiration for, and a criticism of life; and at the same time brings that other fourth of life, quite as necessary as conduct, Beauty. "The need for beauty is a real and now rapidly growing need in man." Part of this was supplied by the poetry of the church liturgies. But there are other beauties as well, some most intimate. "It is a great error to think that whatever is thus perceived to be poetry ceases to be available in religion. The noblest races are those which know how to make the most serious use of poetry."

There has been much ink needlessly spilt over the question what Arnold meant by the phrase "poetry is a criticism of life." But when he tells us that by its service to Culture it lights up morality, giving it beauty and emotional flavor, he is in effect putting it into the place once occupied by religion, whose theologically derived moral code can no longer serve as a guide for and a judgment on life. Religion once had its judgments on life; and its commandments, thou shalt and thou shalt not, were the implications of a God of love and justice whose will it was that love of justice should prevail among men. With the waning of belief in the personal God his commands lost their transcendent and central authority, with the result that anarchy came to prevail and men were lost amid the multitudinousness of conflicting human wills. Again to give direction and unity to life, and the necessary inspiration for conduct, and restore the beauty of harmony, Arnold offers his idea of poetry with its appeal to the mind and imagination, these to serve now as critic and judge.

The cult of beauty, not as an aesthetic escape from the multitude of the commonplace into an ideal realm, as with many a romantic, but as a moral code to cope with the multitude of the commonplace, to illuminate it, and give it rich meaning, this is Arnold's creed for the poet and his belief in the poet's high calling. Poets "must begin with an Idea," he wrote once to Clough, "of the world in order not to be prevailed over by the world's multitudinousness: or if they cannot get that, at least with isolated ideas: and all other things shall (perhaps) be added unto them." To discover and abide by the central issues of life, in their light to discover harmony in the world, and the tradition of excellence, and in his poetry to make this known, this is to be the critic of life and to serve in the eternal warfare to make the will of God and righteousness to prevail.

There is, then, in this new religion offered by Arnold, as a substitute for the old, a new trinity. Culture, Morals, Beauty. Culture, the harmonious state of mind, the perfection and balance of all faculties, trained and disciplined by the study of the tradition of human excellence; morals, the active faculty as a motive for life; and beauty, the inspiration and illumination that gives value to conduct. And for poetic myth, with its charm for the imagination, which all religion has employed to fortify religious belief, there are the *Aberglaube*, the half-beliefs and half-superstitions which as Goethe says are the poetry of life. For these there are the poetic narratives that strew the early path of every religion and are expressed in its liturgies. These are like the vines that adorn the walls of ancient castles, lending to their austere and ruined grandeur the charm of life. They are allegories of human worth and aspiration, and serviceable to the ministration of poetry.

The new Humanism is the phrase that has more than once been applied to the striving for human excellence and culture, and the effort to establish a harmony in life. For an example of what human nature unaided by supernatural aid might accomplish, it looked with admiration to classical Greece. Here were the beginnings of the great tradition of man, sound in all faculties, gazing unafraid upon a human universe which it was his moral duty to reduce to intelligible order. In these our later days of threatened chaos there is the renewed duty that man set his house in order, looking only to the tradition of human excellence and his place in that tradition for aid.

What has been Arnold's influence? How large has been his following? What he wrote of himself and his beloved Oxford is as true today as when he wrote it:

"We have not won our political battles, we have not carried our main points, we have not stopped our adversaries' advance, we have not marched victoriously with the modern world; but we have told silently upon literature and upon the mind of the country, we have prepared currents of feeling which sap our adversaries' position when it seems gained, we have kept up our own communication with the future."

XVI. THE IMMANENT WILL
AND ITS DESIGNS

HARDY

We know that even as larks in cages sing
Unthoughtful of deliverance from the curse
That holds them lifelong in a latticed hearse,
We ply spasmodically our pleasuring.

Winter Words

THOMAS HARDY is not easy reading, even now, for those of tender conscience. In 1870, when yet a young man, when people's imaginations were fired by the Franco-Prussian war, he had been deeply impressed by the stolid persistence of an old peasant, in spite of war and invasion, turning the furrows of his ancestral acres. The picture came vividly to memory in 1914; and he gave us one of his greatest poems:

Only a man harrowing clods
In a slow silent walk
With an old horse that stumbles and nods
Half asleep as they stalk.

Only thin smoke without flame
From the heaps of couch-grass;
Yet this will go onward the same
Though Dynasties pass.

Here is one side, and a very significant one, of this poet. There is another poem, a very different one, which

331

gives another. It has the innocent title of *Panthera*. It is
the story of an old soldier, who had served in the various
Roman campaigns of the first century, A.D.

> "One in youth-time graced
> With indescribable charm, so I have heard,
> Yea, magnetism impossible to word."

But his age was bent by a hidden remorse. It is the story
of his son, as he fancied, told to his friend who longed for
a son in whose advance he could secretly joy.

> "Cancel such wishes, boy!
> A son may be a comfort or a curse,
> A seer, a doer, a coward, a fool; yea, worse—
> A criminal."

For in his best young manhood he had served in Judea,
and as subcenturian had led a company of soldiers from
Judea north to Tyre. They had paused in the beautiful
valley of Galilee at a little village called Nazareth to rest
the ailing soldiers. There at a well where the maidens
came to draw water he had met and loved

> "a slim girl, coy
> Even as a fawn, meek, and as innocent."

They had loved, and then the soldiers passed on.

Thirty and more years later again he is in Judea as
commander of the garrison. The Jews are restless and
sullen. There are to be some punishments, the crucifixion
of one who had raised some heat among the populace,
and to assure the peace of the city he goes with a company of soldiers to guard the scene. There among the
crowd pressing about the cross he sees the victim's mother,
"a weeping woman whose stained countenance . . . was
mocked by the crude rays of the afternoon." He recognized her; it was the woman he had known as a girl; and
the one on the cross, the criminal, was their son.

"And when he had breathed his last
The woman went. I saw her never again. . . .
Now glares my moody meaning on you, friend?—
That when you talk of offspring as sheer joy
So trustingly, you blink contingencies,
Fors Fortuna! He who goes fathering
Gives frightful hostages to hazardry!"

Here is something startling in the turn it takes, giving
an angle to the tragedy quite away from the routine, and
doubly ironical because so intimately personal. The first
poem is more easy, for it throws against the clash of
dynasties and the changing drama of history the one
thing that persists, the plodding will to live. But both of
these are Hardy; and it is this range that makes it easy
for the tender conscience to label him as pessimist and
faith-snatcher, lacking in a healthy joy and acceptance of
life. For Hardy takes a very large and unusual slice of
life for his theme, he is utterly modern in his thought, and
yet he has a universality in his emotions that makes him
also a poet for all time.

Yet his attitude toward life is elusive. It seems to
differ from that, let us say, of Tolstoi or Dostoevsky,
with whom we are right in comparing him, who seem to
clasp and hold it tight until, like Proteus, life has revealed
its true nature. Rather we might say that Hardy prefers
to see it in its Protean shapes, all of which seem as startlingly strange or unexpected to the tender conscience as
the two poems cited, and as destructive to any naïve faith
in the excellence of human destiny.

Excellence of human destiny—Tolstoi had sought it
in the Will of God, the Creator and Maintainer of this
world, and in the love for man. He still, in spite of his
conviction of the reality of evil, preserved the naïve faith
of Rousseau that man is by nature good, though the false

issues of society may turn him from the path of righteousness. Dostoevsky, as sincerely as Tolstoi, perseveres in his faith that humanity is sound and its destiny, at least in part, of its own making, if only the right action can be discovered which shall reconcile the inner conflict of emotion and impulse, and give an undivided motive for life. And in consequence both put man near the center of the universe of action and moral conduct, with the balance always tipped sharply in the favor of man. If there is a God—and both are devoutly convinced of his moral necessity—his powers are allied with that of man in the campaign to make righteousness prevail. Man is by no means secure, but the spiritual powers are moral and benign, even intelligent, and with right human effort, the tradition of human excellence at least is secure. Even suffering, for Dostoevsky, is its very vindication.

Arnold in his long campaign for culture to make righteousness and the will of God prevail finds his cause beset with embattled ignorance and half-knowledge. His moral discipline is more than half an intellectual one, and against such human excellence are arrayed the besotted Populace moved only by instinct and appetite, the healthy Barbarian whose culture is only superficial, and the complacent Philistine whose ignorance is the more appalling because it is self-confessed as knowledge. Against such foes, active or unconscious, the cause of Excellence is ever a perilous one, an island of light threatened by an ocean of darkness. The illumination of human history, the triumphs of human genius, have been only at the times when the keepers of this light were unsleeping in their devotion. Without them the tradition would have been lost; and they are the critics of the present and the guardians of the future. Arnold still retains a hope; if one must use the word, he still has a vein, though perhaps slender, of optimism in his creed. A remnant shall be left, and to them humanity must look for salvation.

But with Hardy, as one reads his novels, and much more important, his poems, one has the feeling, at the first approach, of an adventure along the face of a moving glacier. The path is terribly narrow, the ice caves, that are given the adventurer to explore, are exquisite in the elusive tints of beauty, the slowly moving mass has a serene grandeur inexpressible, indefinable, unhuman. But its movement is unpredictable and remorseless. The path narrows, the adventurer turns in startled surprise. And the end—one more illustration of man's futility—an impersonal, uncalculable, and yet an utterly and devastatingly fascinating world of mute power. It is a world that knows not man, and yet draws man with compelling power to give his all. It is an adventure that beckons irresistibly, and yet one which never can be compassed. It is a game played by wavering intelligence against omnipotent Nescience, a partnership between flickering mind and the great Inane, between morals and One to whom the meaning of conduct is unknown; and there are no rules for the game, except as man makes and obeys them, no articles in the partnership save as man writes for his own edification. His partner is "the Immanent Doer that doth not know." And the story of humanity is strewn by wrecks of thoughts of human significance, once great and moving, but now abandoned.

> "Fill all your cups; feel no distress;
> 'Tis only one great thought the less.
> Fill full your cups; feel no distress
> At all our great thoughts shrinking less;
> We'll do a good deed nevertheless!"

It is no wonder, though these verses were written near the end of his long life, when this startling view of man's place in nature, and his cosmic irrelevancy, first was urged on contemporaries who had not yet lost their faith in at least man, that there arose the horrified cry of protest, and Hardy was branded as a pessimist.

But to call him pessimist is to take only a partial view of Hardy's significance to us and to his own time, and to forget the last line, and the most important, in the *Drinking Song*. For, he wrote in *In Tenebris*, "if way to the Better there be; it exacts a full look at the Worst." Hardy was all his life a deep student of human nature in history and literature, as well as in his daily inter-course with people of all sorts and conditions. He was also more, by poetical insight, as well as by study; he was a student of the best of human thought, and, above all, of the thought, science, and philosophy of his time. He was able, especially in his poetry, to blend these—a rare gift for even genius—into a complete philosophy of life, a philosophy of life we are challenged to explore.

Again, Hardy seems to belong rather to our time than to the end of the nineteenth and beginning of the twen-tieth century, as he seems least of all interested in any social problem, or plan for social uplift, or the lot of the forgotten man, or schemes of social justice. Singularly for his age, he never seems to think of society, the thing we spell with a capital S, the thing that is the theme of most of Ibsen's plays. In its place his poetic intuition gropes persistently for a definition of reality, the im-manent essence behind and beyond all things individual and whose Will governs the all. It is man's relation to this, as well as man's relation to man, individual to in-dividual, a relationship that does not change in spite of changes in time and space—man's eternal debt to the universe and man's debt to his neighbor—these and their

consequent emotions are the large theme of the best in
Hardy's prose and poetry. For

> "this will go onward the same
> Though Dynasties pass."

In consequence, more than any of his contemporary
novelists and poets of the first rank, Hardy is philosophic in outlook. Yet again this statement must not be
taken too literally. For again and again he warns us
that he has no philosophical system to exploit, and that
his thought is never to be taken as more than tentative
views on the meaning and value of human life and conduct. He writes to this effect in the "General Preface"
to his novels and poems. "Positive views on the Whence
and the Wherefore of things have never been advanced
by this pen as a consistent philosophy. Nor is it likely,
indeed, that imaginative writings extending over more
than forty years would exhibit a coherent scientific theory
of the universe even if it had been attempted. . . . But
such objectless consistency never has been attempted, and
the sentiments in the following pages have been stated
truly to be mere impressions of the moment, and not convictions or arguments." They certainly are not arguments, and by saying that they are not convictions he is
by no means implying any lack of depth or sincerity. He
is a philosophic poet but not a philosopher; his "impressions" have utter sincerity, but are not set forth in any
philosophic creed. If they are impressions of the moment
the moments are neither occasional nor fleeting, for they
are also his poetic intuition.

To say this is not to discount Hardy's prose. Yet from
this distance I think it is safe to assert that the future
will know him rather as the poet, and his prose as the
running comment and elaboration of his inexhaustible

interest in life, in its variety and strangeness, which he illuminates with dramatic suddenness in his narrative verse. He was a poet who never ceased to wonder; and a novel, like *Tess* or *The Return of the Native* is only the exploration of the object of his wonder in the panorama to its last details, which in the *Trampwoman's Tragedy* or in *Squire Hooper* is etched with only the barest of bold outlines. It is the same hand with the same poetic intuition of life's ironies that did both. The *Trampwoman's Tragedy* could easily be expanded into the central theme of a novel, or the central theme of *Tess* or *Jude the Obscure* be reduced to the compass of a ballad— but only by Hardy.

Poetry lay closer to Hardy's genius than prose—an amazing fact in this our century of prose—it was his first affection, and to it he returned when his fame as a novelist had been securely established, and into it he distilled the richest of his experience. He confesses that in it is "the more individual part of my literary fruitage," and in a letter written at his request we are told that "speaking generally there is more autobiography in a hundred lines of Mr. Hardy's poetry than in all the novels." They best give us those glimpses of reality, his poetic intuitions, whether of the ultimate nature of the power behind life and nature, or of the inner conflict of the perplexed human soul, or of the compensation within the scope of man in an ironically unfriendly universe. To discover his answer to these three problems is to discover also the significance of Hardy for our century.

> "Perplexed in endeavor to balk future pain
> By uncovering the drift of the drama."

Such became the dominant motive of his search. And what did he, even early, find? The drama of life, with the mysterious producer and author behind and unrevealed, what is He or It? The mystery of human consciousness, the still greater mystery of the human conscience and its insistence upon justice and plain dealing, the greatest mystery of man's demand for an intelligible plan in this universe, that somehow it should be consistent with his conscience and his reason. From somewhere, somehow, somewhen, these seeds were sown in conscience and intelligence, that were not satisfied with their own little world of human thoughts, human conduct, human emotions, but demanded, quite without reason, that beyond man there should be a power that moves for righteousness, whose conscience is like that of man, only universal, whose intelligence should be like that of man, only having within its scope the starry heavens. Is there a cosmic drama, like the human, directed to some transcendental, yet moral and intelligible end; and within this drama does man play a rôle, no matter how minute, so long as it is also like the whole, tinctured with cosmic morals and intelligibility?

The answer to this question, that either assumes an intelligible plan in the universe, or ignores the possibility of unintelligibility, seems to Hardy the most incredible of all human conclusions, drawn from an utter absence of evidence. It is as though an aërolite had come to earth from the depths of space, regions where "no distress had means to mar supreme delight," and had infected all human nature with thoughts and ideals of the benign nature of things that were wholly unwarranted.

> " 'How shall we,' then the seers said,
>   'Oust this awareness, this disease
>   Called sense, here sown,
>   Though good, no doubt, where it was bred,
>   And wherein all things work to please?' "

The disease seems just one of nature's sports, like the leopard's spots, pretty, no doubt, but of no consequence to reality, for nature is not sentient, it is not moral, it is not intelligent. But as a cosmic jest, when there were none to laugh, an accident that marred no plan, for there was none, it came and grew and bore fruit, man's intelligence and moral conscience; and these because they seemed, or are good bore further fruit in a demand that the universe as a whole should be created in man's image, sentient, and rational, and moral—a tragic, ironic jest, a practical jest with man its victim.

But man, wholeheartedly and sincerely, played the game whose rules were only in his mind and conscience—of his own creating—and for the other player created Deity in his own ideal image, in the place of "the Immanent Doer that doth not know."

> "Wherefore, O Man, did there come to you
> The unhappy need of creating me—
> A form like your own—for praying to?
>
> My virtue, power, utility,
> Within my maker must all abide,
> Since none in myself can ever be."

For man has been "tempted to create One whom we can no longer keep alive." And now after science has shown His futility man is slowly pacing in the procession of *God's Funeral.*

> "So, toward our myth's oblivion,
> Darkling, and languid-lipped, we creep and grope
> Sadlier than those who wept in Babylon,
> Whose Zion was a still abiding hope."

Such is the ironic tragedy of man; to this absolute doubt of any reality that makes for cosmic righteousness has man been reduced, now that his eyes have been opened. Such is Hardy's celestial vision of the earth as "a welter of futile doing," and man an ironic jest, in a universe unconscious of the jest, in an infinitesimal fragment of the universe. The thought is appalling. But not so to the poet:

> "Black is night's cope;
> But death will not appal
> One who, past doubtings all,
> Waits in unhope."

It is this growing conviction of man's futility in the face of a cosmic destiny of unreason, that shows itself stronger and stronger in his novels from the *Mayor of Casterbridge* to *Jude*. In the first the balance is held almost even. But with the *Return of the Native* and *Tess* the inscrutability of the inscrutable becomes a deeper and more mysterious power, until it seems almost to become the prime agent in human tragedy. It is the same in the poems. A careless jest in the *Trampwoman's Tragedy*, and lives are ruined and sacrificed. The horror of war at the taking of *San Sebastian*, a soldier's lust, and the reproachful eyes of his victim will always look out at him from the loved face of his daughter. The Turnip-Hoer saves a woman's life in a runaway, and he is lost forever by the thrill of her touch. The theme is endless and always ironic.

The very nature of life is tragic.

> "Yea. Tragedy is true guise,
> Comedy lies."

The conflicts in the human heart, the result of an unsentient universe, are always ironically potent for tragedy. How ephemeral is joy and even love, and how quickly forgotten.

"Oh, are you digging on my grave
My loved one?"

No it is not the loved one that remembers, nor the nearest kin, nor an enemy, prodding sly. It is only the little
dog.

"What feeling do we ever find
To equal among human kind
A dog's fidelity!"

But even that scant of happiness is too much:

"Mistress, I dug upon your grave
To bury a bone, in case
I should be hungry near this spot
When passing on my daily trot.
I am sorry, but I quite forgot
It was your resting-place."

How often even the best of intentions brings the most
amazing ironical results. As an illustration, see the
Curate's Kindness. It is a poor old man speaking, with a
closet full of little skeletons of family unhappiness. He
is now being shipped off to the workhouse, and though
he feels keenly the disgrace, contents himself with the
hope of peace at last.

"Life there will be better than t'other,
For peace is assured.
The men in one wing and their wives in another
Is strictly the rule of the Board."

But just at that moment the parson steps up to encourage
the forlorn pair. They will not be separated; the rules
have been set aside. Poor old man:

"I thought they'd be strangers aroun' me,
But she's to be there!
Let me jump out o' waggon and go back and drown me
At Pummery or Ten-Hatches Weir."

Trifling things these, but of their texture is the texture of life, as Hardy sees it. And the eminence or lack of eminence of the unfortunate does not increase or lessen the pain.

The wise man therefore will expect little of life, will cut no antics on its treacherous ledge, for at best it can hold out few promises.

> " 'I do not promise overmuch,
>   Child; overmuch;
>   Just neutral-tinted haps and such,'
>   You said to minds like mine.
>   Wise warning for your credit's sake!
>   Which I for one failed not to take,
>   And hence could stem such strain and ache
>   As each year might assign."

Such Hardy found it and lived it, and with these words he greeted his eighty-sixth birthday. The Deity's plaint to man who created him ends with something of the same advice.

> "The fact of life with dependence placed
>   On the human heart's resource alone,
>   In brotherhood bonded close and graced
>   With loving-kindness fully blown,
>   And visioned help unsought, unknown."

Brotherhood, human-love, these are the one great, perhaps the only compensation Hardy finds for the iron world of despair without. It is only this that can re-illumine man's pilgrimage. For these are the precious by-product of human consciousness, so ironically bequeathed by the unconscious Will of the universe. Few, I believe, seeing the poems of doubt and questioning and what looks like blank despair, catch the full significance of Hardy as a love poet and the sincerity of his love. It is a love of the im-

agination and of the senses at the same time, and it is
quickened into intense fervor by the oddest of experience.
The plunge of the arms into the cool water of a basin calls
up the picture of an August day long ago of a little water-
fall where his love and he had painted and picnicked, and
under whose pool their drinking glass had disappeared.

> "There the glass still is.
> And, as said, if I thrust my arm below
> Cold water in basin or bowl, a throe
> From the past awakens a sense of that time,
> And the glass we used, and the cascade's
>   rhyme.
> The basin seems the pool, and its edge
> The hard smooth face of the brook-side ledge,
> And the leafy pattern of china-ware
> The hanging plants that were bathing there.
>
> By night, by day, when it shines or lours,
> There lies intact that chalice of ours,
> And its presence adds to the rhyme of love
> Persistently sung by the fall above.
> No lip has touched it since his and mine
> In turns therefrom sipped lovers' wine."

Happiness is fleeting, though sincere, and love the most
fleeting and most sincere. But it, if not expended unwisely
or prized too highly, brings life's only worthy compensation.

But with love for human beings goes also the poet's
love for all animate nature, and his sensitiveness to its
charm. This went so far on one occasion, at least, as to
lead him to approve in the main of the principles of the
antivivisectionist society. And above all, perhaps, Hardy
is a lover of the more intimate things in nature. Not a
boisterous love shouting from the mountain tops, nor a
philosophic love that sees in nature the mysterious gar-

ments of Deity, but the quiet assured love of one who feels nature, like man, to be part of the unconscious process that works through all. Nature like man knows also the irony of existence and feels its pain; and, also like man, flashes with the brief occasions of accepted but unexpected joy.

The future? Will the future, as the past and the present, be the unconscious groping of blind Will? Hardy's argument is by analogy, but perhaps we need better to call it faith. Out of the lifeless in nature in the blind process of time evolved life; out of life evolved consciousness and conscience at the price of tragedy. Can it be possible that "the Great Adjustment," sometime somewhere in the blind future, may in the fulness of time replace Nescience by Knowledge? In the dreary procession of *God's Funeral* the chosen few see distant on the horizon a light.

"Whereof to lift the general night,
A certain few who stood aloof had said,
See you upon the horizon that small light—
Swelling somewhat? Each mourner shook his head."

The miracle, so far, of consciousness has only made man aware of his moral discomfort of living in a universe blind to conscience and knowledge. But can the blank Inane be transformed into conscious judgment? Hardy, contrary to rigid scientific postulates, hopes.

"And they shall see what is, ere long,
Not through a glass, but face to face;
And Right shall disestablish Wrong:
The Great Adjustment is taking place."

It is so rare, this poetic hope, that it seems inconsistent with the Hardy who can face even blank despair with quiet fortitude, that in a lesser or a less sincere poet it would be a faith like that of the ancient Christian, *"Credo quia impossible est,"* I believe because it is impossible, and imply a looking for a miracle. It is a fringe, and a golden one, on the edge of his tapestry of life, but as a fringe affects in no wise the texture or the pattern of its weaving.

The theme of his novels and poems then is the reconciliation, if one can be found, between the way of the world and the reactions of human nature; how human nature bears its destiny. It is nearly always the tragic irony of man's futility in conflict with pity aroused by his fate. Such is the attitude left the reader as he follows the struggles of Eustacia to free herself of the incubus of her environment in *The Return of the Native*. It is for this reason that he entitles the novel of *Tess* the story of "a pure woman faithfully presented." What counts in character, what makes character, is motive; but it is something utterly uncontrollable that twists this motive to an incomprehensible fate. So as we read we are charmed by the lovableness or fastidiousness or sympathy of the character, and dismayed by the untowardness of its harvest.

Interest in human nature, interest in its cosmic background, this is Hardy's divided interest—these two forces seemingly pitted against each other from the beginnings of human time. In none of his works has he so graphically balanced these interests as in the epic-drama, *The Dynasts*. Here each visibly plays its rôle, with human nature in general on the side-lines, edified and edifying, passing judgment and gaining understanding of the issues involved. It was, as a poem, Hardy's katharsis of the bewilderments and doubts, and the clear emergence of his final conviction of man's place in nature. Here against the background of the Napoleonic wars one can study human nature and its reactions in the large, and see the potency of the Immanent Will as it plays with dynasties. "To be sure," he wrote, "one might argue that by surveying Europe from a celestial point of view—as in *The Dynasts*—that continent becomes virtually a province—a Wessex, an Attica, even a mere garden—and hence is made to conform to the principles of the novels, however far it outmeasures this region." But though surveyed from a celestial region—as it must be—the European scene from Trafalgar to Waterloo loses none of its human significance, and still less its cosmic. It is a world drama whose central character is forever Unknown, the fate of whose pawns and knights and kings rouses us to deepest pity; the poem is a study in human motives whose results are nearly always futile, but the persons who give them birth are in their action monumental.

It is only too easy to find a way to criticise so vast a theme for its flaws, and Hardy anticipates the faultfinders: "Critics can never be made to understand that the failure may be greater than the success. It is their particular duty to point this out; but the public points it out to them. To have strength to roll a stone weighing a hundred weight to the top of the mount is a success, and to have the strength to roll a stone of ten hundredweight only half-way up that mount is a failure. But the latter is two or three times as strong a deed."

All his life Hardy had been obsessed by the Napoleonic wars; his poetry is full of the accounts of its soldiers he had known in their old age. He devoted years to the study of its politics and battles. He writes as the third part of the poem is going through the press, "in two or three days I shall have done with the proofs of *Dynasts III*. It is well that the business should be over, for I have been living in Wellington's campaigns so much lately that, like George IV, I am almost positive that I took part in the battle of Waterloo, and have written it from memory." The idea or plan behind the poem is to give a modern scientific, or philosophical interpretation of history, a "modern expression," as he put it, "of a modern outlook." As it is history with scattered and only remotely connected episodes, "no attempt has been made," I again quote Hardy, "to create the completely organic structure of action, and closely-webbed development of character and motive." This last is only partly true, for he is interested only in those phases of the characters that appear in the historical episode; but add them together, the weary Pitt, the patient Wellington, the dominating Napoleon, and the result is a history galvanized and vocal, and a living panorama.

The chief character is the Immanent Will, invisible, unconscious, but remorselessly working behind every individual. Hardy represents it at times as a cosmic brain and nervous system of which Europe as a whole is the organ.

"The nether sky opens, and Europe is disclosed as a prone and emaciated figure, the Alps shaping like a backbone, and the branching mountain-chains like ribs, the peninsular plateau of Spain forming a head. Broad and lengthy lowlands stretch from the north of France across Russia like a grey-green garment hemmed by the Ural mountains and the glistening Arctic Ocean.

"The point of view then sinks downwards through space, and draws near to the surface of the perturbed countries, where the peoples, distressed by events which they did not cause, are seen writhing, crawling, heaving, and vibrating in their various cities and nationalities.

"A new and penetrating light descends on the spectacle, enduing men and things with a seeming transparency, and exhibiting as one organism the anatomy of life and movement in all humanity and vitalized matter included in the display."

This is the anatomy of the General Will. When our interest in the fate of characters and peoples leads us to question Fate and Absolute Justice, this insight into the nature of things will come again to check all protest.

For the visible characters in the huge drama there are the kings and princes of the earth, Austria, Prussia, Russia, England, their generals, statesmen, courtiers, hangers-on, relevant and irrelevant. There are soldiers, cowards, weaklings, women, peasants, those who think they know what it is all about, and those who will never think. There is Napoleon who had disturbed the peace of Europe, fancying himself, as he is, an instrument of inscrutable fate. There are his generals, there is his wife, the Empress Josephine, who when time is ripe must be tossed aside, and a princess of royal birth installed in her place. There are sailors, Nelson and his tragic opponent. All Europe passes in review in the list of the characters that played their part in the meaningless drama, that meaninglessly distributed tragedy and fame. It takes no long reading to tell us that it is an Englishman, born in Wessex, the county of Nelson's flag-captain, himself also a Hardy, who has written this English epic-drama, with the pride of an Englishman in his country's part in the struggle. But as a poet he knows too the insignificant significance of the play.

Then there are other characters that sit and explain, or cry out in judgment against the action. These are none of them supernatural, though they may seem to be people of the over-world. There is the Earth, patient, long-suffering nature, the nourisher and the victim of the human drama. There is the "Spirit of the Years" and the "Chorus of the Years," who are "the passionless insight of the ages," "the best human intelligence of their time," a human insight that has gained true knowledge

and does not waste its time in futile sorrow, for it knows
the lessons of history.

> "Rather they show that, like a knitter drowsed,
> Whose fingers play in skilled unmindfulness,
> The Will has woven with an absent heed
> Since life first was; and ever will so weave."

There are the "Recording Angels," the recorders of true
history, again purely human, and assessing neither praise
nor blame, spirits of understanding. There are the "Spirit
of Rumor" and the "Chorus of Rumors," the intelli-
gences, again human, that convey the news; and it is
their function to keep the "Spirit of the Years" and the
other spectators informed of such doings as are not openly
displayed on the stage.

There are then the "Spirits Sinister and Ironic," again
human, with their Choruses, examples of human attitudes,
Mephistophelian or worse, to whom the human drama has
lost human semblance of respect.

> "My argument is that War
> makes rattling good history;
> but Peace is poor reading.
> So I back Bonaparte."

These are the clear-eyed, hard souls who have knowledge,
and knowledge has bred contempt, irony, or even mis-
anthropic hatred. They are also a necessary and ever
present comment on all human history. Opposed to
these, and more consistently human, are the "Spirit of
Pity" and the "Chorus of the Pities." These are the
"Universal Sympathy of human nature," "humanity with
all its weakness," conscious of and shrinking before the
spectacle of human irrelevance and cruelty, and ever lifting their hands in supplication to the unheeding Will. It
is to these that the spectre of the Will must ever be re-

vealed. But it is also these, after the tremendous drama has unrolled to its single ending, the crushed and baffled Napoleon, that hymn the hope of the "Day of Adjustment." They are humanity's perpetual challenge, addressed to the future against "this viewless, voiceless, Turner of the Wheel."

The First Part begins in Wessex with England's decision in 1805 to enter the war against Napoleon. The French response is to try to send Nelson off on a false trail so that the French Army at Boulogne may be quickly put across the narrow channel. The action here as elsewhere goes by dialogue when the decisions demand it, or by Dumb Show, when it is only mass action. Napoleon is crowned Emperor in Milan, and thrusts quickly at the Austrians with the victory of Ulm. Then comes the counter with Nelson's victory at Trafalgar; England is saved, but she loses her greatest hero.

> "Humble and affectionate he is ever
> Does love die with our frame's decease,
>   I wonder,
> Or does it live forever?"

Napoleon's character has its charm too, that "strange suasive pull of personality." Part One closes with the tremendous Battle of Austerlitz, Napoleon's greatest victory, and Europe's greatest defeat. Pity would read a lesson in the dreadful carnage. But the Chorus of Years chants disillusioned:

> "Our overseeings, our supernal state,
>   Our readings Why and Whence,
> Are but the flower of Man's intelligence;
> And that but an unreckoned incident
> Of the all-urging Will, raptly magnipotent."

Part Two begins with Jena and Tilsit in the next year, 1806. Then two years later, with the beginnings of England's campaign in Spain, it takes us to Coruña. Here we have the desperate retreat of Sir John Moore, the lot of his ragged soldiers and deserters, his mournful death and burial—a campaign and a general thrown away only to exhibit the worth of the sacrifice. Then Wagram, that bloody battle, under the walls of Vienna. Back again to Spain and Wellington now. And the act closes with England's first victories on land, Talavera and Torres Vedras. And ironically the glorious news of England's effort is carried to George III, England's King, now crazed and pathetically forlorn.

> "He says I have won a battle? But I thought
> I was a poor afflicted captive here,
> In darkness lingering out my lonely days,
> Beset with terror of these myrmidons
> That suck my blood like vampires! Ay, ay, ay!"

Part III is the climax and conclusion of the great drama of dynasties. The brilliant beginnings of the Russian Campaign, that is to make Napoleon the master of all Europe; the burning of Moscow; the horrors of the retreat: "Even the Army which once was called the Grand, now in retreat." Even Greek tragedy never wed pity and terror more remorselessly.

"What has floated down from the sky upon the Army is a flake of snow. Then come another and another, till natural features, hitherto varied with the tints of autumn, are confounded, and all is phantasmal grey and white.

"The caterpillar shape still creeps laboriously nearer, but instead of increasing in size by the rules of perspective, it gets more attenuated, and there are left upon the ground behind it minute parts of itself, which are speedily flaked over, and remain as white pimples by the wayside."

"SPIRIT OF THE YEARS
> "These atoms that drop off are snuffed-out souls
> Who are enghosted by the caressing snow.

"Pines rise mournfully on each side of the nearing object; ravens in flocks advance with it overhead, waiting to pick out the eyes of strays who fall. The snowstorm increases, descending in tufts which can hardly be shaken off. The sky seems to join itself to the land. The marching figures drop rapidly, and almost immediately become white grave-mounds.

"Endowed with enlarged powers of audition as of vision, we are struck by the mournful taciturnity that prevails. Nature is mute. Save for the incessant flogging of the wind-broken and lacerated horses there are no sounds."

Then the great battle of Leipzig where the Emperor at last meets defeat at the hand of man. The rejoicing that follows is broken by the irrelevancy of the Prince Regent of England's marital infelicities—a thing to this ruler of as great importance as or greater than the destiny of nations. English peasants celebrate by burning the Emperor; one, who has run himself out of breath is disappointed that it is to be only in effigy. Such anti-climaxes are set against the tremendous battle of Waterloo; and as a climax to the horrors of the war are shown the sufferings even of the least of animate life. Thus all nature is confounded in the human catastrophe.

> "The mole's tunnelled chambers are crushed by wheels,
> The lark's eggs scattered, their owners fled;
> And the hedgehog's household the sapper unseals.
>
> "The snail draws in at the terrible tread,
> But in vain; he is crushed by the felloe-rim;
> The worm asks what can be overhead,
>
> "And wriggles deep from a scene so grim,
> And guesses him safe; for he does not know
> What a foul red flood will be soaking him!
>
> "Beaten about by the heel and toe
> Are butterflies, sick of the day's long rheum,
> To die of a worse than the weather-foe."

"War

> "Plied by the Managed for the Managers;
> To wit: by frenzied folks who profit naught
> For those who profit all."

And what was its profit? Here are Napoleon's last words:

> "I came too late in time
> To assume the prophet or the demi-god,
> A part past playing now. My only course
> To make good showance to posterity
> Was to implant my line upon the throne.
> And how shape that, if now extinction nears?
> Great men are meteors that consume themselves
> To light the earth. This is my burnt-out hour."

And to this the "Spirit of the Years" makes answer:

> "Such men as thou, who wade across the world
> To make an epoch, bless, confuse, appal,
> Are in the elemental ages' chart
> Like meanest insects on obscurest leaves
> But incidents and grooves of Earth's unfolding;
> Or as the brazen rod that stirs the fire
> Because it must."

Is this all? Napoleon was followed by Metternich, and the clock was set back for the Dynasties, and all that had been since the Revolution, Europe set its head to forget. Is man growing nobler and wiser? The "Chorus of the Pities" at the conclusion chants the hope. But in 1914 the renewal of the European struggle startled even Hardy. He abandoned his old theory of the gradual ennoblement of man and the hope of ultimate wisdom. Even this faint hope of the Pities perhaps is a vain aspiration. Should not the "Spirit Ironic" or even the "Spirit Sinister" have the last word?

What emerges from the meaningless welter of human life, when one sees it against the background of Immanent Will? Direction, progress, evolution toward something more intelligible? Risings on stepping stones of dead selves to higher things? All that the Pities can hold out, and they represent human aspiration as well as human weakness, is that in time somehow, somewhere, the Will may grow conscious, and then a new day dawn. Is this all? Is present humanity to live only in expectation of a doubtful future humanity? There is little comfort in so distant an ideal, a cold fire before which life must warm its hands.

The only other compensation, and it is far richer, is human character and human affection. It is for this reason that Hardy has enriched these lines with the large variety of humanity and human endeavor, human loyalty, human affection: the deserter catching at a moment's love in a hovel as a refuge from the harshness of the campaign, the fortitude of woman who shares the danger of her warrior husband, the loyal love between Hardy the flag captain and Nelson the admiral, Wellington touched during the crisis of battle by a companion shot down at his side, the crazed George III seeking in vain in the garden for his dead princess. Humanity finds compensation or consolation in the sentiment of humanity. These affections persist in spite of History and Dynasties. Without these

"Thought's the slave of life, and life time's
fool."

At the beginning of the century another English poet wrote a cosmic drama celebrating the triumph of human emancipation. Shelley's *Prometheus Unbound* surveys man and nature, and finds both animated with one vast motive that works for righteous intelligence. Tyranny, Ignorance, Superstition: these are the vices that keep man from his rightful heritage and postpone the golden day of freedom and harmony. Now at the end of the century, with a science that has seen more deeply, there is an outlook pitifully circumscribed. Let me quote from Hardy's own Apology:

"Pain to all upon it, tongued or dumb, shall be kept down to a minimum by loving-kindness, operating through scientific knowledge, and actuated by the modicum of free will conjecturally possessed by organic life when the mighty necessitating forces—unconscious or other—that have 'the balancings of the clouds,' happen to be in equilibrium, which may or may not be often."

The Immanent Will leaves man a trifle of freedom when the powers that have the "balancings of the clouds," when natural forces happen to be in equilibrium, or when the Will relaxes its unconscious power. Is this the end of the century of search, and will this be the final answer?

Hardy rightly comes at the end of an epoch, an epoch that began with a Great War and ends with The Great War, an epoch that began with faith and ends with disillusionment. Science had seemed to build a blank wall against human aspiration, and Hardy cheerfully accepts the only possibles left and cultivates these diligently. We may be unable to mould dynasties, our fates may be ever inscrutable, but we have in our hands a humble happiness as a compensation for our fatal knowledge. The larks may be forever prisoners in latticed cages, but they have yet the gift of song, and in this happiness can achieve forgetfulness.[1]

[1] How much more sober and universal is Hardy than Anatole France, who has much the same philosophic background, and human, too, I might add.

XVII. NEW ISSUES

CONCLUSION

The Devil—"The truth is, you have—I won't say no heart; for we all know that beneath all your affected cynicism you have a warm one."

SHAW—*Man and Superman*

IN scattered jottings of *Thoughts* that were to make a book, jottings rich with insight, and that deserve to be read more assiduously today than in the seventeenth century when they were written, Blaise Pascal startled himself and now us with one of those flashes of illumination of man's fatal and naked insecurity.

"For, finally, what is man in nature? A zero in comparison with infinity, an infinity in comparison with zero, a middle ground between nothing and all. At an infinite distance from understanding finalities, the ends of things as their beginnings are for him invincibly hidden in an impenetrable secret; equally incapable is he to see the zero from which he is drawn and the infinity in which he is engulfed. . . .

"Behold such is our true estate; this it is that makes us incapable of certain knowledge and of absolute ignorance. We waver over a vast middle ground, ever uncertain and ever adrift, driven from one course to the other. Whatever the bourne where we think to find rest and a firm refuge, it gives way and eludes us; if we follow, it evades our grasp, and slipping from us, escapes in an eternal flight."

A zero in comparison with the infinite universe which his science has allowed him to see outrolled as a cosmic pan-

orama; an infinity in comparison with the zero, again revealed by his science, of the cosmic dance of electrons and
protons. And the most recent chapter of his science has
brought home, not to savants alone and mathematicians,
but to each thinker, that its hypotheses, where he thought
to find rest and a firm refuge, have a habit of giving way
and eluding him. Truth seems ever to evade us, slipping
from the grasp and escaping in eternal flight.

Even this middle ground which we seem to occupy, this
practical world of human actions, is also none too secure
and always unpredictable. And the story of the nineteenth
century is that of its growing complexity and discomfort.
It has been a Proteus constantly changing shape, and refusing, like the old mythical monster, to answer questions; for who, like the antique hero Menelaus, has the
power to seize and hold it fast and force an unwilling
response? Each generation of the century has seen a
transformation in the ideas and appurtenances of life,
a transformation that in previous epochs would not be
known in centuries. "Off with the old, on with the new,"
"the king is dead, long live the king," are cries that have
been a constant din in the ears. Restless, footsore, eager
for change, bewildered and wearied by the constant new,
beginning to master a new toy just when it is outmoded
and tossed aside for the unexplored new, the years between the French Revolution and our latest revolutions
have been the story of hope, trial and error, bewilderment,
near-despair, and new hope, new experiment, and new bewilderment. But it has been an interesting story.

It has meant, beside, a changing humanity, modified
profoundly by the changing environment. The science of
genetics, though it can speak with some statistical certainty of inherited characteristics, like the color of the
eyes and the texture of the hair, has yet no formula that

can describe the more profound psychological effects of changes in environment, though it recognises their importance. How different, then, must be the state of mind today from that at the beginning of the nineteenth century. A relatively stable population then, largely rural: an unstable population today, the majority urban. Communication then slow and difficult and newspapers scarce and treasured: today we live instantly in every quarter of the globe and hear its most irrelevant gossip. Hand labor then, today the age of the machine, and the laborer rapidly displaced by the mechanical robot. How far all this has gone to transform character we can only guess; but we look in vain about us for parallels for the national traits as they were described when the century began.[1] And the story of the gradual transformation is told us again in the story of the century's literature. Human nature in its fundamentals may yet be human nature; but its character, its motive for conduct, and its philosophy of life, the story of the changes in these is the inner biography of the nineteenth century seen in its greatest thinkers and writers, the men who knew the hope, or trembled in expectancy before the experiment of the new, or stood baffled by its failure.

A new age, such was the promise of the French Revolution, and the imagination of youth and age thrilled at the prospect, a promise of liberty, equality, and fraternity, by the simple device of a regenerated will, by what in good evangelical Methodism would be called conversion. Man is by nature good, so it was confidently believed; and if a true direction can be given to his will, man's inherited evil can be overthrown as easily as the Bastille, the symbol of dead tyranny. How distant, and impossible that bright

[1] I am thinking of Carlyle's description of the patient, studious, philosophical German, whose kingdom was that of the "air." Jean Paul Richter invented the phrase.

hope appears today in the light of new revolutions again planned to secure the happiness of mankind. Soviet Russia no longer talks of man's natural goodness, or expects much from his moral will even where untempered by tyranny. It substitutes the virtue of organization and obedience, and calls for the superman, the dictator. It is the century of change that has transformed even the motive for revolution, in which liberty, once so ardently desired, nay, demanded as the first human prerogative, now is the first victim to be laid on the altar as a sacrifice for human regeneration.

Faith in man's natural goodness, the faith affirmed as a religion by Rousseau, transformed into idealistic poetry by Shelley, sought in the democracy of America by Whitman, how this faith glows, wavers, flickers, and finally is quenched by the damp of doubt as the century narrows to its close. Already before the nineteenth century has turned its first quarter Manzoni finds it only in the natural piety of the unspoiled peasant. If others are good it is the triumph of righteousness through austere discipline. To Tolstoi it is the fruit of ignorance, almost; and if achieved by others is the result of ascetic denial of the joy of living. Ibsen searched for it all his life amid the illiterate as the cultured, and found in its place only folly or obliquity, and that all virtue, as all vice, is in the last analysis only relative. Indeed as we come to the end of the century the very words good and bad lose all their old firm outlines as descriptions of conduct or character, and in their place there is set up another standard of value, that of survival.

The good is that which survives, that which brings disintegration and desolation is bad. Here is a definition which has its precise analogy in the world of biology. Mrs. Alving, in Ibsen's *Ghosts*, who followed painfully in the old path of orthodox virtue, raised a tempest of tragedy in her household beset with malevolent ghosts of the past. Raskolnikoff in Dostoevsky's *Crime and Punishment* found his way to salvation only over the corpse of his victim. This study of the relativity of good and evil finds its logical conclusion in Hardy, for whom in the last analysis it is only the motive that counts; for the action lies beyond man's power in the inscrutable will of Nescience. It is only the quality of the human emotion that counts in this cosmic game in which men are only conscious pawns:

> "But helpless Pieces of Game He plays
> Upon this chequer-board of Nights and Days;
> Hither and thither moves, and checks, and slays,
> And one by one back in the Closet lays."

So the century, which began with profound faith in moral human nature, with its ideal religiously conceived of moral liberty, closes in a growing cloud of doubt of both morals and liberty.

What has then become of the early nineteenth century trust in democracy? Shelley and Whitman were its triumphant poets, but with a difference: Whitman robust and trusting in the unspoiled goodness of the American pioneer, a pioneer in a new world with forests to be felled and mountains and rivers to be conquered, but a pioneer also in a new social world, building in a new land a new civilization. In the pre-Civil War America it was not difficult to proclaim this robust faith. Its fruits could be anticipated without the prophet's vision. But Shelley came to an England and Europe in reaction against the liberalizing Revolution, and his prophetic power sees a new people springing to life in a valley of dry bones. His creed has more of Plato, and is inspired with the new philosophy of evolution. When man's faculties have been harmonized and trained, then he can rightfully step forth to claim his heritage. This is a more difficult optimism than Whitman's.

But by the end of the century these calls of faith in the brotherhood of man and human equality have lost their novelty and much of their power. The new science has not been of the aid the earlier prophets had hoped; and the later theories of survival have caused more talk of class wars than brotherly love. Even Tolstoi with his great commandment can hardly be called upon to pinch-hit in the cause of democracy. His constitution for the state or for the world is rather one of benevolent anarchy than of popular assemblies and courts. And Ibsen's comment on the "compact majority" is a description of a creature with long ears, unmusical voice, and hind-legged obstinacy.

If faith in equality and fraternity have thus lost their bright hues with the loss of faith in man's natural goodness, what then of the last of the trinity, liberty? All great literature from Homer to Dante to Montaigne to Goethe has been the search for the price man must pay for this the most precious, and the most elusive of human treasures. Rousseau reads the lesson of history as the gradual enslavement of the individual by the favored few of a corrupted society. He would transform society to break these chains and allow the Son of God his native endowment. At the end of the century Zola, his last disciple, with the aid of the weapon on which Rousseau contemptuously turned his back, Science, proclaimed anew an Age of Gold and liberty for all. The discipline that will achieve this conquest is the discipline of the instrument of the human reason, which shall one day transform the human environment, and allow man to develop to his full stature, and be free. There may be many yet who have some of the Zola faith, but their voices have difficulty in making this faith heard.

There are others, like Arnold, who follow the sterner discipline of the new Stoicism, and set the prize of liberty only for the few who can follow in the hard tradition of human excellence and culture. These are the remnant that have in every age been left, of those who have refused to bow the knee before the shrine of the popular Baal. Reason, righteousness, culture, the vision of life true and whole, and its end spiritual and moral emancipation, all this is the still small voice that sounds only to their ears. There are some yet, not many perhaps, that can breathe this rarefied atmosphere, hold themselves aloof, and yet fear neither loneliness nor hate human weakness. Theirs is a species of unacknowledged aristocracy—to the uniniti- ated it will always appear cold, uninviting, even intel- lectual snobbery.

Is there any faith left? For without faith what motive is there left for life?

> "For doubt is a sea without shore,
>   And Faith is a rock that abides;
> But her ears are vexed with its roar,
>   And her face by the foam of its tides."

To Hardy, our latest comer, faith, as a reality, is quite unnecessary in the urge of life to prolong itself; its idols are as meaningless as the unknowable mystery of its being. The vital urge is enough, it may cast up in its career faiths innumerable, it may leave its victims with blanched faces, but its unfeeling fingers play on, and man perforce acts, and with his accident of a moral con- sciousness strives to read a pattern in the action. But it is as unnecessary to strive to read, as it is impossible ever to read aright. If this is the last word of the century, is it also the only significant word?

Even Nietzsche, who pushed the ideal of human personality to the pinnacle of the superman, the being self-sufficient and self-directing, beyond Good and Evil, the breaker of tables, and the maker of new laws, gave no coherent answer to the final question, to what end? The essential reality to him, as to Hardy, is the unmeaning urge of existence itself, Primordial Being, in which finally the individual finds himself engulfed. The only reality is this primordial urge to activity, and the superman shares according to his stature this urge of spontaneous activity; but even in his highest state he is only a creature of Maya, illusion. Is there a world progress? Is humanity moving toward some goal? Is the tragedy of the superman to some end? And again to these Nietzsche can give no answer.

The century began with a metaphysical faith in evolutionary progress, it ended with a metaphysical doubt in man's reason. From Kant to Bergson is the journey from the pole of faith in a human universe, to the pole from whence the universe is described only as an unmeaning *élan vital*. The only thing we can now say of it, says Bergson, is that it is not reasonable, and our science can give no clue to its nature.

There have been vigorous protests. The tradition of humanism will proudly affirm that it is not concerned with the essential reality, which, by our very nature, we can never know. It is the excellence and reasonableness of the human world that counts in the long run, the middle region of human experience; and of this we have evidence, that we disregard to our sorrow, in the tradition of human excellence. The values discoverable here are those and only those that the human mind can recognize. All without that tradition is written in a strange cipher to which we can never have the key. The beauty and reasonableness of human affections and institutions, sweetness and light in conduct, we can never escape the charm of these. To us, constituted as we are, these are the only realities, they and their opposites with which we are in eternal conflict.

And the scientist speaks a not dissimilar language, changing for his purpose its theme. The formulas of science may be far from corresponding with the essential realities. Not only are they hypotheses, and as such subject to constant verification; but that in any imaginably distant future they will describe the lineaments of reality, such a thought never enters his head. They are formulas, and only such, expressing discoverable relations in experience, be metaphysical reality what it may; and we discard them at our peril. With the same peril we discard the tradition of human excellence in the practical world of human conduct.

But this is to bring us back again to a faith not wholly unlike that of Dante, a faith in a knowable universe, within the limits of the human reason, a universe of human conduct and of a nature which is its theatre. Dante lived in an age of little natural science, but strong faith in human reason and the potency of the human ideal of righteousness. He asks no question of ultimate beginnings nor of ultimate ends.[2] It is easy to ask unanswerable questions —any child can put wisdom to flight—it is very much harder, and more vitally human, to look upon the face of Dante's Deity and see that it is human. And though not with his triumphant success, for the nineteenth century

[2] I am quite aware that in this I shall rouse the opposition of all who read Dante's cosmic drama as a poem based on a rigidly held metaphysics and physics made to blend with as rigid a theology.

world was a far more novel and complex world than the environs of Italy in the Middle Ages, some of its poets and novelists have, waveringly or boldly, looked in the same human reason for the illumination of conduct, and refused to be troubled by the meaningless rumble of Primordial Will or Immanent Reality. The metaphysical search may after all, of the infinitely great as of the infinitely small, though an intoxicating adventure for a philosopher, be also a dangerous pastime. It is the middle region that is the domain of human conduct.

Now what of our contemporaries? What are the leading lines of the story written since the war? To those who were young in 1914 the war came as a shock, the shock of unexpected and painful reality. As in Thomas Mann's *Magic Mountain* it awoke youth, that had been living in a world of fancied realities, to a reality that demanded immediate action and admitted no compromise. It left in its wake a feeling of insecurity, painful self-consciousness, a desire to cling to life, and yet a conviction of its remorseless elusiveness. The years of the war were the end of one epoch, and the beginning of a new. One could hardly feel otherwise after the visitation of so monstrous a cataclysm. But perhaps the most painful of all of its results was a sharpened sensitiveness, a quicker alertness of every sense to the fugitive impression that might so easily be sinister in its consequence. Tranquillity, reflection, these old sources of poetry require the cultivation of habit; how could this generation, that had known years of nervous strain and torture, ever again discover the meaning of peace?

Peace, to some, can be discovered only in the future. The past has died in the war, the present is an ill-defined transition—the Future!

"Morto è il Passo, e con baionette
Stiamo uccidendo il Presente
per mettre in trono il Futuro."

So shouted an Italian poet. "The Past is dead, and with bayonets let us stand slaying the Present so that we may set on the throne the Future." As one surveys the new poetry and the prose of Europe during the first ten years after the war, the story is one of weariness, disillusionment, sensitiveness, enthusiasm only for the future. There is little humor, much cynicism. It is only the figures of the preceding generation, those who had begun and been well established before the outbreak, who recovered and carried on in the earlier tradition. But it is of the new that I am now speaking.

The war brought home, as a wholesale experience, the fragile nature of the thing we call civilization. Fragile it seemed not only in the externals of culture and refinement, but fragile—and this is far more important—in its tempering effects on human character. After centuries and millenniums of instruction in the virtues of peace and good-will, man again emerged, the primitive beast, using his much vaunted science to satiate his lust of blood. A universe gone mad with mutual slaughter, to which there seemed and still at times seems no end. The thought is sobering and disillusioning.

To this has been added the growing conviction that the ultimate bases of science are fragile, with its shattering of trust in the human reason. Professor McDougall calls the new physics "a sort of mystic chant over an unintelligible universe." Professor Einstein has confused all but hard-boiled professionals with the jumble of space and time, until the conviction seems growing that man in searching for realities comes only upon the evidence of his own limitations; that all experience is somehow subjective, or, what seems infinitely worse, that things, and these, undiscoverable and indeterminate, are masters complete, and human behavior the complex of the drama of the endocrine glands.

All this, and then add the rapid changes in modern life. The nineteenth century had seen celerity, but with these last decades the pace has become a stampede. Our folkways are for children to resemble their grand or great-grand parents. A modern child does not acknowledge its parents, and parents cannot recognize their own offspring. A new world, a rapidly changing world, a brutally indifferent world, an elusive world, is it any wonder that many writers of the present scene, like the writers of every period of transition, give up the hope of permanence or of final excellence that once dominated the tradition of literature?

As a result this is a period of tentative effort, of experiment, and of experiment pushed to extremes in a resolute desire to *know*. What is human nature in fact, if not in essence, and what is this thing called the world of human experience? In this quest the writer will, so far as he can, be hampered by no postulates or theories, or inherited beliefs. "Put off holiness, put on intelligence." Armed thus, the adventure is the search for the secret of personality and experience. Or if the writer returns to tradition and belief, his return will come as the result of the quest and conflict, after he discovers in belief new and more vital issues of life and conduct.[3]

There is above all in the present the resolute desire to explore the reality of consciousness. This may be, or may

[3] In what follows, as well as in what has gone before, I am by no means trying to summarize all of the movements in letters of the last twenty years. Such an attempt would take a separate volume—the task would be intriguing. It is only a few lines of contemporary thought that I try to describe, and these without identifying them with their authors. There must be limits to the size of a book.

not be, the result of the new psychology. Certainly in this day one still hears the names of Freud and Jung, and their ideas have had many repercussions in the new art of fiction—as new as anything can be under the sun. The stream of consciousness novels did not begin with Proust, but he did much to make it popular. It did not come to its climax with Joyce's *Ulysses,* but it there showed that a novel could be written without an idea, though it might be a flux of ideas. *M. Teste,* of Paul Valéry gives its theme: "It is the obscure (*inconnu*), the unguessed, in me which makes me what I am." And it is to follow the hints of this *self,* the essential constitution and the processes of the mind and of the emotions, that has given present day fiction and even poetry its major quest.

One can criticise the quest easily, as Rivière does after reading Marcel Proust. "I feel myself literally in a world depopulated; what I wish to say is that contemporary literature offers itself to me like a palace without inhabitants; at least I see myself surrounded by phantoms who enter and leave by the windows as easily as by the doors. I search in vain for anything concrete." But, perhaps, it is because this world, of the consciousness only, has nothing of the concrete that it is to some the more alluring. And then below the conscious is the subconscious, that sub-liminal self of which Freud has taught us to catch hints in involuntary impressions and dreams. Perhaps this shadowy self is as real, or more real, than the self of will and action and reason.

Perhaps, and this thought is the more startling, there are more selves in this mystery of the essence of the human personality than our crude science can ever reveal. A conscious self and no end of unconscious selves that can displace the conscious, or at odd times play the most fantastic tricks with otherwise orderly lives. Or again, is the idea of an orderly life after all not much more than a conventional fiction? *Notre âme total n'a que une valeur presque fictive.* Our idea of a total personality has not much value beyond a fictitious one. It is a startling thought, when once long ago we used to read of dual personalities as a sign of mental derangement. But here comes Pirandello and gives it currency in his dramas, as, for example, in his *Henry IV*. Or, what is still worse, is the word fictitious itself, as I have used it, fictitious? Do not fictitious personalities, after an author has created them, find themselves possessed of an essential reality? Read his *Six Characters in Search of an Author*. What is consciousness, where does it consist? What is reality, where does it consist? The answers, as the questions, can induce vertigo; and there have been vertiginous plays and novels in these our later years.

It was the desire to express the inner experience in its essential reality that led to that extravagance, now past, that called itself Expressionism, and to its illegitimate frantic daughter that called herself Dadaism. There is no time nor place here to describe their extravagances, but their motive was as serious as their votaries, who found in them a new artistic religion—an escape from objective reality that is crude and forbidding. "The drama is in our own minds," writes an Italian, "the decent thing to do is to subdue it by expressing it." *Hors du monde, n'importe ou*, cries out a Frenchman. "The world is there," writes a German, "it would be absurd to reproduce it. The greatest task of art is to search out its intrinsic essence and create it anew." Thus to them a landscape is not a picture of some objective scene that might be recognised, but a symbol of the state of mind roused in the painter by the object. A laborer crushed under his load is not the picture of a man overburdened but is the symbol of the mood his misery arouses. Of course the fact that often such pictures, as such poems, are unintelligible to the uninitiated is no argument to such religious faith. For unintelligibility itself can be a very great virtue. "Writing is not an art of words but of things." "We write without taking into consideration the meaning of words." To this there is no answer—in words.

But this desire to explore the inner experience as the only reality has led also to some vital and vivid poetry and prose. The world of the five senses at least has impeccable reality. To explore it and make its poetry and prose vividly and sensuously alive is no small accomplishment. Joyce has done this in his *Ulysses*. Language must be recoined to rouse the sensuous response, and new metaphors and new uses for old words. It is again the old protest against stereotyped diction, and these poets are battling anew shoulder to shoulder with Wordsworth. To live in the world of the senses; and in pure sensitivity to discover a fleeting but vivid reality, not ideas or intellectual images, but sensations.

But again, like all else, this attempt to capture a world of sensation has its excess in the poetry of sur-realism, the search for a higher reality whose clue one finds in the fleeting sense impression. Is it a dream world? Perhaps. Certainly it is an inner world, or as one of its devotees calls it, "outward reality inwardly transformed." It comes from a spontaneous hint, an intuition, and there follows the revelation of a reality in a higher dimension, fantastic perhaps, but not fantastic as an escape from reality, but fantastic because it is a higher reality. Here is something that escapes the ordinary mind, it is unstable because we lack the mental forms to hold it, and it transcends the intelligence to conceive it, or words to express it. The redoubtable Bottom once had just such a vision.

"But man is but a patched fool,
If he will offer to say
What methought I had.
The eye of man hath not heard,
The ear of man hath not seen;
Man's hand is not able to taste,
His tongue to conceive,
Nor his heart to report
What my dream was."

Nor can ours. For Bottom is really in a higher dimension.

In this moment of intense and sometimes clear impression, in this *sentiment*, in the French, the new realism, sane or exaggerated, finds its new absolute. The realism of the sentient moment. Proust's novels are its search and its episodic story. Others modify it slightly and find it in the moment of intense sensuous action, sometimes called the *acte gratuit*, the action devoted to no intelligible end, but a thing for its own sake. These are the moments when through all its avenues life is manifesting itself, and giving a hint of its eternal riddle. It is to discover these that the more typical of the contemporaries have at one time or other devoted their search.

There have been those in revolt against this contemporary trend. Rilke in Germany devotes himself to a newer and fresher attitude toward objective reality. There have been many who, confused by the tumult of jarring cries, have turned to orthodoxy and religion and the Church. There are those who call us back again to the Tradition. The new experiments have been valuable, as they have revealed new human powers and old human limitations. The attempted synthesis with science is an effort that deserves full credit. The desire to reconcile literature and life, interrupted by romantic vagaries, is in itself an effort to pick up again the thread of the literary tradition. Above all, possibly, the refusal by most of today to make literature the handmaid of some social or political theory is beyond praise. This and the downright seriousness of all today in the pursuit of letters, the steadfast desire to see life as it is, and to know its ultimate constitution, are full of promise for the future.

The nineteenth century was a century of bewildered, perhaps, but always exciting search. In its quest it covered as extensive a field as the range of human life and interest. The twentieth century, this our second quarter, sees this field daily enlarged and as full of interest and downright adventure. Doubtless we are again on the threshold of another century of search. Without the interest and the adventure, and the attending danger, life would be a drab affair indeed.

THE END

A BRIEF BIBLIOGRAPHY

THE purpose of this is to guide the reader, who wishes to carry his search farther, to the most available books of the authors and to the critical comment that seems to offer most. No mention is made of the works of authors whose novels and poems are well known. For writers in a foreign language reference is made to works in translation, except as with Ibsen, Tolstoi and some others, where editions are numerous and easily available.

GENERAL

Brandes, G.: *Main Currents in 19th Century Literature.* Macmillan.
Magnus, Laurie: *History of European Literature.* Ivor Nicholson and Watson.

ROUSSEAU

Babbitt, I.: *Rousseau and Romanticism.* Houghton, Mifflin.
Cobban, A.: *Rousseau and the Modern State.* Allen and Unwin.
Faguet, É.: *Vie de Rousseau.* Société Française d'Imprimerie.
Hendel, C. W.: *J. J. Rousseau, Moralist.* Oxford Press.
Josephson, M.: *J. J. Rousseau.* Gollancz.
Morley, J.: *Rousseau.* Macmillan.
Wright, E. Hunter: *The Meaning of Rousseau.* Oxford Press.

CHATEAUBRIAND

Sainte-Beuve, C. A.: *On Chateaubriand*—in English, translations of his Selected Essays.
Chateaubriand: *Atala,* tr. into English. Stanford University Press.
Chateaubriand: *Genius of Christianity,* tr. into English. Murphy, Baltimore and New York.
Chateaubriand: *Memoirs from Beyond the Tomb,* tr. into English. Freemantle.

SHELLEY

Clutton-Brock, A.: *Shelley the Man and the Poet.* Methuen.
Dowden, E.: *Life of Percy Bysshe Shelley.* Kegan, Paul.

Elton, O.: *Shelley.* Edward Arnold.
Grabo, C. H.: *A Newton among Poets.* Univ. of N. C. Press.
Maurois, A.: *Ariel, the Life of Shelley.* Appleton.
Peck, W. E.: *Shelley, His Life and Work.* Benn.

MANZONI

The Betrothed, Manzoni. tr. into English. Bell. tr. into English
with an Introduction by D. J. Connor. Macmillan.
Croce, B.: *A. Manzoni,* Saggi e Discussioni. Laterza.
Gentile, G.: *Manzoni,* Studi e Lezioni. Laterza.

WHITMAN

Burroughs, J.: *Whitman, A Study.* Houghton, Mifflin.
Morris, H. S.: *Walt Whitman, a Brief Biography.* Harvard University Press.
Perry, B.: *Walt Whitman, His Life and Work.* Houghton, Mifflin.
Rogers, C.: *The Magnificent Idler.* Doubleday.
Sherman, S. P.: *Whitman in America.* Scribners.

HEBBEL

Hebbel: Three plays translated into English. *Maria Magdelene,
Herodes and Mariamne, Gyges and His Ring.* Everyman Library.
Agnes Bernauer: tr. into English, in *Poet Lore,* 1909.
Campbell, T. M.: *Life and Works of Friedrich Hebbel.* Badger.
Purdie E.: *Friedrich Hebbel, Study of His Life and Work.* Oxford
Press.

TOLSTOI

Baring, M.: *Landmarks in Russian Literature.* Heinemann.
Heller, O.: *Prophets of Dissent—Essays on Nietzsche and Tolstoi.*
Knopf.
Maude, A.: *Life of Tolstoi.* Dodd, Mead.
Nazaroff, A. I.: *Tolstoy—a Biography.* Stokes.
Rolland, R.: *Tolstoi.* tr. into English. Dutton.

DOSTOEVSKY

Berdyev, N.: *Dostoevsky,* tr. D. Atwater. Sheed, Ward.
Carr, E. Hallet: *Dostoevsky, a New Biography.* Allen and Unwin.
Meier-Graefe: *Dostoevsky, the Man and His Work.* Harcourt.
Murry, M.: *Fyodor Dostoevsky.* Dodd, Mead and Company.
Schestov, L.: *Dostoevsky and Nietzsche,* tr, into the German.
Marcan.
Yarmolinsky, A.: *Dostoevsky.* Harcourt.

NIETZSCHE

Nietzsche: *Thus Spake Zarathustra,* tr. into English. Macmillan.
(With the translation of his other works.)
Abraham, G.: Nietzsche, *Great Lives.* Duckworth.

Archer, William: *Fighting a Philosophy.* Oxford Press.
Knight, A. H. J.: *Some Aspects of the Life and Work of Nietzsche.* Cambridge University Press.
Salter, W. T.: *Nietzsche the Thinker.* Holt.
Wolf, A.: *The Philosophy of Nietzsche.* Constable.

IBSEN

Brandes, G.: *Ibsen—Critical Studies.* Heinemann.
Ellis, H.: *New Spirit,* Constable.
Gosse, E.: *Studies in the Literature of Northern Europe.* Kegan, Paul.
Koht, H.: *Life of Ibsen,* tr. into English. Allen and Unwin.
Shaw, G. B.: *The Quintessence of Ibsenism.* Brentano.
Zucker, A. E.: *Ibsen: The Master Builder, a Biography.* Holt and Company.

ZOLA

Zola: *The Downfall,* tr. into English. Macmillan.
Zola: *The Dram Shop.* Chatto.
Zola: *Germinal,* tr. into English. Knopf.
Zola: *Nana,* tr. into English. Modern Library.
Zola: *Paris,* tr. into English. The Macmillan Company.
Barbusse, H.: *Zola,* tr. into English. Dent.
Ellis, H.: *In Affirmations.* Houghton, Mifflin.
Josephson, M.: *Life of Zola.* Macaulay.
Vizetelly, E. A.: *Émile Zola, Novelist and Reformer.* Lane.

ARNOLD

Brownell, W. C.: *Victorian Prose Masters.* Scribners.
Chambers, Sir E.: *Matthew Arnold.* Oxford Press.
Kingsmiell, H.: *Matthew Arnold.* Duckworth.
Walker, H.: *The Greater Victorian Poets.* Macmillan.

HARDY

Abercrombie, L.: *Thomas Hardy.* Martin Secker.
Fowler, J. H.: *The Novels of Thomas Hardy.* Oxford Press.
Hardy, F. E.: *Life of Hardy,* two volumes. Macmillan.
McDowall, A.: *Thomas Hardy, A Critical Study.* Faber.
Symons, A.: *A Study of Thomas Hardy.* Charles J. Sawyer.

INDEX

As in *The Golden Thread* the index below is planned for those who wish to discover the topics treated in the chapters of the book, and the places where they are treated at length. They are grouped under the names of the various writers. Names of persons or places that are merely mentioned, for illustration or for reference, are not noted here.

379